FEROCIOUS WARMTH

PRAISE FOR FEROCIOUS WARMTH

'Ferocious warmth leadership is relevant and needed now more than ever. This book not only inspires but successfully pokes and prods our thinking within a supportive framework, just like a Ferocious Warm leader would do. It is easy to read and cleverly structured with features such as: 'reflection pauses' which could be used for conversation starters in team meetings or professional reading book clubs. Continual references to other notable leadership thinking and practical authentic examples of warm, ferocious leadership complement Tracey's narrative and ensure that it is a valuable reference book too. Most importantly a warm, ferocious leader has students at the centre of everything they do, and the links that Tracey shares to promote increased student voice and agency are clear and powerful. I "dob in" Tracey for writing an uplifting and truly inspiring book. Priority reading for 2021!'

Coralee Pratt, *President, ACEL Victoria*
(Australian Council for Educational Leaders)

'This book is deeply insightful and provides a window into the mind, heart and soul of effective leaders. Whilst evidence based and research informed, it is highly actionable and incredibly readable. *Ferocious Warmth* cements Tracey Ezard as a powerful voice in the space of leadership effectiveness.'

Debra Punton, *Deputy Director,Catholic Identity, Leadership, Learning & Teaching Diocese of Sale Catholic Education Ltd*

'I needed this book well before I had the privilege to read it. The best educational leaders are always an indefinable mix of firm and fair. And for decades, various scribes have attempted to decode and strategise this concept as though discovering a generic formula for school leadership will somehow make a difference. As Tracey points out, it won't. The resultant Ferocious Warmth from the right balance of firm and fair is far more an act of art, than it is of science. It's less strategy than it is permission – and that permission is to be more human and more just in our leadership. This isn't a book that disrespects as to instruct or to script you, but it does rely on your determination to lead with both your head and your heart. On the other side of that worthy assumption, Tracey invites us to work toward purpose, to live our beliefs and to lean on each other for mutual growth. Every aspiring school leader needs to devour *Ferocious Warmth* and to reflect on its message as they seek to mobilise others behind their vision for a better school.'

Adam Voigt, *CEO and Founder, Real Schools*

'Many books have been written portraying skills such as setting strategic direction, prioritizing goals and systems thinking as essential to success in leadership. In *Ferocious Warmth,* Tracey Ezard offers a compelling argument that while these skills are necessary, the work of a leader is in fact much broader and complex. Tracey puts forward a model of an infinite cycle that balances Ferocious and Warmth as the real world in which leaders work and thrive. Examining Emotional, Strategic and Learning Intelligences, Tracey breaks these domains into Expansive, Connection, Courage and Authentic skillsets. *Ferocious Warmth* is relevant and practical. Through her powerful use of story, Tracey illustrates how leaders in a wide variety of contexts have used the principles and skills of Ferocious Warmth leadership to better the lives of young people and adults working in ever increasingly complex circumstances. In an era where people are seeking not only direction but connectedness and purpose, this book is not only relevant but timely. The world needs more Ferocious Warmth!'

Piet Langstraat, *Former Superintendent of Red Deer,*
Alberta and Victoria, British Columbia.

'The Priory Federation of Academies is so fortunate to have connected with Tracey and the concept of Ferocious Warmth at this point in our organisational expansion; it will be essential reading for our growing teachers and leaders. As emotionally compelling as it is intellectually fascinating, there can be no headteacher past or present who will fail to find resonance in this exploration of leadership behaviours. We are moved to confront and challenge the enduring polarity, so frequently accepted, between results-driven accountability and the obligation to foster human relationships.

'This book could not have come at a better time. In this period of global turbulence, Tracey offers hope for the school leaders of the future and aspiration for the young people in their care. The reader is called upon to identify and name their default mindsets through the synthesis of eminently human narratives and academic insight. Tracey's articulation of powerful models provides a blueprint for personal, professional and organisational growth and a lexicon with which to choreograph the "dance to balance ferocity and warmth.'

Andrew Chisholm, *Director of Teaching*
Nicki Shore, *Researcher in Residence (former secondary headteacher)*
Priory Federation of Academies, Lincolnshire, UK

'I love the elegance and nuance in the label 'ferocious warmth', the determination and compassion this directive holds seems perfect for leadership in the now. *Ferocious Warmth* takes leadership from a theory or capability and gives it life. Ferocious warmth walks the line between conviction and curiosity, between courage and compassion, a line that defines the leadership experience.'

Matt Church, *Author 'Rise Up; an evolution in leadership',*
Founder Thought Leaders

'Tracey offers school leaders an approach to help us reimagine education. Learning for these changing times demands a new narrative, a challenging of the status quo of schooling. She explains the need to look beyond the dichotomy of 'results' or 'relationships' and presents a model to help us effectively change the story of schooling. The use of real examples from the profession makes this an important read.'

Dr David Turner, *Director of Professional Learning, QASSP*
(Queensland Association of State School Principals)

'If you are looking for a practical book that just 'makes sense' - that gives you reflective questions, ideas to try and strategies to implement to establish and grow a high-performing collaborative team in an educational setting, this latest book by Tracey Ezard just hits the mark. *Ferocious Warmth* is an easy (very worthwhile) read and can be picked up and re visited a number of times, each occasion finding a new gem, an alternate perspective or just reminders of a very common sense approach to leadership. So many examples of real leadership in practise, through challenges and opportunities. What stands out once again is Tracey's ability to connect with such a range of vibrant people and her ability to share/celebrate their journeys to aid others!'

Sandy Cartwright, *Principal, Alawa Primary School Darwin NT*

'Developing the concept of 'Ferocious Warmth' Tracey Ezard has tapped into Jung's concept of the tension of opposites. Who would have thought you could be, or even needed to be, both ferocious and warm at the same time to be a transformative leader? Brené Brown in her recent podcast with Barack Obama described his holding the discomfort of paradox as one of his most important leadership skill sets. Tracey's evocative descriptions of Ferociously Warm leaders will prompt us to reflect on our own leadership, and grapple with the paradox to become transformative in our actions.'

Sue Bell, President, *VASSP*
(Victorian Association of State Secondary Principals)

'I often write that each person in our schools is home to a life. In *Ferocious Warmth* Tracey Ezard explores this construct through the lens of remarkable educational leaders, individuals that operate from a deep sense of self in the service of the other. Ezard takes us on an important journey through the key elements of transformational leadership, inviting the reader to explore the necessary *expansive* (open minded and curious), *connected* (deep consciousness of self and the other), *courageous* (conviction and bravery) and *authentic* (keeping it real) character dispositions for ways to learn, lead, live and work.'

Adriano Di Prato, *Founding Partner, a School for tomorrow*

Author: Tracey Ezard

Title: Ferocious Warmth: Schools Leaders Who Inspire and Transform

ISBN: 978-0-6487931-2-0

Cover design: Kieran Flanagan

Illustrations: Sherrill Knezel of Meaningful Marks

Graphic images: Jaiden Gusti

Edited by: Ann Bolch

Typesetting: Lu Sexton

DEDICATION

One of the biggest influences in my journey was a great man, Hans Keuffer, a Ferocious Warmth leader and the principal where my children went to primary school in Melbourne, Victoria. He passed away in 2009, tragically and too soon. This book is dedicated to him and the legacy he left for his community and his colleagues.

This book is also dedicated to one of the shining examples of Ferocious Warmth leadership. Claudine Moncur-White, a principal from Townsville, Queensland, was a constant light through the journey of writing this book. Her approach to life and leadership inspired me to unpack the Ferocious Warmth approach. She was a fierce advocate for all students. The world is a better place because Claudine was in it.

To all of the Ferocious Warmth leaders who have inspired me, supported me and challenged me over the course of my life. I am lucky to count many of you not only as clients, colleagues or mentors, but also my friends.

Heads and Hearts

TRACEY EZARD

FEROCIOUS WARMTH

*School leaders
who inspire and transform*

FOREWORD

Dr Barbara Watterston

Ferocious Warmth leadership is testament to Tracey's talent to craft a narrative underpinned by her constant focus on authentically engaging in learning with others, enriching her language and repertoire of examples so that we too can be inspired in our learning and growth.

As is evidenced in all of her work, and now *Ferocious Warmth*, Tracey has the unique ability to capture the essence of a concept and eloquently explore it in great depth to inform and empower others. As a generous, energetic and collaborative author and consultant, her work is grounded in theory and evidence-informed practice and equally, enormously accessible to test and apply. Her choice of words and nuanced use of phrases immediately get to the heart of the matter in a way that we can all understand and relate to, stimulating reflection and impacting on our practice.

The interdependency of Ferocious Warmth leadership takes us from polarity to duality, from an either/or to a both/and focus on leading for results *with* compassion and vulnerability. This approach is informed by a rich tapestry of case study and academic research, with scenarios and gems of personal experiences and observations within and beyond the education sector.

Tracey has provided a transformative space for readers to challenge, interrogate and acknowledge all that they bring to their leadership. As I turned the pages of *Ferocious Warmth*, I smiled, reflected, questioned, admired and celebrated the messages, research and stories that Tracey has woven in such a way that resonate so viscerally. Leadership and learning are inextricably linked. There is no one size fits all.

Tracey guides us into crafting our own leadership identity in recognising our strengths, being open to wisdom and feedback, *and* compassionately caring for self and others to provide the enabling conditions for all of us to do our best work. She illustrates this through the push and pull of the infinity symbol. Where polarities nestle together providing balance and perspective to making the right choice at the right time to enact leadership most effectively; 'knowing when to lift the bar, knowing when to deeply listen and hold the space'.

Tracey speaks of enlightening moments with others that sparked her thinking and tingled her senses. Prepare to be motivated and inspired. The sparks will continue as you take the journey through the pages of *Ferocious Warmth*.

Dr Lesley Murrihy

Kia ora koutou

Ko Putauaki tōku maunga

Ko Tarawera tōku awa

Ko Ngati Pākehā tōku iwi

No Kawerau ahau

Ko Blakely tōku whānau

Ko John tōku tane

Ko Demelza ratou ko Nadia, ko Aaron, ko Sebastian, ko Melissa, ko Natasha, ko Zara, ko Serena āku tamariki

Ko au te tumuaki of te kura o Amesbury

Ko Lesley Murrihy ahau

Nō reira, tēnā koutou, tēnā koutou, tēnā tātou koutou

My name is Lesley Murrihy and this is my pepeha. This tells you how I am connected to the land (through my mountain – Putauaki, and through my river –

Tarawera, and to Kawerau, the small North Island town in the Bay of Plenty, New Zealand, in which I was raised). It also tells you a bit about who I am connected to – my husband, John and our eight children, from Demelza who is the oldest and to Serena who is the youngest. I am from the Blakely family. I am a European New Zealander (Ngati Pākehā) and I am currently the principal (tumuaki) of Amesbury School. Therefore, I greet you all.

During lockdown I spent more time on social media than usual and I became not only incredibly frustrated but genuinely sick at heart. So much so that in the end I had to avoid social media altogether. Our country was doing well dealing with Covid-19 compared with much of the rest of the world and yet there was so much negativity against the people who I felt were doing their best and learning as they went along to protect our country during this unprecedented threat. After weeks and weeks of being Covid-free in the community, we had a small outbreak and the backlash was fevered. There seemed to be no middle ground – people were on one side or the other and they were often personally attacking in the way they expressed their views. Recent events in America have shown a similar trend but on a much bigger scale, more extreme and with shocking results.

It seems to me that there is nothing more important for our world right now than moving beyond Piaget's formal reasoning which includes binary logic and analytical thinking. This has been the dominant way of thinking of the 20th century and has led to the great scientific and technological achievements of the industrial society – achievements that have contributed so much to the evolution of human civilisation. But it is no longer serving us well and it *has* to become a global educational priority today for those in education to evolve their ability to think, but also to lay the foundations for an education that ensures our children and young people develop as both/and, integrative thinkers. Einstein said, 'The significant problems we have, cannot be solved at the same level of thinking with which we have created them.' We need a new way of thinking.

Ferocious Warmth focuses on just this issue and this reason alone would give me sufficient cause to write in support of this book. But wait…there's more. It is also warmly written with captivating stories and illuminating themes. I was particularly drawn in by the story Tracey tells of her own experience of loss and grief. As I read this portion of the book, I lost all sense of time and place, and I found myself reflecting, as she does, on how my leadership has been shaped by every experience, every encounter, not just the professional ones or the nice tidy ones, but by all of the messiness of my whole life. Stories are woven through the book to provide practical illustrations of Ferocious Warmth leaders that each of us will be able to identify with but also be challenged by. NZ school principal, Sarah Martin (Chapter 10) and I meet together regularly to share our developing thinking about education and I can assure you that you will be hard pressed find a better example of a Ferocious Warmth leader. So please do take note.

Though *Ferocious Warmth* is written with warmth, humour and heart, Tracey Ezard is refreshingly blunt and tells it like it is, exposing the elephants in the room for all to see. I laughed out loud when she used the term 'Spoilt Brat Syndrome' to describe a tendency by some teachers to expect high levels of support but only accept low levels of challenge. She playfully suggests raising expectations and then watching 'the fast and furious push back'. I have noticed this phenomena, but I have never had a label for it. Neither did I quite have the courage to actually say it out loud in public. Thank you, Tracey, it had to be said and now you have given me permission to also speak out this truth.

But to the crux of the matter. In his book *The Courage to Teach*, Parker Palmer said, 'We distort things...because we are trained neither to voice both sides of an issue nor to listen with both ears... It is rooted in the fact that we look at the world through analytical lenses. We see everything as this or that, plus or minus, on or off, black or white; and we fragment reality into an endless series of either-ors. In a phrase, we think the world apart.' Ferocious Warmth leaders are those who have learned to think the world back together again. They use heart and head to ensure wise leadership decision-making. They use both high support and high challenge so their staff don't end up with 'Spoilt Brat Syndrome'. They use cognitive and emotional intelligences to enable balanced outcomes. They are brave and vulnerable at the same time and evidence-based and innovative. Ezard describes this weaving of what appears to be polar opposites as a dance, 'blending moves from both ferociousness and warmth'. In actual fact, they are not polar opposites but rather they are simply parts of a whole. I applaud Tracey Ezard for challenging a still pervasive siloed view of the world and of leadership and for presenting in its place a holistic, multidimensional view which will not necessarily be understood by all, will certainly be challenging to implement for many, but which will make all the difference if we succeed.

I have been a school leader for nearly two decades and I have written about leadership from many different perspectives. But as I approach my twilight years in leadership, *Ferocious Warmth* has inspired me to do better, to be better – to be more courageous, to better balance my tendency to use my head by paying greater attention to what my heart is saying. As I have already done while reading the book, I will be sure to use the questions to reflect on my practice and to try the strategies outlined with staff. Though the ideas in the book are theoretically based, it is above all a book for practitioners. A book for you and me to build our skills so that we can more gracefully blend ferocity and warmth in the dance of a Ferocious Warmth leader.

Ngā mihi nui ki a koutou

THE WORLD NEEDS MORE LEADERS WITH THE FEROCITY TO LEAD TRANSFORMATION,
AND THE WARMTH TO INSPIRE AND CONNECT PEOPLE.
IT NEEDS YOU.

ACKNOWLEDGEMENTS

This book was written on the land of the Wurundjeri people of the Kulin Nation, where I also live. I first and foremost pay my respects to their elders, past, present and emerging. I acknowledge that this beautiful land was never ceded. It always was and always will be Aboriginal land.

Many people have had impact on the development of the Ferocious Warmth concept over the years. Some I have only met briefly, but my Ferocious Warmth senses tingle as I see and hear them in action. Others have shaped my thinking more directly.

My great appreciation to those who willingly were interviewed for this book, or allowed me to share their stories. While many names are mentioned throughout the chapters, there are also a number whose leadership approach, and discussions informed my thinking, even though they are not mentioned by name within the text. Heartfelt thanks to all of you: Professor Judy Atkinson, Vicki Baylis, Sue Bell, Pitsa Binnion, Tracey Breese, Sandy Cartwright, Aderyn Chatterton, Nathan Chisholm, Meagan Cook, Kaye Corcoran, Adriano Di Prato, Jane Gibbs, Philip Hughes, Peter Hutton, Keith Jessup, Maria Karvouni, Dr Stephen Kendall-Jones, Julie Kennedy, Dr Jane Kise, Piet Langstraat, Aine Maher, Justine Mackey, Sarah Martin, Jennifer McCrabb, Claudine Moncur-White, Liz Pringle, Coralee Pratt, Debra Punton, John Richmond, Dr Briony Scott, Associate Professor Elizabeth Sigston, Julie Symons, Professor Helena Teede, Adam Voigt, Dr Barbara Watterson, Penny Weily.

Others have shared their thinking anonymously and are within the chapters with changed names – you know who you are and I thank you for your trust in me with your stories and lessons learned.

My huge gratitude to the people who reviewed the book and gave feedback along the way. Thank you for 'seeing' Ferocious Warmth for what it is and the support to get it into the world. Thank you especially to Dr Barbara Watterston and Dr Lesley Murrihy for providing the foreword and to Sue Bell for providing Ferocious Warmth feedback.

My business would not hold together if not for my business manager Suzie Leyden. Suzie keeps me on track and is committed to this work and our clients in a way that I am so appreciative of.

The incomparable Kieran Flanagan for her design work on this book. I am lucky to count Kieran as a friend and mentor, as well as my designer! Kieran's eye for design and message is legendary. Thank you Kieran for collaborating with me on this project.

Sherrill Knezel of Meaningful Marks has brought the Ferocious Warmth concept to life through her beautiful graphics. I have admired Sherrill's work for many years now and was so excited when she was able to work with me on this project.

To the production team: Ann Bolch my editor, thank you for your perseverance and belief in the concept of Ferocious Warmth. Jaiden Gusti for his graphic design and Lu Sexton for her layout and proofing work. What an awesome team!

To all my clients and those who are in the education field in general. I admire your skills, perseverance and love for the job you do. It is joyful to work in a sector so committed to those who are our future.

Thought Leaders Business School and the brilliant people within continue to give generously both professional and personal sustenance. So many fabulous relationships, so many enlightening moments to spark thinking. Thank you everyone for what you give to me so freely. Thank you to Matt Church and Pete Cook for what you created, and to Lisa O'Neill, Kim Cox and Col Fink for your continued care of us all.

From a personal perspective, my shout outs go far and wide to those who support me and love me for all my flaws and good bits. I am grateful for all the different network of friends I have and the alchemy we create.

The two most important people in my life: Conor and Layla – so much love for you both. Thank you for always supporting me through everything. You are amazing and unique human beings and I love what you bring to the world. We are an awesome fambam. 'Relax, yeah.'

My mum and dad, Keith and Robyn Jessup, who's love and support I have been blessed to have all my life.

Karin and Adrian White, my anchors. Open 24 hours. No more needs to be said. (xoxo yuk as usual)

Justin, who remains a strong and constant support in all that I do.

My squad: Maree Burgess, Lynne Cazaly, Donna McGeorge. There are peeps in life that elevate you. Your thinking, your connection and your trust in yourself. These three have been all of that to me over many years and I love our 'thing'.

CONTENTS

COURAGEOUS

AUTHENTIC

INTRODUCTION

Ferocious Warmth is firmly and unashamedly a book to celebrate the humanness seen in educational leaders everywhere. The time is ripe for education to transform in all manner of ways. The Ferocious Warmth approach creates cultures of learning, connection, thriving and innovation.

In the most complex of times, how do leaders stay balanced to deliver results and transformation yet maintain and grow relationships? How do they involve their people to transform education in a way that inspires and motivates? How can they have expertise in both enacting strategy and building culture. How can these be in concert, rather than in polarity as they often are?

Ferocious Warmth leadership blends the duality of leading for results and leading with compassion. These should not be mutually exclusive but often our more negative experiences of leaders are of one or the other. Ferocious Warmth combines outcomes with heart, rigour with connection, high challenge with high support. It's brave and vulnerable, evidence and innovation, cognitive and emotional. The junction of ferocity and warmth is the sweet spot needed to transform the way we work and find even better ways to provide education that is relevant, accessible and fit for purpose amid the swiftest context changes the world has ever seen. A great leader can access all of these and make it look like a dance, blending moves from both ferociousness and warmth. They build strong commitment and trust with those they lead, working in authentic collaboration, not unchallengeable authority. A Ferocious Warmth leader connects to the students with an enviable professional intimacy. They push the students in their care to aspire to greater heights, while holding the space for compassion and open conversation.

Unfortunately, the leadership many people experience is far from this. Have you worked with a leader who everyone hides from when they walk down the corridor? One that makes people quake in their boots when they call them into their office for a meeting? On the other extreme, a leader who is so embedded in the emotional lives of their people that they forget to also focus on what needs to be achieved? They stay too long at the barbecue or at Friday night drinks? One extreme is focussed only on results, the other only on relationships. They both sit at the edges of leadership, yet too often they are the default.

Over the last eighteen months I've interviewed leaders who have led at least one of three significant shifts:

1. Transformed outcomes in the education setting with their teams.
2. Shifted culture over a short period of time.
3. Currently lead dynamic environments that continue to evolve.

I wanted them to describe what's important about leading, about people and about education. In Australia, I've spoken with school leaders from rural, regional and metropolitan state schools, and metropolitan independent and Catholic schools. I've spoken with principals in New Zealand, and system leaders in both Australia and Canada. Each interview was a joy and a privilege. Ferocious Warmth leaders are voracious learners, and so eager to unpack ideas and discuss thinking and beliefs. You'll hear some of their stories through the pages of this book. I have used this case study research as well as academic research to inform and interrogate the Ferocious Warmth leadership approach.

Over the past fifteen years, since leaving the education system in Victoria, Australia, where I was an assistant principal in a primary school, I have worked with leaders to help them reflect and grow their leadership. I've been influenced by great researchers and leaders in the middle of this work and have always sought learning both within and outside the education sector. People who've helped uncover some of the nuances of great leaders, such as Dr Ben Palmer and Professor Con Stough with emotional intelligence, Don Beck and Chris Cowan of Spiral Dynamics, Neuro Linguistic Programming leaders John Grinder and Marvin Oka, as well as Professor Amy Edmondson, Brené Brown, Rita Pierson, Amy Cuddy and many more have all fed into my thinking and reflection on leadership. Education leaders such as Professors Michael Fullan, Andy Hargreaves, Dylan William, John Hattie, Viviane Robinson, Dr Lyn Sharratt and Peter DeWitt and more have helped inform my work and thinking. More recently, Thought Leaders Australia has provided me with an amazing array of people to hang out with. They elevate my thinking and provoke me to delve more deeply into the elements that help people be their best to make a dent in the universe.

Every year I come across hundreds of school leaders in all education sectors across the country. All of them doing one of the most complex and confounding jobs around. The job of an educational leader constantly mixes joy and challenge, reactivity and proactivity, forward momentum and backward slides. I admire these leaders for their tenacity and intent, and am truly grateful for the trust they put in me to work with them and their teams to create momentum and deep collaboration.

I have always been an observer of leadership. Like a beach comber collecting treasures of shells and beautiful stones along the shore, I've been fascinated to watch the little and big things leaders do in the name of their craft that build strong culture and transforms students' experience of school.

When I look back on my career, I can see that my love for leadership was created way back in my primary and secondary school years, mainly through playing in bands and orchestras as a flute player. I was surrounded by people who encouraged me to put my head up and push myself further, especially when I was coasting on my talent.

I've been lucky enough to work and learn under a number of larger-than-life leaders, even as a student. My Grade 5 teacher, Mr Savage, created a following of musicians who could, by the time we left primary school at the age of 12, play all the recorders from sopranino through descant to the bass recorder, and sight-read complex Baroque and Elizabethan music. Every day before school we gathered to play in a portable full of orchestral marimbas, xylophones and vibraphones that he had purchased for us to use. Doug Heywood, my high school music teacher and university lecturer, still leads the choir at the televised popular Melbourne Carols by Candlelight at the Sidney Myer Music Bowl every Christmas Eve. A group of us still catch up with him a few times a year to reminisce and celebrate his influence on us, forty years on. His impact on music teachers throughout my state of Victoria, Australia, is well known.

Mr John Savage was pretty ferocious (oh the irony!). He was quite scary and yet we still wanted to work like crazy to improve. He tapped into a part of us that straightened our shoulders and got us thinking 'I can do this'. Our standards lifted way above the average musical skills of primary school kids and we were proud of ourselves. So ferociously devoted to performing well, I felt too scared to let Mr

Savage know before an important concert performance that I was busting to go to the toilet. He was focussed on what we had to do; we were in the stage wings and had to be dead quiet as the group before us finished performing. My need to speak up about the urgency was overpowered by my fear of letting him down and looking silly in front of everyone for not having thought of visiting the toilet earlier. On we went to perform our piece at the Oxfam concert. And on I went to pee my pants, on a stage in front of hundreds of people, as we valiantly played all the way through a Telemann recorder quartet.

Doug was more of a softy. His rapport with the music kids at school was legendary. As with Mr Savage, Doug imparted great knowledge and wisdom, and gave us latitude to develop as individuals. We felt cared for, trusted and respected by him, and gave that back in spades. He cared for us even when it was not his responsibility. After I had sat my Grade 7 flute exam and got an A, Doug said to me, 'Trace, you know you didn't deserve that mark. You didn't do the work.' He was right, of course. My teacher hadn't pushed me or held me to higher account about my slackness when it came to practising and doing my scales. (Urghhhh!) I needed pushing. My internal motivation was very dodgy in some areas and developing more tenacity around the 'boring' stuff is probably something I could have developed with the right guidance and push. (I can guarantee my accountant wishes the same thing!) It wasn't Doug's job to do this as he wasn't my direct flute teacher, but I do wonder what might have happened to my journey if I'd learnt it back then? Maybe I would have got that gold flute my dad promised me if I made it into the Melbourne Symphony Orchestra! I probably wouldn't be here writing this book though. Sliding doors.

Both John and Doug were strong leaders in their own way and both impacted my own leadership approach. My study of leaders has shown me it's possible to combine the two: the ferocity and the warmth. Doug did this in the most endearing manner. His purpose was clear and his expectations were high, while maintaining relationships and really *seeing* individuals, their strengths and foibles, and still loving them for who they are. Leadership expert and author John Maxwell's 'treat them not as they are but as they could be' is a great example of the Doug-style Ferocious Warmth leader.

Through my teaching career and stints in the automotive and restaurant sectors, my leaders did amazing things as I watched and experienced their leadership. One of my earliest education leaders moved swiftly from being a new principal, through the education system right up to the CEO of a leadership institute. Another led a national training board. Yet another created a fine-dining restaurant that still delivered exquisite quality for diners some 20 years after opening, and grew a number of Australia's well-known chefs. From all of my leaders I discovered gems about leadership, and some strong messages of what not to do as well...

When I presented a wise and esteemed principal of many years with some concepts, she advised me: 'Never forget, Tracey, that I am an English teacher at heart. Give me practical, actionable tips that I can take away and try that will make my leadership better, just like I would give practical feedback advice to a student essay.' Other leaders like a more theoretical exploration of the challenges and concepts, drawing from journal articles and research to guide their learning. Common feedback on my first book for education *The Buzz – Creating a Thriving and Collaborative Learning Culture* is around its practical nature and the way research is drawn from but does not overwhelm the writing. I have strived to keep that balance here.

This book uncovers the patterns of thinking, beliefs and approaches that Ferocious Warmth leaders use to lead and remain in balance between the two. Not bounce between extremes – too harsh or too soft, too analytical or too emotional. It highlights the challenges of being out of balance and the impact this can have on ourselves and others. Throughout the book there are reflection opportunities, where I encourage you to put the book down to consider the concept being discussed. This is also a time to identify the thinking, beliefs and approaches that you put out to the world.

I hope this book gives you an opportunity to celebrate the skills you already possess and builds new ways to step into the equilibrium of the Ferocious Warmth leader. Many people have lent their thinking and insights to the development of the Ferocious Warmth concept over a number of years. I've observed some in action in their 'native habitat' (I do feel like Sir David Attenborough sometimes) and interviewed about leadership and life.

I am incredibly grateful to every leader and others for allowing me to test my theories and willingly delve into the whys and hows of their thinking, feeling and behaviours. Some of these people are found in the stories of this book, others greatly impacted the conceptualisation of this approach, even though their name may not appear through the text. I thank you all for your wisdom and openness and for being my guinea pigs!

chapter one

THE WORLD NEEDS MORE COURAGEOUS AND CARING LEADERSHIP

Leaders who can balance results and relationships are needed now more than ever. The stakes are high. Quality wellbeing and learning outcomes for students, educators and support staff, schools and systems, not to mention leaders themselves is becoming more complex. High levels of mental health issues and disengagement are changing the dynamics of classrooms and the role of the teacher. The democratisation of knowledge and increased learning occurring outside the classroom via technology, mounts pressure on teaching and learning within the school system to remain relevant and engaging. Education is at a time of immense and needed change. It takes both courage to address these wicked problems, as well as deep understanding of how humans work and what we need to thrive in change. Creating this change as a collective is critical to dealing with our most pressing challenges:

- Up to 40% of our students are disengaged in learning.[1]
- Youth mental health issues are continuing to rise, as is youth suicide.[2]
- Disadvantaged students are more likely to experience inequity in educational opportunities and outcomes.[3]
- Youth unemployment is at the highest rate in twenty years.[4]
- Families disenfranchised from school lower student outcomes.[5]

- Lack of student voice and agency increases disengagement in learning.[6]
- Education that helps students thrive now and in the future beyond school requires three types of skills: social and emotional, cognitive and meta-cognitive; practical and physical skills. Fostering these authentically is a challenge for both schools and systems.[7]

As education is essentially about learning and growing, it's ironic that most schools and school systems have not evolved much over the last 150 years. The move to remote learning during the 2020 COVID-19 pandemic has seen the biggest radical shift in education delivery since schooling began. Some schools found it a perfect opportunity to learn new ways of working and connecting with students, the community adapting as they learnt about what worked and what didn't. The audacious shift of education to deal with the context was exciting to witness, as it showed just how adaptable and responsive educators can be.

I am privileged to be exposed to many leaders and teachers who are continually evolving learning and teaching. They are pushing against 'the way we've always done it' to grow strong learning cultures that are not prepared to accept the status quo. They are true learners in partnership with their students, co-constructing a teaching and learning environment responsive to the Imagination Age, the age of entrepreneurial opportunity and a democratisation of knowledge. They are ferocious about this purpose, and have the warmth and belief in people to create a movement towards a different paradigm. You'll find some of these leaders and teachers within the pages of this book. Yet there are many more out there who are, together, fuelling a movement to provide education that not only helps our young people gain the skills and attitudes they need for a fulfilling life in a complex world, but also experience joyful, connected relationships and learning along the way. They are courageously pushing against the comfort zone in a way that compels others to join. I call them Ferocious Warmth leaders.

Ferocious Warmth leaders help those around them lift the quality of daily interactions in schools to transform education. Ferocious Warmth leaders aim to eradicate mediocrity. Beige thinking and relationships do not sit well with Ferocious Warmth leaders.

How do you spot mediocrity? Researchers in the Netherlands used the term 'mentality of mediocrity' when identifying factors in higher education students described as 'strategically exerting the minimum effort necessary to get passing grades.' [8] This was found to be a strategy utilised by students to get the grades good enough to get through, perhaps reducing cognitive dissonance, and not an indicator of their abilities, or their learning regulation. It also showed that the students used this approach strategically depending on the perceived importance of the task. If you put the lens over your school, can you sense a 'mentality of mediocrity' where you don't believe it's appropriate? Are there educators that accept mediocrity for their teaching practice? Do too many of your students aim for 'just good enough'?

The word mediocrity doesn't fit the purpose of schools. It doesn't serve education or quality relationships. Ferocious Warmth is about rejecting cognitive or emotional 'average'. Cognitive and emotional mediocrity won't help us deal with the big challenges we face.

Cognitive mediocrity is feeling comfort with the status quo: happy with the strategy and thinking that keeps us stagnant or, at the very least, only just keeping up with what society needs from us, rather than leading the education directions that respond to a changing world. In this realm we are OK with underperformance or teachers who don't really want to be there, content to keep doing things the way we've always done.

Emotional mediocrity is being satisfied with low levels of trust and empathy in our cultures, punitive management of behaviours and poor adult performance. It's leadership that gets results via emotional negligence or emotional manipulation. It creates an environment where the professional relationships are parent/child-like rather than adult to adult. Relationships between students and teachers are aloof, disconnected and based on content rather than learning.

To get to extraordinary in both emotional and cognitive approach, you need both courage to lift the bar and care to support a culture of wellbeing.

WHAT IS YOUR EXTRAORDINARY?

As a leader, what would you do if you and your team were bolder? What is your vision? What transformation, shift of the status quo or rise above mediocrity are you leading? Is it teaching and learning or relationships and culture? Perhaps it's all of these? Is it building professional trust to learn more from each other or implementing a new approach to literacy or numeracy? Or perhaps it's time to innovate into the next phase of 21st century learning? What big picture impact do you want for your students? What do your students want for their learning?

> WHAT IS EXTRAORDINARY FOR YOUR SCHOOL AND COMMUNITY? WHETHER IT'S A SMALL EVOLUTION OR A LARGE REVOLUTION, FEROCIOUS WARMTH PROVIDES THE BALANCE YOU NEED TO HAVE THE COURAGE FOR CHANGE AND THE PROFESSIONAL TRUST TO ENABLE THE MOVEMENT.

If you haven't thought much about your 'extraordinary', I encourage you to imagine where you would take your school with the momentum, strategy and commitment to get there? What are you ferocious about? Committed to? How can you co-create this vision with your community? Have you the trust and relationships to get there? Do people see both conviction and connection as your strengths? Are you ferocious and warm?

LOOKING WITHIN

Leadership is messy. School leadership is especially so. Everyday there are myriad cross relationships and interactions that go on in classrooms, staff rooms, corridors and playgrounds. Leading in the messy middle is hard work, constantly pulling us in one direction or another. Our ability to lead with balance and calmness can be a daily challenge. Yet many of us walk through the world totally unconscious of the affect our leadership has on others.

While self-awareness is usually first on the agenda for many leadership programs, these often do not go deep enough, failing to open our eyes to the internal drivers of our underpinning, often unconscious beliefs.

Leadership is about a way of being, not doing. It's nebulous, nuanced and elusive. It is as much to do with feeling and energy as thinking and planning. It's contextual and responsive, and can never be one size fits all.

When you meet a Ferocious Warmth leader you know it. You feel the vibe. When I share the Ferocious Warmth approach with others, many can immediately name one or two leaders who fill the criteria outlined in this book. These leaders have built more leaders through an environment characterised by high challenge and high support. They have brought together community and school, mended broken trust and lifted outcomes for students. They've instilled hope and joy in those they lead and created a collaborative culture that fronts up to the hard conversations. Ferocious Warmth leaders also have a Ferocious Warmth leadership team. If they move into a school without one, building leadership capacity in others is one of their first strategies.

Yet, too often more people have experienced leaders who've led in an unbalanced and uncentered way, focussed too much on results or too much on relationships. This is not useful to anyone. One is a win-at-all-costs approach, the other usually entails indecisive direction and a greater focus on the welfare and relationships of the teachers over the good of the students.

Leanne was a deputy principal in a primary school. She often felt caught in the vortex of having to play the other half to her principal. Leanne's principal was a person with strong compassion for others who listened deeply to what others thought. Unfortunately, though, when inappropriate staff behaviours occurred, Leanne was called in to deal with it. This became a good cop/bad cop exercise that no one won. Highly stressed by this, Leanne felt her principal was not standing up for what she believed. In private to Leanne, the principal would acknowledge what she thought the teacher should do, but not say it directly. This was left up to Leanne, while the principal herself made overtly empathetic acts to the teacher without mentioning the actual issue. Apart from an unfair responsibility on Leanne to hold the person to account, this also created a habit of leadership that expected one person to be responsible for accountability and the tougher conversations.

Others have the opposite situation. Joe was a fearsome leader who was so focussed on data and student outcomes that he badly affected morale and staff engagement. Joe was acting principal at a school that had focussed clearly on their professional culture, and teaching and learning practice. During the two years prior to Joe's arrival, there'd been a positive shift in attitudes to school, collaborative culture and consistent pedagogy. But over a six-month period, it seemed as if a systematic destruction of the work they'd done took place. After actively building professional trust and breaking down silos with the previous principal, this leader rarely had the staff meet together. There was a divide and conquer approach. People no longer felt safe to open their mouths. Unbelievably, one person was terminated in front of others. Implausible, but true. The acting principal continued on, obsessing over results and displaying abysmal emotional intelligence, while staff morale went from 98% the previous year to 48%. When the principal returned, she had to lead the rebuilding. Fortunately, she is a Ferocious Warmth leader.

FOCUSSING ONLY ON RESULTS

Leading a results-at-all-costs culture at the expense of support and empathy ends in cultural and wellbeing demise. How do we inspire our people for the stretch that transformational work requires while providing the safety nets to thrive and grow? More broadly: how do educational leaders ensure we zero in on results that matter, wider than the narrow definitions the media and bureaucracy encourage the community to focus on?

There is incredible pressure on school leadership to lead a school that performs. As it should. No one wants to send their children to a school with unskilled educators or who don't care about student wellbeing. Unfortunately, our measurement systems are geared to a narrow concept of success, characterised by a snapshot assessment of literacy and numeracy in the form of standardised testing leading to the pointy end of a university entrance score only useful for a small percentage of university courses. While many schools believe that this one-eyed focus is in no small measure killing the major purpose of education, and needs to change, it is still the predominant way schools and student learning are assessed.

When schools are structured around control, standardisation and compliance, among the first things to lose are trusting, meaningful relationships.'

Michael Wehmeyer, Yong Zhao, 'Teaching Students to Become Self Determined Learners[9]

When we focus too much on the standard results of targets and well-worn standards of achievement levels, we stay firmly stuck in the old paradigm of education, which is out of date and not relevant. From a human leadership point of view, we lose the heart and soul of education: students who thrive and contribute in a complex and challenging world. Not just in the future, but now. We need Ferocious Warmth leaders at a system level and a school level for the shift to happen in earnest, from policy to implementation.

FOCUSSING ONLY ON RELATIONSHIPS

Yet we also have leaders who maintain goodwill and harmony over the need for robust dialogue, hard decisions and shift. This is a tricky position. In some cases, I've worked with leaders unaware that their 'trusting' relationships were stopping the school moving forward. They were stuck, not wanting to speak their truth to people for fear of causing a massive blow up or a passive-aggressive reaction of snide comments and being 'frozen out'. The personal trust did not create the environment of rigorous conversations. This can lead to complacency, avoidance and a 'digging in' when true transformation is required to achieve results. Open discussion and lifting the bar is seen as conflict, even unfair.

We end up with The Spoilt Brat Syndrome – high levels of support expected but low levels of challenge accepted. In some schools, the time, resources and support teachers get is incredibly generous, yet the expectations for growth and continued transformation are low. Then watch the fast and furious push back when expectations are raised by internal change, the system or the community.

THE GOLDILOCKS OPTION

The conflict of courageous and compassionate leadership – stay a course of action or back away – is real. As is the overwhelming pressure on educational leaders to be all things to all people. Every day brings the need for swift and brave decision-making while leading strategic shift, coupled with deep empathy to ensure the wellbeing of our people. The not-too-tough, not-too-kind but just right approach.

I recently coached a senior executive within a large education system. She is well respected by her peers and those she leads. Yet she felt that around the executive table she needed more courage to speak with conviction about the skills she brought to the table. Her strengths lay on the 'warm' side – deep listening, empathy, emotional awareness. While her senior colleagues are open and respectful in lateral relationships, she feels that her executive colleagues are cold, aloof and hierarchical with those they lead. She believes they're not getting the best out of everyone, due to a lack of empathy, collaboration and collective orientation. Staff survey results support her concern. Here is her challenge: to influence her executive peers to see that the warmth side of leadership is just as important as ferocity.

Do you see both sides as critical? Or do you think that the warmth of leadership is just 'soft and fluffy'?

Jacinda Ardern, Prime Minister of New Zealand leading during one of the most challenging global and local periods, is a well-known example of these two characteristics. Leading with compassion through earthquakes, volcano eruptions, terrorist attacks and a global pandemic, people were quick to try to put Ardern in a box that she was too soft to lead well. Her response to a question on leadership on the US Today Show[10] on NBC in September 2018 went viral:

'I really rebel against this idea that politics has to be a place full of ego and where you're constantly focused on scoring hits against one another. Yes, we need a robust democracy, but you can be strong, and you can be kind.'

Leadership requires us to pull from our strengths, values and contextualise these in the moment. It is this adaptive ability that helps Ferocious Warmth leaders do the dance between ferocity and warmth. The concept has been captured in such approaches as adaptive leadership and transformational leadership. Ronald Heifetz and his colleagues argue in the book *The Practice of Adaptive Leadership*, that adaptive leadership is a practice not a theory, defining it as the 'practice of mobilising people to tackle tough challenges and thrive'[11] The same is true for Ferocious Warmth. Mediocrity and status quo are the antithesis of this type of leadership. Action makes all the difference.

Our general leadership history is one of logic, cognition and technical skill, focussing on results at the expense of the people doing the work or receiving the service. It's a more 'masculine' energy view of leadership that minimises empathy, feelings and connection. A top-down hierarchical structure where our 'level' within an organisation defined our voice and value. You could fill a library with books written about leadership full of war stories and leadership lessons glorifying hero leadership and a 'command and control' approach. To make it as a leader, competition, sabotage and a dog-eat-dog climb to the top. This may seem overly emotive, yet walk into many organisations in the legal, financial or medical sectors and you will see this type of culture alive and well. The research clearly shows that amid this predominant style, disengagement, mental health issues and low morale are rife.

The last twenty years has seen research delve further into the impact of the concepts of trust, empathy, warmth and joy in the workplace. Neuroscience and the use of fMRIs (functional medical radio imaging) is unearthing more connections that show that these things impact the neural pathways our brains use and the engagement of the more evolved part of the brain, the prefrontal cortex. The connection and interaction of the prefrontal cortex and the limbic brain is impacted by a huge variety of factors, such as context, trauma, environment and connection. We will explore these findings further in the book as we explore the elements of Ferocious Warmth.

THE IMPACT OF THE EXTREMES

Through the COVID-19 lock down in March 2020, I had the privilege of working with a number of leadership groups as they steadied themselves through the rollercoaster of each week, each day. The stories of how they, with their teams, made swift and massive shifts come with inspiring examples of leaders connecting, supporting and leading strategically. Educators led the way with this 'pivot', moving to online learning in a matter of weeks. The whole of society learnt so much about how we individually deal with immense pressure and the need for quick action and 'building the plane as it's flying'. Not all leadership stories are like this.

As restrictions eased in my home state, I grabbed the chance to hang out with a couple of my friends. We shared stories of what was happening in our lives and I heard two very different leadership tales.

One of my friends works in a health network, with thousands of workers on the front line of COVID-19. They were swiftly mobilised to be ready, armed for pandemic proportion health impacts if needed, as well as creating a safe and functioning workforce. The other friend works in a small company that supports businesses, which has a workforce of around 50 across a large geographical distance.

Here are the two scenarios (summarised and in no particular order). Can you guess which is which?

SCENARIO 1

1. No acknowledgement from leaders as to the challenges people are dealing with at home, including children at home learning, compromised immune systems and general stress and anxiety.

2. Little interaction from senior management in how to deal with the challenges of the new situation.
3. No external display of support and compassion for the tough times experienced by either the team or the clients.
4. A requirement that all normally expected KPIs (key performance indicators) would be met during this time.
5. No regular check-ins or connection from the senior leader to team members on a personal level.
6. No special professional learning put in place to help people cope more effectively.

How does my friend feel? Disconnected, unseen, undervalued, burnt out, angry, untrusted and untrusting.

Leadership approach: we've got work to do. I don't care about the pain you might be in – get on with it. That's the very extreme of ferocity – it's fearsome.

SCENARIO 2

1. Planning from the outset as to how the pandemic would affect those they serve and the workers.
2. Twice weekly online forums with an open invitation to all.
3. Executive present at both forums to answer questions.
4. Feedback loops so that unanswered questions are responded to.
5. Next-level leaders maintaining high levels of communication with their teams.

How does my friend feel? Connected, heard, in the loop, valued, able to contribute, committed, understanding and understood.

Leadership approach: we've got work to do so let's do it together. That's Ferocious Warmth.

Scenario 1 is the smaller organisation. It could be easy to assume that the smaller the organisation, the greater the compassion, support and connection people would feel from the leadership team. The easier the direct contact should be, the greater insight into personal situations. It is distressing to see a friend who I know gives her all to her clients and works hard, feeling so disheartened and stressed.

In scenario 2, the executive led the complex organisation with positivity and appreciation, transparency and accessibility through the most major crisis to hit us in a couple of generations. Did they get it right all the time? Probably not, and hopefully they'd see any missteps (trials, pilots, experiments) as learning, acknowledge it and shift to try another tack. Agility and flexibility have, at their roots, a deep learning foundation, one that takes on continuous feedback and shifts to respond. This was unchartered territory. We needed leaders willing to let us sail into new waters and test out what works.

The other? Well, I'm wondering what was happening for the leadership of that business. As leaders, our role is to support our people to be their best, not beat them into the ground with a results-at-all-cost approach, especially in times of extreme crisis challenging every person one way or another. While tough decisions need to be made at this time, in this case there seems to be little thought about the support people need from their leaders to manage as best they can.

Do you have the balance of Ferocious Warmth to be able to get people there? We need ferocity to even contemplate our aspirations and turn them into action. But more than ever we also need warmth to authentically convey: I care for you as people and I'm here by your side every step of the way.

chapter two

FEROCIOUS WARMTH

I want to share with you the elation I feel when I discover a Ferocious Warmth leader. I can spot them from a hundred paces. I can feel their passion through the newsletters and videos on the school websites before I even meet them. I can hear it in the language they use as we speak via email, over the phone or virtually. I experience the connection they have with their students and staff as we walk through the school. I hear the belief and love they hold for those they serve expressed in their words. I can feel the psychological safety in place for people to raise and discuss ideas, differences of opinion and share personal challenges with them. I feel the sense of trust, fun and hard work that goes on in the halls and rooms of the school. I see them reflect with deep self-awareness on their own growth. I see the transformation they are leading within their community, how they lift expectations and build momentum to achieve the results and changes required. I hear the reputation they have within their collegiate networks. I see people walk away from working with these leaders just that little bit taller, ready to make their own ripples on the world.

Let's look at the two sides of Ferocious Warmth. Great leadership never uses them in isolation. The strengths come from both sides.

FEROCIOUS

There is a fierce congruence in this side of Ferocious Warmth leaders. They are focussed on their clear purpose of providing high-quality education for their students and courageous in making hard decisions along the way. They are strong advocates for their students, staff and their community. Most importantly, they challenge assumptions on how we 'do' education, whether it be shifting the structures, innovating practice or lifting out of complacency or mediocrity. They are fierce in their belief that education, as traditionally provided, needs to evolve. In some circumstances, these leaders are leading system revolution not just evolution.

WARMTH

Ferocious Warmth leaders work with compassion as a base for all relationships, regardless of who. From the student in the yard to the teacher in the classroom to the parent in the corridor, people feel connected to these leaders. People know they have their back in good times and in challenging circumstances. These leaders genuinely love people. I never hear them speaking anything other than constructive and positive comments about their staff, students and parents. Even those causing them stress and taking a lot of energy are treated with empathy and a real belief in the growth and positive intent of that person. Don't get me wrong, the leader still needs to debrief and sometimes gets blindsided by the behaviours of others. But the way they handle it comes from a position of compassion, not anger.

When we're at our best, ferocity and warmth, courage and vulnerability, results and relationships, head and hearts, need not be polarities, but nest inside each other. They support each other in every decision we make. If we are focussed on strategically achieving our purpose, and constantly building our emotional intelligence to understand how to best serve our people, they go together hand in glove. Our challenge is staying in balance when the going gets tough and ensuring the blend is right.

Figure 1. Ferocious Warmth – Drawing from Both Sides

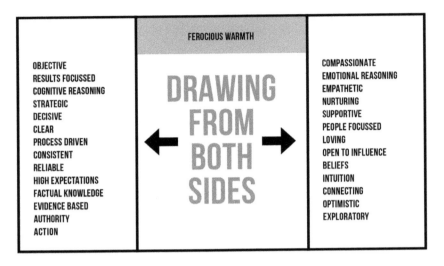

BE THE BLEND

As I was blogging about the emerging concept of Ferocious Warmth, an assistant principal emailed me describing her principal:

'I am wanting to "dob in" my Principal. She is definitely the Ferocious Warmth leader you are talking about. That person who stands out amongst all leaders.

In Term 4 of last year, she was appointed Principal and I was appointed Assistant Principal. At the beginning of this year, two more Assistant Principals and two more Learning Specialists were appointed. As you can imagine establishing trust with a brand new leadership team is a difficult thing to do but this was made particularly difficult given the history of the school where four years ago some of our staff members were subjected to trauma at the hands of a previous leadership team. The ripples of this can still be felt.

Ellen has that magic mix of warmth and ferocity and it is quite amazing to watch. She treats everyone with respect and connects with them on both a personal and professional level. She speaks kindly to all members of the community from the Foundation child to the difficult parent. She also gets things done – quickly, efficiently and will leave no stone unturned when there is an issue that needs to be resolved. I love listening to some of the most crucial conversations that have the ability to leave people feeling slighted or offside, but she turns them around so that people are prepared to work for the greater good. Although it is taking time, you can definitely feel the beginnings of a cultural shift in our school community.'

What a beautiful example of the leader who knows that the recipe is not the 'head' or the 'heart', but a *blend* of these. Knowing when to lift the bar, knowing when to deeply listen and hold the space. This is the magic of the Ferocious Warmth leader. Of the leaders I interviewed, many mentioned the intuitive way they lead. In our discussions, I sought to unpack this intuition and create some frameworks that underpin the approach, which we explore throughout the chapters.

All of these leaders deeply believe that relationships are the critical piece to develop. This certainly doesn't mean they ignore getting the work done. The work is their driving purpose. But they share the need to get beyond the 'technical' descriptions of leadership and into 'feeling' – the empathy, connection and humanness of leading. A sense of being that is deeply connected to those around.

TO BE, NOT TO DO

Research into leadership beyond what to 'do' towards how to 'be' in education is somewhat limited. It can seem intangible and elusive – something science can find hard to pin down. Discussions about characteristics, personal effectiveness and culture can be presented in rather unfriendly and hard-to-access language. One of the many things I admire about global education leader Professor Michael Fullan is his ability to write in a way that captures our heads and our hearts, while drawing on the evidence base. His 'sticky messages' come through in both his writing and presenting. Artful curation of academic leadership research, accessible and practical is a wonderful gift for time poor school leaders. The late Sir Ken Robinson influenced so many of us as educators in his life-long crusade against boring education fitting a 19th century paradigm. His message was made more powerful by his storytelling, viral TED talk and the visual animation that accompanied his talk – all making links between theory and practice. I also unashamedly look beyond education to research and application in the areas of neuroleadership, courage, shame, learning cultures, and emotional and conversational intelligence. People such as Professor Amy Edmondson, Judith E. Glaser, Brené Brown, Amy Cuddy, David Rock and Daniel Goleman have all straddled the difficult chasm of translating research around leadership 'being' into practical, accessible approaches.

Our leadership learning should never end. In the thousands of leaders I have met and worked with over the years, the most inspiring leaders are those who are explicitly still learning their craft. Still making mistakes, trying new things, reflecting and adjusting. They are the true embodiment of Fullan's 'lead learner' label. Not leading learner from the stance of an expert, but a co-learner. Always reflecting, learning, expanding.

Some leadership approaches suggest your leadership teams should contain people who 'balance you out', once you learn your 'leadership style' during a leadership program. To me this totally misses the point of leadership development.

> SCHOOL LEADERS WHO ARE LEAD LEARNERS SEEK TO FIND AND DEVELOP THE LEADERSHIP THAT CREATES THE MOST IMPACT AND TRANSFORMATION.

Therefore, our task is to keep learning what makes the best leadership in education, schools and systems at any given time, and build that capability. But the intricacy and duality of many of the leadership tensions people face every day, sometimes a number of times an hour, is not prescriptive. Nor is it an easy formula.

The answer lies in the Ferocious Warmth approach.

THE KEY PIECES OF THE FEROCIOUS WARMTH FORMULA

- The Infinity Symbol – a visual that brings the concept to life.
- Three Intelligences – areas of thinking and skill development that, when blended, form Ferocious Warmth leadership and create buy in, continuous improvement and potential.
- Four Elements – underpinning ways of being that serve as the foundation of Ferocious Warmth leaders.

THE INFINITY SYMBOL

If you were to visualise Ferocious Warmth as an image, what would it be? The words are a metaphor in themselves. They evoke the lioness, holding her cub in her mouth protecting it from prey, while at the same time pushing the cub to take a risk by standing on its own paws. I recently saw a video of a giraffe being born. As it lay on the ground, seemingly not breathing, the mother stood next to it, licking it and pushing it until the baby took a breath. Within a few minutes, the mother was nudging the baby to get up on its legs. It stumbled and fell over. Again, the mother pushed. The baby managed to move towards its mother, hoping to take refuge against the mother's legs. The mother shoved it away until it got the idea and moved by itself. Cruel? No of course not. It's the only way the baby giraffe will survive in the wild. The mother was there protecting and pushing. Stretch and safety. Ferocity and warmth.

The infinity symbol defines the constant push and pull that leadership requires. It also suggests the duality and paradox of drawing from ways of thinking and feeling that seem diametrically opposed – courageous yet vulnerable, strategic yet people centred. It invokes the flow of the Yin and the Yang, the masculine and the feminine.

Figure 2. Ferocious Warmth Symbol

The power of this symbol sits in the centre, the overlap, where we stand with conviction, balanced with both sides at play. We draw in energy from both sides to create a leadership approach that is adaptable and responsive.

'In the past, I felt I ran the infinity laps. Now I feel I stand in the middle leaning left then right. Then a new day starts and I do it again – breathe, balance and believe.'

Ainslie Peszynksi, Regional Leading Teacher

When I speak about the Ferocious Warmth symbol, I cannot help but move my body from side to side in a rhythmic flow drawing from left and right, visualising the internal dance great leaders make as they go about their work.

> THE DANCE IS CONSTANT IN THE FEROCIOUS WARMTH LEADER. THEY ARE NOT STAGNANT OR STILL. ALWAYS MOVING WITHIN THE CONTEXT, BUT ALIGNED TO THEIR VALUES AND PRINCIPLES.

Imagine Mr Miyagi in Karate Kid teaching his student how to 'wax on and wax off'. Poised, focussed, committed.

THE THREE INTELLIGENCES OF FEROCIOUS WARMTH LEADERS

Woven through the chapters of this book are areas of skill that pull from three intelligences, which, when used together, create the platform for the Ferocious Warmth leader. These intelligences focus on three areas: the people – emotional intelligence, the purpose and plan – strategic intelligence, and building the potential of all – learning intelligence. Below I list some examples of characteristics of each.

EMOTIONAL INTELLIGENCE — THE PEOPLE:
- Managing self and others
- Buy in and commitment
- Self-compassion and empathy
- Values and ways of being
- Building and connecting community
- Emotional reasoning.

STRATEGIC INTELLIGENCE — THE PURPOSE AND PLAN:

- Systems thinking
- Vision
- Purpose
- Strategy
- Mental models
- Goal clarification
- Prioritising
- Resourcing
- Action.

LEARNING INTELLIGENCE — THE POTENTIAL OF ALL:

- Growing a professional learning community
- Leader as learner
- Collaboration and collective efficacy
- Innovation
- Agility and flexibility
- Conversations that matter.

Figure 3. The Three Intelligences of Ferocious Warmth

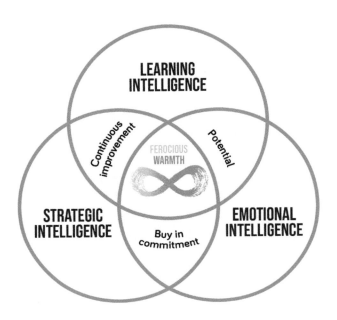

EMOTIONAL INTELLIGENCE — THE PEOPLE

In 2007, I was accredited in the emotional intelligence tool created by Professor Con Stough and Dr Ben Palmer – the Swinburne University Emotional Intelligence Tool, now known as the Genos tool and used globally to build emotional intelligence in workplaces. I've always found their first definition of emotional intelligence one of the most accessible and concise explanations of the term:

Emotional intelligence refers to the ability to perceive, understand and manage emotions in self and others. [12]

Ferocious warmth is deeply steeped in emotional intelligence. Our emotional awareness of others gives us the insights to shift our leadership to meet the needs of those we lead. It also reminds us to focus on self-care and compassion. The skill of emotional self-awareness is step number one for all leaders. Starting with self is the step towards growth.

'It's not always easy to reckon with our own and others' emotional lives. But when kids and adults are given the permission to feel all emotions,

and learn how to manage them, it opens doors to collaboration, relationship building, improved decision-making and performance, and greater wellbeing. Almost all the essential ingredients for success arise from emotion skills.' [13]

Professor Marc Brackett's book *Permission to Feel: Unlock the Power of Emotions to Help Our Kids, Ourselves, and Our Society to Thrive* offers five key emotion skills:

- I am able to accurately recognise my own and others' emotions
- I am aware of the causes and consequences of my own and others' feelings
- I have a refined emotion vocabulary
- I am skilled at expressing the full range of emotions
- I am skilled at managing my own emotions and at helping others manage theirs.

The Ferocious Warmth themes of perception, understanding and managing emotions come through these statements. Professor Brackett shares the experience of running an intensive for a school district. The course included a principal initially resistant to the concepts. By the end of the course the same principal, when asked what he thought now about emotions and integrating emotional skills into his school, answered: 'I realise now that I didn't know what I didn't know. The language of feelings was foreign to me. So, thank you for giving me permission to feel.' This is a school leader stepping into the warmth side of his leadership with more mindfulness.

If you know that integrating feelings into the way you lead and work in the world is a challenge, keep an eye out for the emotional intelligence woven throughout the stories and thinking in this book. Being able to bring these into your leadership is the main intelligence that will help centre you in your Ferocious Warmth. The four elements of Ferocious Warmth – expansion, connection, courage and authenticity – are full of emotional-intelligence skills. Like the delicious Italian dessert tiramisu, layered sponge cake soaked in coffee and marsala, all of these elements are soaked in emotional intelligence. It's learnable and makes a greater difference to leadership outcomes than IQ.

There are many excellent resources available to help build these emotional intelligence skills, such as Professor Brackett's book *Permission to Feel.* Daniel

Goleman's *The New Leaders* was one of the first leadership books that gave an accessible and practical overview of emotional intelligence in action. A book I highly recommend is *Step In, Step Up* by Jane A.G. Kise and Barbara K. Watterston.[14] Kise and Watterston are highly experienced educators and leadership development experts. The book is full of insightful activities to build your emotional intelligence. It's written for women in education leadership, but the theory, application and activities are applicable to all.

STRATEGIC INTELLIGENCE — THE PURPOSE AND THE PLAN

Do you know the people in your school with a strategic mind? Those who can rise above the details to see the key questions to ask, the major strategies to address? Many school teams suffer from confusion and burn out due to the lack of focus on thinking strategically about where to leverage and effect change. A leader with strategic intelligence forges a path that sets out the stepping stones to our vision. Strategic intelligence connects the what to the how to the why. We don't get far if we don't have a purpose and a plan or if we can't connect the work we're doing to a strong why that goes far beyond 'to improve student outcomes'. This is an outcome, not a purpose for education. Strategic intelligence takes us from the high-level vision to the action to get there. It takes in the resourcing needed, clarifies the goals and shapes the future.

Strategic intelligence is also understanding the mental models we use to view the world. Often these mental models are totally unconscious. Peter Senge is a global expert on systems thinking and organisational strategy. His book *The Fifth Discipline: The Art and Practice of the Learning Organization*[15] is one of the most influential strategic culture books ever published. He believes that mental models are one of the key definers of strong organisational culture, summarised below:

'Differences between mental models explain why two people can observe the same event and describe it differently; they are paying attention to different details. But because mental models are usually tacit, existing below the level of awareness, they are often untested and unexamined. They are generally invisible to us – until we look for them. The core of this discipline is bringing mental models to the surface, to explore and talk about them with minimal defensiveness – to help us see the pane of glass, see its impact on our

lives, and find ways to re-form the glass by creating better mental models that serve us better in the world.'

Ferocious Warmth leaders seek to unpack their 'models of the world' and shape their thinking and approaches strategically. We are surrounded by mental models that have shaped our world. Recently I talked with a school principal who'd gone through a leadership program I ran over a decade ago. She told me that some of the mental models we explored through that program were still her 'go to' models when she needed to do some deep thinking. Models such as Argyris' Ladder of Inference, Heifetz and Linksy's Balcony and Dancefloor, and the Johari window by Joseph Luft and Harry Ingham. Some of these models are over 50 years old, yet they stand the test of time for smart leaders.

LEARNING INTELLIGENCE — THE POTENTIAL OF ALL

The last intelligence is the intelligence of growth, for both the individual and the organisation. It's the ability to be a learner and create a learning culture for those we lead. Learning intelligence has three levels – self, team and school. At a team and school level this learning intelligence is what I call The Buzz. It is the essence of a strong collaborative professional learning culture. My first book *The Buzz – Creating a Thriving & Collaborative Learning Culture* was dedicated to unpacking the three pillars of The Buzz – mindset, environment and authentic dialogue. It focussed on three levels for an effective learning culture:

'Learning intelligence needs to be evident at three levels for a school to create a truly thriving professional learning culture. These three levels are like the layers of an onion. In the centre is the individual. The strength of learning intelligence in each individual member affects the quality of the outer layers. The middle layer represents all the teams within the school structure and the way they work together. The outer layer is the school unit as a complete, thriving learning organisation. If one of these levels is not pulling its weight in regard to learning, the outcomes are not as strong.' [16]

SELF

Leaders with a strong learning intelligence thrive on being out of the comfort zone and in the learning zone. They are voracious learners. The Ferocious Warmth approach to learning is one that is antifragile, instead of being resilient with change and arming ourselves against what might happen, Ferocious Warmth leaders face the oncoming storm and yell 'bring it on', revelling in the challenge and the opportunities to innovate, shift to get better outcomes and continually evolve.

Nassim Taleb defines antifragility as:

'Some things benefit from shocks; they thrive and grow when exposed to volatility, randomness, disorder, and stressors, and love adventure, risk, and uncertainty. Yet, in spite of the ubiquity of the phenomenon, there is no word for the exact opposite of fragile. Let us call it antifragile. Antifragility is beyond resilience or robustness. The resilient resists shocks and stays the same; the antifragile gets better.' [17]

Now perhaps we could redefine antifragile with one number: 2020!

Even amidst the challenges and stresses, did you approach the world during 2020 as a learner? With a focus on the opportunities as well as the realities of leading through it? 2020 gave us lived experience of being in the learning zone… were you thriving or just surviving?

TEAM AND SCHOOL

Schools are in the business of learning, yet developing and maintaining a staff culture of learning is a challenge for many schools. The Buzz diagnostic survey has been undertaken by over 8000 educators and 280 schools over the past two years. Using The Buzz pillars of mindset, environment and dialogue, it asks participants to reflect on their own learning and contribution to the learning culture. It also asks them to assess the school's learning culture. The results clearly show that the most difficult part of building learning intelligence is taking the culture of learning to the collective. For schools with a low collaborative learning culture, the difference between how individuals see their own learning skills and how they see the school's is stark. Many see themselves as strong individual learners, but that the team culture is not a collective learning environment. Moving a learning culture from 'I' to 'we' is strategic work, yet it's often left to chance or done at a surface level.

Part of the work of learning intelligence is creating psychological safety, encouraging voice and contribution. We'll discuss this further in the chapters ahead – it is a critical piece of this puzzle. Above all else Ferocious Warmth leaders are committed to growing their people and themselves. They tap into and encourage the skills and talents of others. James Kouzes and Barry Posner, authors and leadership professors at Leavey School of Business, surveyed thousands of people about the 'worst' and 'best' leaders they had ever had. They asked 'what percentage of your talents (skills, ability plus time and energy) would you say each of these leaders brought out?' They then asked them to give a percentage from 1 to 100. When it came to the worst leaders, the answers ranged from 2% to 40%, with an average of 31%. In contrast, those labelled the 'best' leaders brought out between 40% to 100%, with an average of 95%.

'There's clearly a difference between people's worst and best leaders. The best leaders bring out more than three times the amount of talent, energy and motivation from their people compared with their counterparts at the other end of the spectrum.' [18]

Emotional, strategic and learning intelligence. These three intelligences work together to support the Ferocious Warmth leader and curate buy in, commitment and continuous improvement.

Figure 4. Ferocious Warmth Leadership

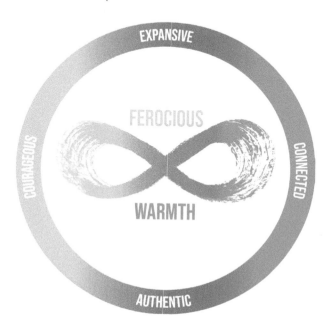

THE ELEMENTS OF FEROCIOUS WARMTH

Through both my work with Ferocious Warmth leaders and interviews during the writing of this book, four clear elements stand out from these great human beings. Though explored more deeply in the chapters beyond, through some Ferocious Warmth exemplars, the essence of these elements is:

EXPANSIVE

I am open to evolving my thinking, to disruption and innovation. I love learning with others and co-creating future pathways. I challenge my own thinking and other's. I see the world with optimism and possibility. I build collaborative learning cultures with others. I have high levels of self-awareness.

CONNECTED

I have a love for others. I believe and love the work I do and the people I work with. I approach people, no matter their circumstances, with a belief in their positive intent and inherent worth. I believe all people deserve kindness, compassion and empathy.

COURAGEOUS

I know what I stand for and my moral purpose. I am willing to make tough decisions based on my values and principles. I work with my people to address the hard challenges. I stand for what I believe in.

AUTHENTIC

My ability to lead is based on connection and collaboration with others. I let others see both my vulnerability and courage through authentic relationships. I use power to make the world a better place. I am who you see.

Figure 5. Ferocious Warmth Elements

I am open to evolving my thinking, to disruption and innovation.
I love learning with others and co-creating future pathways.
I challenge my own thinking and other's.
I see the world with optimism and possibility.
I build collaborative learning cultures with others.
I have high levels of self-awareness.

EXPANSIVE

FEROCIOUS

WARMTH

I know what I stand for and my moral purpose.
I am willing to make tough decisions based on my values and principles.
I work with others to address the hard challenges.
I stand for what I believe in.

I have a love for others.
I believe in & love the work I do and the people I work with.
I approach people, no matter their circumstances, believing in their positive intent and inherent worth.
I believe all people deserve kindness.

AUTHENTIC

My ability to lead is based on connection and collaboration with others.
I let others see both my vulnerability and courage through authentic relationships.
I use my power to make the world a better place.
I am who you see.

FEROCIOUS WARMTH IN ACTION

The elements and intelligences of Ferocious Warmth all work in concert, overlapping and informing each other at an almost unconscious level. Here's an example of the Ferocious Warmth approach in action.

Meagan Cook is a school principal I've known for over a decade. In 2017, Meagan moved from being an assistant principal and integral part of a well-connected leadership team, to becoming principal in a K-12 school. A few years prior the school had emerged from a challenging amalgamation of the local primary and high schools. Even with the best intentions and strategies of the merger school leaders, many of the staff did not want the amalgamation. They were anxious about it. And the high school's staff were traumatised by a particularly distressing school review prior to the merger. The college lurched through the first four years, not quite able to build strong connectedness, trust and community. Merging school communities is one of the hardest cultural undertakings to lead. The toll on school leaders and teachers doing this work can be difficult and exhausting.

Three years into her principalship I found a strong example of a Ferocious Warmth leader in action. As well as knowing that Meagan fulfils 'the goods' of Ferocious Warmth, two staff members from her new school emailed me to 'dob her in' when I called for nominations at a leadership conference. What follows is a powerful story from her first year at her school.

Meagan arrived just as the school had been reviewed. Not just the content, but also the way the report was delivered left the staff traumatised and demoralised. Many of you would have experienced the different ways a school review can unfold. Fortunately, through learning and processes evolving, most school reviews are thorough, robust explorations of both a school's strengths and its areas of growth. Data analysis and strong collegiate conversations within the school review panel, often with an experienced principal from another school as well, are coupled with conversation with the staff to ascertain where the school is at. System leaders have worked hard at reviewing their part to play as partners, not judges, in this process. At its worst though, when hard realities need to be faced in an already de-moralised culture, an external school reviewer when sharing the findings and the final report can inflict trauma, leaving leaders to pick up the pieces.

Meagan told me, 'I think I spent a lot of time wondering what I'd done, because the stories that came out in response to me taking this job on were around, "What the hell are you doing?" and "Why would you go there?" or "It's a really tough gig."' The review had shattered the staff and the organisation.' Meagan also believed that some of this reaction stemmed from staff experiences prior to the merger.

Reflection pause ...

Let's take a moment to identify the Ferocious Warmth elements involved in Meagan's approach. Even with this small window into her actions, we can observe the following:

Ferocious: courage to have potentially difficult conversations.

Warmth: empathy to seek to understand perspective and hold the space for people to be vulnerable. When we come from a curious and empathetic stance, people felt connected and not judged, exploration could then occur.

Meagan again. 'I also met with the reviewer who gave me some context. I felt her to be a pretty aggressive person. I met with the previous principal and got context from that perspective as well. I met with staff individually just for coffee and conversation. They talked about their history in the school, who they were out of the school. All of them turned to that review as part of that conversation.

'The school was not performing well in terms of the data that was examined. I got the sense through these conversations just how hurt people were. If you've been in a school for a year, you don't really own the data yourself, but even the people that had been there just that year were broken as a result of what had happened through that process. Just about every single one of them, at some point, brought up how they felt through the process of review. This was prior to us even getting the report. I heard all those stories. I heard about the trauma that had happened in the previous review prior to the merger and how they felt cut down to size. They really had the finger pointed at them, that it was their fault and they weren't good enough at the work they were doing. And so on. The stories were consistent. People that had been here for less time, were less invested, but still saw and experienced the angst.

'These conversations also brought out how upset people were with leadership. A lot of staff that had come into the amalgamation didn't want it and had used that as an opportunity to really go hard on the leadership of the school at the time It was an opportunity to have a go and say "it's their fault, not my fault". The previous leadership had to deal with some less-than professional behaviour.'

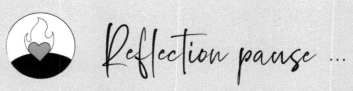

Reflection pause ...

Emotional and Strategic Intelligence guiding the Ferocious Warmth Leader's Reflection:

What is the context I am leading in?

What are people's emotional needs and current reality?

What strategic approach do I need to take to a) get this school moving forward strategically?

b) get this school moving forward culturally?

What does this community need from me as a leader right now?

How do I acknowledge the positive intentions and attributes of my predecessors?

FEROCIOUS ADVOCACY

Meagan was kind and frank in her dealings with everyone. 'I sat down with the reviewer and said, "The manner you have dealt with them so far has hurt them. When you present this report, it needs to be in a way that empowers them to move forward, not slapping them back to the ground." ' (Author's two cents worth... you'd think this would be in School Reviewer 101, wouldn't you? But over the years I've worked with too many schools that have suffered from fearsome feedback rather than Ferocious Warmth feedback from reviewers.) Meagan admits to being quite blunt in this conversation, but feels she had to be. The reviewer's PowerPoint presentation's footer claimed: '[this school's] kids fall behind' on every single slide, for council and for staff. In this statement, she invalidated everyone.

Meagan continues: 'That was a really interesting moment in the journey. I let her walk out the door that day and I rang my boss and said, "She's not coming back. I don't care how many hours we're meant to get from her. She's never walking back in this door again." I wrote to our community, both the school councillors and the staff: "What we heard is what we heard. Let's break it down to what we're going to do something about." I said that we weren't going to be beaten around the head about what we haven't done in the past. We were going to look towards what we could do in the future. It was time we advocated for our community.' Meagan also looked deeply at the data and found much more nuance, as well as growth that had not been highlighted by the reviewer and made sure to share this with the community. 'Because if you'd sat in that council, you would have pulled your kid out. I said, "We've heard a story but we're more than those bits of data that were highlighted. Let's move forward."'

Reflection pause ...

The image of Meagan standing there, essentially saying, "Back off, you are not helping. I'm protecting my staff. We'll do this work, but you're not helping," is incredibly powerful. Can you hear the Ferocious Warmth conviction that Meagan brings? She knows what she stands for and that her job is to look out for her people and community, just as much as to look out for the outcomes. Results and relationships. The school needed a strong advocate and got a principal that was prepared to have everyone's back, as well as lifting the bar.

This strong and courageous advocacy stance, coupled with intense listening and empathetic curiosity, led to strong trust in Meagan as the new principal. To do this with conviction, Ferocious Warmth leaders draw from their personal principles to keep that stance strong.

Does Meagan get it right all the time? Of course not. But she's on the ground, doing the work.

I asked Meagan to tell me about one of her most important principles when it comes to leading:

'I think it's about always assuming positive intent, regardless of what's being said or done. I don't believe anyone in schools, your own staff in particular, are out to get you or out to make things harder for anyone. We all make mistakes. Just asking a question can change our insights and understanding. A lot of people came to my door during the first year and said, "Apparently so and so did so and so." My first response is always: "Let's ask them." It took people time to realise that hearsay and one-sided commentary wouldn't cut it with me. I would say to my leaders: ask the question, and I also modelled that. Because often you find that apparently so and so isn't actually what's happening. So, my advice is, "Just ask the question." Then I'd ask the other person involved. They'd say, "Oh well, yeah. That's partly right but this is the rest of the story." It gives you a clearer picture. It also models the principles of restorative justice, which we enact throughout the school.'

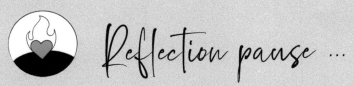

The principle of positive intent is a great example of the Ferocious Warmth element of CONNECTION. What are your stories of stepping into Ferocious Warmth? If you shared your story with others, could they identify the fluidity between ferocity and warmth? Would they hear the principles and values that underpin your leadership? Would they feel the connection to your purpose and the people you lead?

In contrast, the school review in 2020 was a very different experience. To start with the process has evolved since 2016. But the four years had also seen strong, strategic work in building a culture of connection and learning. There was a positive increase in all areas of the staff opinion survey, with all targets exceeded. At the beginning of the process the reviewer asked the team to write down what they hoped to achieve through the review. This is a powerful activity, which sets a frame of inquiry and openness at the beginning. Meagan wrote, 'To restore community confidence in the purpose and process of a school review and to celebrate the work that has been done.' Meagan saw this as an opportunity to again advocate for the community and challenge perceptions happening in the classrooms. This was definitely achieved through the review process.

Meagan: 'We know we still have a long way to go when it comes to improving academic outcomes for all students; however, we now have the preconditions in place to achieve this and the right mindset amongst staff to do the next layer of work. I have moved away from saying that we are lucky not to have blockers within our staff. It hasn't been luck. It's been the plan to develop a positive staff culture. We have invested in it, recruited for it, built structures to support and engage staff in the way forward and challenged it when it isn't being demonstrated.'

WHAT ABOUT TRUST?

Professional trust is one of the outcomes of Ferocious Warmth leadership. It can't be created by strategy, but through the concepts and elements we have just been introduced to. Meagan, for example, has built strong levels of trust in a short amount of time. Yet trust is not a *project*. It is a way of being. It's embedded in every behaviour, interaction, structure and process that surrounds leadership. It requires fine-tuned self-awareness and capacity building in both relational and professional competency.

In a literature review undertaken for the Australian Institute of School Teaching and Leadership in 2013, Dr Jessica Harris, Professor Brian Caldwell and Ms Fiona Longmuir[19] summarised their findings on trust:

'There are two especially noteworthy conclusions. The first is that trust does not stand alone as a discrete capacity: it is the lifeblood of success in virtually every structure and process that involves the principal and other school leaders. It is for this reason that one-off efforts to create trust are unlikely to succeed. Similarly, a contrived project, even if sustained, may breed distrust.

Second, while a headline finding that the quality of relationships is central to the creation of trust, the extent of that quality is influenced by many factors, including the competence of the leader: trust will be lost very quickly if a leader is perceived to be incompetent. It is therefore important to build strength in and draw on intellectual or professional capital in establishing relational trust.'

The critical statement here is: 'Trust does not stand alone as a discrete capacity: it is the lifeblood of success in virtually every structure and process that involves the principal and other school leaders.' In my book, *Glue – The Stuff That Binds Us Together to do Extraordinary Work*[20], I use a framework of Connection, Compassion and Conversation to guide leaders wanting to reflect on their organisational trust.

- Connection: to purpose, people and the work
- Compassion: people are seen and valued with empathy
- Conversation: dialogue is open, two way and about sharing and discovering.

All of these concepts are found in the stories throughout this book. Remember, Ferocious Warmth trust comes from head and heart, strategy and culture, character and competence.

chapter three

THE PARADOX OF YET

'Paradox: a statement that is apparently contradictory or absurd and yet might be true.'

Penguin Concise English Dictionary

'The test of a first-rate intelligence is the ability to hold two opposed ideas in mind at the same time and still retain the ability to function.'

F. Scott Fitzgerald

Leadership is full of contradictions. Without them, leadership would be a walk in the park. We could make decisions quickly and easily, as the answer would be straightforward. Yet I know every person reading this book understands the complexity of leading. We need to draw from both our ferocity and our warmth to balance results and relationships. The visual image for Ferocious Warmth is the infinity symbol. Every moment of the day we draw from our head and heart, the evidence base and the beliefs, the cognition and the emotion. Blending apparent opposites makes ferocious warmth a powerful leadership approach as it builds the capability to ride the 'yet' of perceived dichotomy.

DANCING WITH PARADOX

At the centre of the infinity loop lies the 'yet'. The yet gives us permission to hold the paradox of:

- Explicit, yet empowering
- Strategic, yet people focussed
- Challenging, yet providing psychological safety
- Director, yet co-creator
- Compassionate, yet with high expectations
- Courageous, yet vulnerable
- Open to influence, yet with purposeful intent
- Focussed, yet open to ambiguity and flexibility
- Realistic, yet optimistic.

Simultaneously reflecting on both sides of the equation takes curiosity and skill. If we're driven by a strong set of principles that centre us, we can bring this duality together. Like an artist mixing two seeming opposing colours together, we end up with a third choice. It becomes a richer choice that incorporates strengths from both sides. It becomes what my mentor Matt Church, founder of Thought Leaders Australia, describes as 'non-dualistic' peace. He encourages us to think about the tyranny of the 'or' and step into exploring the nuance of the intersection of two seemingly opposing ideas. It's the opportunity that the 'and' and 'yet' and 'and also' provides us. Matt's thinking on the exploration and limitations of polarity has greatly influenced my own over the years. His book *Rise Up: An Evolution in Leadership*[21] will take you on an exploration of yourself as a leader that you will never forget. It's a personal inventory on who we are when we lead.

REALIST OPTIMISM

Jim Collins discusses the concept of this duality in his well-known book *Good to Great*.[22] In his description of the paradox and duality of optimistic realism, he names what he calls the Stockdale Paradox. General Stockdale was held captive in the Hanoi Hilton during the Vietnam war for eight years, suffering torture and other immense hardships. Through this time the mental fitness that got General Stockdale through was his faith that he would get out, even though he knew it would be the toughest fight of his life. He forced himself to see the brutal facts of the context and stoically deal with them. He believed he would prevail and that it would be a defining time in his life. The people who didn't deal well with the horrible reality they were living through were those who were in denial of the situation. They kept saying, 'We'll be out by Easter' and 'We'll be out by Christmas'. These milestones came and went, and after a while their empty optimism left them and they 'died of a broken heart'. Research would show that Stockdale displayed optimism that was problem-focussed and emotion-focussed. He engaged with the situation while the others who didn't make it were disengaged from any strategy other than hope.

In stressful times, realistic optimists pull from both the head and the heart in their coping mechanisms. Research and meta-analysis on optimism research by Carver et al[23] found that optimism 'predicted active attempts to both change and accommodate to stressful circumstances, in ways that reflect flexible engagement'. In their meta-analysis of optimism and coping, Solberg Nes and Segerstrom[24] found optimism was positively associated with the two types of engagement-coping responses: those that are problem-focused (head) and those that are emotion-focused (heart). Optimists are responsive to the type of stressor being confronted. Optimists display problem-focused coping with stress that had controllable factors and more emotion-focused coping when faced with uncontrollable stressors (e.g. trauma). This adaptability and flexibility of the optimist is the hallmark of the Ferocious Warmth leader.

Seth Godin, marketing and tribe expert and one of the world's most prolific entrepreneurial thinkers, sums up optimism as a leadership attribute in one paragraph:

'Optimism is an attitude and a choice. It involves context and focus. We're not deluding ourselves with the reassurance that everything is going to be okay (because that's not productive). Instead, we're committed to finding things we can contribute to, work on and improve. We're devoted to seeking out useful lessons and to discovering where the benefit of the doubt might be helpful. Positive thinking doesn't solve every problem. But it's a much better tool than negative thinking.' [25]

THE HUMBLE PERSISTOR

Continuing with the concept of duality, Collins' top leadership level (Level 5)[26] is about the ability to balance two seemingly opposing traits: humility and extreme persistence. An outdated view of leadership would see humility as a weakness, but Collins demonstrates that this humility is supported by strength that can also be forceful and decisive. Either side of this humble/forceful approach is an asset on its own in context, but Collins believes the reason for these leaders' success is the unique combination of the two qualities. These Level 5 leaders also encourage strong robust debate, especially within a senior team, and devolve power from themselves to the team.

Without the blending of the seemingly opposing strengths, we become a victim of extremities. If we are by default always the fearsome leader or the very warm 'enmeshed' leader, everything is out of kilter. If we are only problem-focussed and not emotion-focussed, we respond in ways that don't take all needs into account. We end up making decisions that don't consider a whole lot of perspectives because we haven't listened to them. Ferocity can sometimes take the high road of 'being right'. At the other end, if we default to the warmth side, we might try to keep everyone happy, unwilling to upset the perceived harmony.

POWER AND LOVE

One of my most admired educators is Dr Briony Scott, Principal of Wenona School in Sydney, Australia. She is also convenor and founder of the Renaissance Women's Network. I worked with Briony's school a few years ago and witnessed her start-of-year speech to staff. I was struck by her brilliant oration, one of the most impactful I have ever heard. She inspired, challenged and collected everyone in that auditorium together for the year ahead. Briony encourages the people she leads to work together to continue to raise the bar in their work, while showing authentic and caring leadership. She's also a prolific tweeter.

Twitter is one of the ways to see inside people's heads. What do they share? What commentary do they bring? Briony's tweets are insightful and legendary! This tweet in late 2019 encouraged me to get in touch with her again and discuss all things Ferocious Warmth. It captures the nuance and complexity of leading in schools.

'Another chapter on school leadership that has yet to be written – understanding emotional regulation in communities, when people lose it and why, how to maintain equanimity, how to lead drama free, how to keep your heart open yet protected. School leadership demands connection.'

Briony Scott, school principal, Twitter, 22/1/2019

This is the challenge of the Ferocious Warmth approach. We often need to make strong decisions, sometimes hard decisions, and the best decisions are made from both the head and the heart. Connecting the cognitive and emotive together creates leadership that people are inspired by and drawn to. Yet opening our heart to others can lead to not protecting ourselves from attack or malice, which is why we need to draw on strengths from the opposing side. Questions to consider, include: What is my conviction on this? Am I listening carefully to the meaning behind the words? What values and beliefs are driving the interactions I'm having?

Briony's tweet reflects the challenge of the 'yet' around the heart. How do we remain open hearted yet protected? How do we walk willingly into an interaction that could potentially hurt us personally and professionally? Many readers could think of situations where they have gone in with a very open approach and been blindsided by a harsh, personal attack. We often walk towards conversations with an open heart, yet we can't control where the other person is, what is happening for them and how they see us. I asked Briony how she manages this tricky environment.

'Part of it is not setting up a forced dichotomy. You can have both a personal resolution or a personal strength about what you want. But you know that like an iceberg, at any point in time there's actually very little that we know for sure. As I get older, I get more cautious about being absolute. I'm more determined now about less things. I am more determined now for, example, about the power of kindness – it is such a powerful currency. Yet often this term is associated with weakness. But so much of what we bring to our work is not binary.'

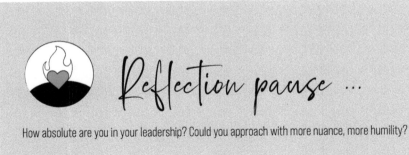

Steve Munby's book *Imperfect Leadership*[27] explores duality under the paradox of power and love. Munby is the former chief executive of the National College for School Leadership in England and the international education charity Education Development Trust. In a speech at the Seizing Success Conference in 2012 he named the great challenge of this paradox.

'As Martin Luther King says: power without love is reckless and abusive and love without power is sentimental and anaemic. I believe that at this time of great change and in an increasingly devolved system, we as leaders should not choose between power and love. We must choose both.'

Munby names four tensions when balancing power and love, which represent a move away from both ferocity and warmth. One from the characteristics of power, authority and decisiveness. The other from love, inclusion and empowerment.

'Being a pace-setter and being a coach.
Being challenging and being open to challenge.
Being competitive and being collaborative.
Being consistent and being adaptive to context.'

Munby's view of power and love 'is that they are false opposites and that the best leadership has both.' Ferocious Warmth leaders understand this.

POLARITY AT WORK

Jane A.G. Kise's book *Holistic Leadership, Thriving Schools*[28] is based on the concept of polarity through the Jungian lens best known via the Myers-Briggs Type Indicator (MBTI). Kise also uses the visual of the infinity symbol with twelve lenses to explore their characteristics and interdependencies. Jane talks in terms of 'and'. Breadth and depth, community and individual, predictability and possibility. She uses the metaphor of breathing to explain the interdependency, the necessary exhale and inhale. Is one better or more important than the other? No, they are both critical and required. One is incomplete without the other. Ferocious Warmth draws from the same conceptual approach. We are richer when we access from both ferocity and warmth 'and yet', together contextually, as needed.

In a discussion with Jane Kise, she shared an example of working with a school superintendent to develop stronger decision-making skills. His default was to put everything to a democratic vote. Momentum was slow. Accountability was dubious. It reminded me of one of my beloved principals. When I arrived as a leading teacher at the school, decision-making was made more complex by his visiting every classroom to discuss each issue with every teacher before he made a decision. The school was one of the most collaborative places I had ever worked, but the process just didn't move us along. Like Jane's superintendent, there was very little forward momentum! As the leader, he had trouble identifying where perspective and insight were needed in the decision-making process and when he needed to make the call. Status quo won as he swayed between different staff opinions. As he built his leadership team, we moved to more transparent ways of making decisions, but it was challenging for him to stay centred and realise when over-consultation was causing chaos.

At a system level, paradox weighs in during transformation. Pak Tee Ng, from the National Institute of Education, Nanyang Technological University, is a Singaporean educator deeply involved in the development of school and teacher leaders. To me he exudes Ferocious Warmth, as he openly speaks of his aim to encourage educators to walk a path not easily travelled, with love, courage and resilience.

His book, *Learning from Singapore: The Power of Paradoxes*[29], published in 2017, tracks the shift to the Singaporean system: learning for life. Rather than learning for exams, this and other systems focus on citizenship and student wellbeing. This shift has required strong development in teacher capability around how they work and what teaching and learning looks like.

Ng writes about the opportunities provided by the creative tension of paradoxes. These paradoxes draw from the 'co-existence of timely change and timeless constraints, centralisation and de-centralisation, meritocracy and compassion, and teaching less to learn more'.

As one of the highest-performing systems in the world, the Singaporean system is continuing to change for the better. Lee speaks of the approach that for many seemed to be 'kicking away the ladder' that got them to these results. They have been mindful of change, whether during something like COVID-19 or the complexity of the world in general. Singapore approaches challenges calmly and with courage to strategically look to the future, deeply investing in the capability of teachers and resourcing the system.

One of Ng's most provocative paradoxes is 'timely change with timeless constants', because change should be moored to something timeless, so it doesn't overwhelm us. This Ferocious Warmth skill draws not only from our strategic intelligence, where we identify our levers for change, but also our emotional intelligence to anchor this change to the foundations that provide the stability to leap from. It combines ferocity as a system for change, transformation and strategy, with the warm heart of focussing on the professionals on the ground. To improve a system, this connection is critical. Ng spoke at the ACEL Global 2020 conference and left us with a powerful statement that captures the balance of policy and implementation in a Ferocious Warmth way: 'Students do not experience policies, they experience teachers.'

Seth Godin, who I believe is one of the world's most provocative thinkers, posts daily. The day after hearing Ng speak at the conference, I received Godin's blog on the arc and the arch in my inbox:

The arc and the arch[30]

They sound similar, but they're not.

An arc, like and arch, is bent. The strength comes from that bend.

But the arc doesn't have to be supported at both ends, and the arc is more flexible. The arc can take us to parts unknown, yet it has a trajectory.

An arch, on the other hand, is a solid structure.

It's a bridge that others have already walked over.

Our life is filled with both. We're trained on arches, encouraged to seek them out.

But an arc, which comes from 'arrow', is the rare ability to take flight and go further than you or others expected.

A Ferocious Warmth leader has their eye on both – the arc and the arch. One holds permanence and years of weathering, the other is light, free and moving with momentum.

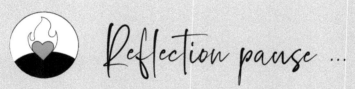

What are the permanent foundations, the timeless arches of your school that you want to maintain? Where are the opportunities to seize the learning and timely change that contexts such as a global pandemic give us?

I see a difference in the momentum built in new leaders who want timely change, but who forget timeless constants. Principals who go in looking only for what's not working and what needs to change should expect warning lights. When we dismiss any of the foundations that hold a school steady, we smash people's faith in our leadership. I saw a high-functioning school plunge into dark morale and toxicity through a new leadership team holding what happened prior to their tenure in seeming contempt. It is devastating. The road to professional trust becomes treacherous and full of huge pot holes, sending the school backwards.

STANDING IN THE CENTRE

How do we stay poised in the moment – able to almost intuitively know where to place our focus or actions? It can be hard for many great leaders I know to articulate the breakdown of their thinking, because they work with unconscious competence. It seems they are in a flow state in this dance of Ferocious Warmth, drawing from where it's needed to get the best outcomes. They identify a few key internal messages as if they're intuitively driven by the four elements of expansion, connection, courage and authenticity. These drive the blend between head and heart and allow them to stay centred more than many others. Many great leaders unconsciously lead in flow, yet, importantly, when the situation is very complex, take the time to pause and consciously draw from these elements.

'Optimal experience depends on the ability to control what happens in consciousness moment by moment'.

Mikalyi Czikszentmihalyi [31]

Psychologist and author Mikalyi Czikszentmihalyi writes of the 'optimal experience' of flow. Czikszentmihalyi developed and researched the concept and theory of flow, which is now used globally in education, business, psychology and the creative arts. Flow is the state we're in when time flies. We're so immersed in what we're doing that nothing else matters – just the activity we're undertaking. When leading in flow, we can draw on and use strengths to sort through the challenges of the context with the skills of a sensei. There's Mr Miyagi again! If you have never watched *Karate Kid*, please do. Mr Miyagi is a great example of Ferocious Warmth leadership.

PULLING FROM THE PARADOX OF YET

A friend of mine rang me recently on her way to a meeting with a principal and a case manager. Rachel works with outreach youth services, helping to get out-of-home youth into school. She was worried about the meeting becoming adversarial with both the school and the youth service talking at rather than with each other. The principal and the case worker's previous interactions had not been successful. She feared that no one would take control of the meeting and it would become aimless and ineffective very quickly. She knew that people were seeing each other as adversaries rather that in partnership.

Rachel understands she is warm and relationship driven. In the past she'd gone with a softly, softly approach, not wanting to upset the delicate tensions or be 'eaten alive'. The challenge of influence without authority was raising its head. Collaboration and partnerships are often stymied by unsaid hierarchical protocols getting in the way. Rachel and I talked about the need to paint a picture of mutual success for everyone in the room and acknowledge the collective wisdom, while being firm that they needed an outcome that worked first and foremost for the student.

When I caught up with Rachel after the meeting, this is what she said:

'I went in and began with naming what was in the room and acknowledged that while in some ways we appear to be at odds with each other on the surface, we were actually working towards the same thing. We all acknowledged that. I asked that we spend time really listening to each other's perspective and understand that we all bring to this situation our own wisdom and practice. A little bit of the work had already happened before I walked in. I was five minutes late and the principal and case worker were already in the room. When I got there, they had been having a conversation about life in general, and the football. I think in those moments they saw their "humanness".'

Two interesting findings in the neuroscience of conversations are painting a picture of mutual success and listening to connect. I learnt this through the work of a mentor, Judith E. Glaser, author of *Conversational Intelligence*.[32] These two characteristics increase oxytocin, serotonin and dopamine levels in the brain and decrease cortisol. When oxytocin is increased, the prefrontal cortex clicks in, which enables collaboration and problem solving. Whereas when cortisol is too high, the amygdala, the reptilian part of our brain, is running the show and we are more likely to experience heightened tension, lack of listening and empathy, and be driven by a need to be right.

Rachel's framing and the willingness of the other members to actually talk to each other in a more relaxed way primed the conversation for partnership, not a battlefield. It created transparency. Rachel took the lead on naming what could potentially get in the way of a purposeful and fruitful meeting. She connected into each person's strengths and opened up the dialogue with a focus on listening deeply. In a short time, there was trust where there hadn't been in the past. She curated the environment where the 'yet' could live – robust yet respectful.

In *Conversational Intelligence* Judith E. Glaser calls this 'taking the lead'.

'Quell the amygdala by talking about the threats and fears that are standing in the way of building trust. Be open and communicate with others to share and quell threats. This sends messages of trust that the amygdala understands: "I trust you will not harm me".'

There are too many meetings held with no time to discuss, listen deeply or connect to our humanity. We are social creatures and our brains are far more able to see and hear the nuance and perspective of a difficult situation when we are connected. Rachel laid the situation on the table at the start with humility yet strength, focussed on bringing out the best thinking in the room for the student and the school. This time, the case manager was able to hear where the principal was coming from, while the principal was able to understand more fully the remit of the case manager. When they had a more complete understanding of these perspectives, they were all able to take those into the decision-making.

Rachel concluded: 'In the end, it was acknowledging that everyone at the table brought their own professionalism to solve the same problem that made the difference. On reflection I realise I would always usually do that but was fearful of being attacked like I had in the past.'

My response to Rachel was that all she needed was to reconnect with her conviction and courage about the work. Her fear and nervousness had put her out of balance. She had lost sight of how to combine the duality of conviction and compassion. A quick discussion got it back. She was able to stand in the centre of Ferocious Warmth and pull from both sides to step into flow.

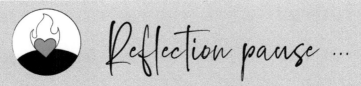

Reflection pause ...

Reflect on a recent conversation that challenged your centredness. Which side of the Ferocious Warmth approach could you have drawn more from to regain balance?

Figure 6. Centred Conversations

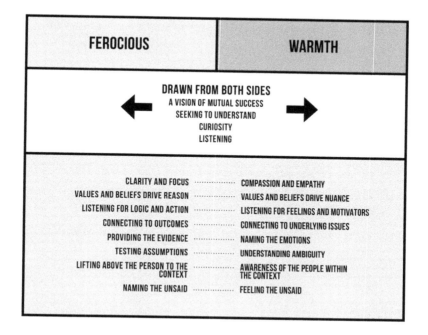

Why is it so hard to hold both sides? Are these things really opposed? I don't believe so. But I do think society is too focussed on being on one side or the other, adopting extremes rather than integration.

Ferocious Warmth leadership seeks to come from a place of balance. Drawing from the facts, the evidence, the logic, while sustaining the trust, relationship building and empathy needed to lead people well and achieve outcomes and wellbeing. This is the power of yet.

Ferocious Warmth leaders are those who straddle the 'yes and' and the 'yet'. This ability to blend seemingly contradictory approaches allows them to step into the power of Ferocious Warmth. They:

- are brave and courageous in the face of big challenges, and inspire their people to come with them on the journey.
- are lead learners who provide the right balance of high challenge and high support. People feel psychologically safe to raise and discuss ideas, differences of opinion and share personal challenges.

- draw from clear evidence base, as well as provide the culture that allows innovation to flourish.
- have strong conviction on their leadership beliefs and discuss them openly with others.
- work from a firm set of values and moral purpose.
- build trust through their ability to empathise and deeply listen, and surf the wave of logically and emotionally based discussion.
- inspire people to be their best self and connect into the vision and purpose of the organisation.
- build deep collaborative cultures and create leaders within their teams.
- lift expectations and give support to achieve the results and transformations required.

Cultivating our skills on both sides of ferocity and warmth is the work to do. How do you identify them?

chapter four

STRENGTH AND SHADOW

Like a tightrope walker high in the air, staying centred keeps us balanced. A tension exists in staying in the duality of ferocity and warmth, which can wear us out if we don't explicitly build our skills on either side.

HEAD AND HEART

One way to categorise Ferocious Warmth skills is through the lens of head and heart. The cognitive work and the emotional work. These extremes were highlighted for me when working with a diverse group in a government transport agency on the keys to being more collaborative. A systems engineer bemoaned that too often problem-solving processes simply ignored the facts about whether something was doable. The customer-experience director responded, 'I find the opposite. Too often the systems and fact-based approaches we use to make decisions don't take into account the end user at all. Then we wonder why they fail.' Two classic examples of project work done by the head or the heart, not the blend. But at least there's acknowledgement that success needs to somehow incorporate both.

Yet most people know they have a bias for thinking more one way than the other when not consciously focussed on it. I remember learning from two of the original leaders of MBTI (Myer-Briggs Type Indicator) in the early 2000s the concept of doing a sort-of type test in the stance of your 'shoes-off self'. We know context matters. Who we're working with affects us, but we also deep down know that when we don't have to worry about anyone else we tend to a more logical, head approach or a more emotional, heart approach. No judgement lies here. It's simply where we like to go when we don't have to think!

Research into decision-making and reasoning has uncovered an intricate dance between our cognitions, emotions and feelings. Matthew Liebermann is a researcher and leader in the science of social cognitive neuroscience. His work demonstrates that the inner workings of the brain sort into an analytical-brain and social-brain response. We also use what he calls social and non-social reasoning. Each handles information quite differently, often at odds with the other. For groups, this is a huge challenge. But then we discover that our own brains also struggle to blend both!

Liebermann was originally a PhD in social psychology yet found brain science fascinating, which he also studied, using both in his research on social connection. Understanding and experiencing the overwhelm we often feel when reading any neuroscientific findings, he sought to demystify academic brain theories. His initial major work on social pain being as significant as physical pain shows our deep need for belonging, and the importance of a culture of inclusion when leading. His books are well worth putting in the 'books I will read' pile! His research into the brain network shows that we turn different parts of our brain depending on the type of reasoning we are undertaking.

'In many situations, the more you turn on the brain network for nonsocial reasoning, the more you turn off the brain network for social reasoning. This antagonism between social and nonsocial thinking is really important because the more someone is focused on a problem, the more that person might be likely to alienate others around him or her who could help solve the problem. Effective nonsocial problem solving may interfere with the neural circuitry that promotes effective thinking about a group's needs.' [33]

Social reasoning is the basis of true collaboration. Is it possible to create that balance of head and heart if we are battling thousands of years of brain development? Yes! Continued evolution comes from our current approach not matching the complexity of the current context. If we are committed to developing our leadership skills, then continuing to build the strengths of both sides is the work to do.

Here is a not-exhaustive list of strengths that could be categorised into head and heart. You might recognise it from our original Figure 1 Ferocious Warmth table in Chapter 2.

HEAD	HEART
Objective	Compassionate
Results focussed	Emotional reasoning
Cognitive reasoning	Empathetic
Strategic	Nurturing
Decisive	Supportive
Clear	People focussed
Process driven	Loving
Consistent	Open to influence
Reliable	Beliefs
High expectations	Intuition
Factual knowledge	Connecting
Evidence based	Optimistic
Authority	Exploratory
Action	Influence

When you look at the list, do you find strengths on one side influenced by strengths from the other? The best strategic 'head' thinking is flawed if it does not use the 'heart' skill of empathy into the strategic process. The 'heart' beliefs we have as educators can be flawed without the 'head' evidence of the impact we're having. It is not an either/or. Hand in glove. Ferocious Warmth.

And.

Yet.

Through the lens of head and heart, you may identify other words that work for you. Which are highly developed strengths on both sides? Which could do with some work? If you see them, I cheer you for your insight! If you're not sure, ask a colleague which they see as your strengths.

PUSHING OUR STRENGTHS INTO SHADOWS

Assessment tools such as VIA Character Strengths[34] and The Cliftons' Strength Assessment[35] are useful for uncovering strengths. I've found going back to my top strengths helped me stay strong through adverse times, such as COVID-19 lockdowns during 2020 and other challenges. Our strengths rise to the top in times of crisis. My top strengths of individualisation, strategic, activator, adaptability and learning allowed me to deal with a complete change to how I run my business and shift the support I offer to the people I serve. It helped me think of and trial different ways of continuing to do this work.

Yet our strengths can also have shadows. The Jungian approach to shadows suggests they are hidden from the conscious mind and are dark and dense. Jungian shadow work takes people through a process of diving into the unconscious mind and bringing these tendencies and fixations to awareness, to integrate them.

If you're thinking I'm about to launch into a Jungian dialogue, don't worry! Let's use the word shadow as simply a way to reflect on ourselves when we get out of balance and our strengths go to extremes. Let's not beat ourselves up when we go to extremes, but look at how we might evolve through our awareness and insight. The MBTI (Myers-Briggs Type Indicator) world calls this 'in the grip' [36], which I think reflects what happens perfectly.

Some examples of strength into shadow:

- Optimism can move to naivety

- Trust can move to gullibility
- Objectivity can become aloofness
- Results-focus can shift to task-only focus
- Cognitive reasoning can lead to being emotionally absent
- Concise strength can lead to being harsh
- Compassion can become rescuing
- Strategic strength can lead to being dominating and disconnected
- Supportive strength can mean doing too much for others.

These are not hard and fast, nor are they the same for everyone. This work is all about self-awareness and understanding our impact on ourselves and those around us.

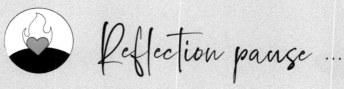

Identify: Make a list of your known strengths

Explore: Reflect on some examples where one of these strengths made a positive impact on the work you do

Stretch: Find times where focussing or pushing this strength too far were less than useful

Stabilise: Look to a strength from the other side of the ferocious-warmth flow. If your extreme strength/shadow was from the head, what heart strength would have helped the situation? Or, if your reflection focussed on a heart strength, what head strength would have been useful to draw from?

Here's an example of being 'in the grip'.

Steven was becoming overwhelmed by doing too much for others and not having enough time to do his own job. As a senior lawyer in a large organisation, his role was designed to be strategic. In his leadership Steven was supportive and open to people's challenges and issues with workload. Unfortunately, this meant he was doing many tasks that were not his. You know that feeling when the email comes in or there's a knock at the door and your inner voice says, 'Again? Is this really my problem?' His team bounced problems up to him instead of using him as a sounding board during challenges. Steven's team took advantage of his compassion, and he let them. Even the experienced leaders shirked their responsibilities, because Steven would deal with them. Soon, other members of his team expected him to take on their trickier situations as well, instead of seeing him as a safety net and mentor.

Among others, Steven's strengths are heart: supportive, empathetic and compassionate, but you can see what's coming, can't you? On the shadow side, these become resentful, walked-over and burnt out. So we worked together on a number of ferocious head strengths to get him back on track.

Reflection pause ...

Where would you suggest Steven move his focus to? What head strength would help him step into more conviction about his role of leading and supporting, not doing?

Steven began a more strategic look at what was going on. Drawing from an objective view, he clarified the roles and responsibilities with his whole team. He reflected on how he delegated tasks and undertook professional learning that improved his delegation skills. When his senior team tried to move things up to him, he supported and coached them to take responsibility. He also provided external training and development for the team to become more proficient at Ferocious Warmth conversations. Most of all, Steven drew from conviction and courage to have the more difficult conversations with people taking advantage of him. He drew a line in the sand.

On the other side of the spectrum, Toni was focussed on shifting the data. Her strong strategic plan was rolling out and her eye was firmly on actions, outcomes and impact. But her team was struggling. The strategy was great, but the timelines were unrealistic. Toni, with her gaze firmly on the outcomes, had forgotten to check on how people were travelling. People were getting burnt out and, as one more email came into the inbox with the next task, some were close to breaking point. One of her team bravely fronted up to discuss the issue. To Toni's credit she diarised time to sit and evaluate where things were at, both individually and with her team. Knowing her strengths were very much oriented to thinking, Toni decided to connect to how people were feeling. She posed questions that asked what was stopping the forward momentum and uncovered how people really felt about the situation. Then she was able to work with the team to correct course.

When the tightrope walker is leaning too far to one side, she or he overcompensates by pulling from the other side to get back in balance. Of course, things get wobbly! When our extremities come out, we need to steady and consider our rebalancing options.

THE BIG WORDS

The four elements of Ferocious Warmth are the key pieces to maintaining this sense of balance and centredness. When we experience *expansion* we create an ever-evolving space of learning and growth. When we maintain *connection* it reminds us of our humanness and our belonging. When we stand in *courage* we draw strength from who we are and what we stand for. And when we connect firmly to our *authentic* self, people are sure of who we are.

We'll dive into these elements soon, but first: what do you do when you shift out of balance?

chapter five

THE IMPACT OF IMBALANCE

Many of us know the feeling. The to-do list is four metres long, everyone is after a piece of you, and you just wish you could get people to move faster, take responsibility, or make the right decisions, but they don't, and you have to step in to fix things. For many of us, our default leadership needle tilts towards the ferocity side of imbalance.

> FOR SOME OF US, AS OUR FEROCITY SPEEDS UP OUR PEOPLE METER STARTS TO DIMINISH.

Our need for action, finalisation, movement, decisiveness means we short circuit our thoughts away from people to hard-edged results. The pendulum swings too far from centre. This is the territory of the results-driven leader. Take it too far and we become the fearsome leader.

For leaders on the other side, as everything speeds up and stress levels rise, our results meter starts to lower and we lose sight of our vision and strategy, our purpose. The volume gets turned right up in our heads and we vigorously defend our people and get involved in stories and dramas – our own and those surrounding us. This is the territory of the relationship-driven leader. It's all pressure and stress. As this rises further, we become the enmeshed leader.

Figure 7. Moving Out of Balance

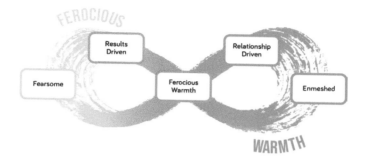

UNDERSTAND YOUR BAROMETER

A barometer measures air pressure. The image that comes to mind when I think of a barometer is a gold-rimmed thick dial with beautiful mix of fonts designating the weather conditions. When the air pressure is heavy the dial turns one way, when lighter it turns another way, the black arrow pointing to the current weather conditions. The measurements range from stormy to very dry. This metaphor is a useful way to describe our popping out of our infinity loop into imbalance. We start drifting to one side or the other.

At our best, we stand in the centre of the infinity loop in calm balance. We stand solidly, drawing on our ability to create strong collaborative cultures built on warmth, trust and connection so that people can thrive. We're also drawing from our ferocity, lifting the bar, asserting boundaries, achieving the measures, and using the evidence base.

Then the pressure rises. We start to swing a little. Our self-awareness helps us understand where we swing by default. Self-awareness is the number-one skill for this work. We build it by focussing our attention out, looking for the outcome.

Is it having the impact that our students and staff need?

Our own families can also tell us with honesty! When things are a little out of balance for you, where do you go? More ferocity or more warmth? More head or more heart? What's your preference? What are the descriptors your team would use when you're under stress? This insight is gold to a self-reflective leader.

SHIFTING OUT OF BALANCE

Figure 8. The Impact of Imbalance

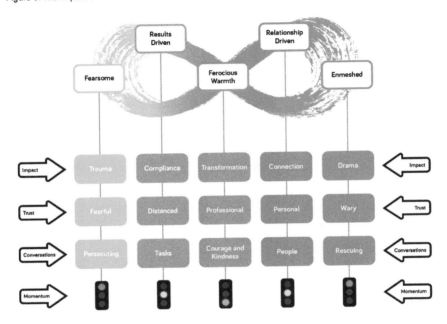

RESULTS DRIVEN

Results-driven leaders get results in many of the performance measurements using 'hard data'. They put task before people, focussed on lifting standards and moving the team forward. Results-driven leaders work from a logic base in their decision-making and are clear and objective in their communications. They can struggle with building trust and having enough empathy for others. Their listening lens is generally from an objective, critique approach. When leading, they need others around them to bring human-centred leadership skills to their attention. Results-driven leaders rely on compliance more than collaboration to reach goals. They concentrate on growth and improvement.

Trust is distanced. The connection between the results-driven leader and the students, teachers and community can be reserved and aloof.

Conversations are predominantly task-driven.

Impact is more about compliance than commitment, due to the interactions being about engaging the head, not the heart.

RELATIONSHIP DRIVEN

Relationship-driven leaders put people over task. They provide a culture of support and create high trust through empathy and connection. Decisions are made with emotional reasoning. They maintain focus on wellbeing and relationship building. Relationship-driven leaders can struggle with holding people to account and increasing ambiguity through unclear expectations. They can rely on others on the team to raise expectations and have the more difficult conversations. Their listening lens is generally from a subjective, emotionally based approach. They maintain focus on support and connectedness.

Trust is personally driven, creating an environment where we trust each other on a personal level, but not necessarily within discussion of our professional growth and areas of development.

Conversations are predominantly people driven.

Impact is more about connection than results.

Knowing our default provides insight into how to get back into balance. Understanding what triggers this imbalance is slightly trickier! Knowing when we're heading towards extremes? This is critical to our wellbeing and the wellbeing of the people we lead.

EXPLORING THE EXTREMES — THE FEARSOME AND ENMESHED LEADERS

Warning label: we're going places that may feel uncomfortable!

Research undertaken by Amy Cuddy and colleagues Susan Fiske, of Princeton, and Peter Glick, of Lawrence University[37], showed that people judged to be competent, but lacking in warmth, often elicit envy in others, an emotion involving both respect and resentment that cuts both ways. When we respect someone, we want to cooperate with him or her, but resentment can make that person vulnerable to harsh reprisal. I know a principal who experiences exactly that. She cares very much for her team, but shows it in actions not warmth.

I feel deeply for her as she continually steps up to provide her people with the support they need, but misses the deeper connection, as it's not her natural style. A number of her staff judge her harshly and she struggles with the loyalty of some of the more influential staff. This small but mighty group seem to sit and wait for her to muck up, so they can heap judgement on her and garner support for disenchantment in her leadership. As she is learning the emotional intelligence skills of connection and empathy, when she does share more of herself with her team, it can come across as martyrdom, sharing the challenges of her role inadvertently indicating that no one really appreciates her.

On the other hand, Cuddy and her colleagues found that people judged as warm but incompetent tend to elicit pity, which also involves a mix of emotions: compassion moves us to help those we pity, but our lack of respect leads us ultimately to neglect them. I have come across a number of leaders over the years who put their heart and soul into their roles yet didn't shift the status quo. They are warm and caring people, but they have not worked on the more ferocious leadership skills they need to lead a complex beast like a school. Competency in both relationships and results is needed for effective leadership. Strong decision-making, technical and pedagogical knowledge are both critical in the world of education. We cannot have one side without the other.

THE FEARSOME LEADER

A few years ago at a conference I found myself standing in line with a school leader who proudly told me that she'd started at a new school and would have half the staff out of there by the end of Term 3, because they were so 'crap'. This leader was passionate about students, but any teacher who showed a belief system or standards different to hers, was wiped as soon as she assumed they were not on her bus. Consequently, school turnover, morale and standing in the community was, indeed, crap. I was astounded by the vitriolic download on her teachers and shocked at how easily she displayed her disdain.

This was all kinds of wrong. How can we be so righteous about our work and the value of putting students at the centre, yet burn and intimidate the people we need to work with to get to there? Ferocity is about lifting our standards and continually improving for the sake of our students, but if we think we can do that by a 'chop off their heads' approach then we've got a long way to go.

When we're stuck in judgement and condemnation, we lead through fear.

We may not want to admit it, but we know that our approach is not bringing out the best in people. It's focussing on what's wrong, not the strengths. We create an environment that people are reluctant to be a part of. Often, we kid ourselves that we're courageous and standing up to those who don't hold up to our levels of professionalism, but, actually, we're creating a space where people are so fearful, their performance will never lift to where we want it to be.

In other cases, we can be seen to be harsh or non-caring when we're actually seeking to make everything OK. Our intent may be caring, but the delivery misses the mark. Simone experienced this recently. She knows that as a leader she needs to focus on the people and heart side, because, if left to her preference, she'd be purely on task. Simone is seeking to build warmth into her leadership and this self-awareness is a big step in the right direction. She has a high achievement belief system but can come across as lacking empathy and insight into her impact on others.

At the end of a particularly stressful and busy term and year, one of Simone's staff members was in a very fragile and exhausted state. His colleagues supported him as much as they could, buffering him from the extreme overwhelm threatening to overtake him. One of the leaders approached Simone and mentioned that he had asked the staff member to go home and take the rest of the day off. Simone walked briskly into the staff room where the person was sitting and demanded his laptop. Looking afraid and bewildered, he handed it over. She then demanded that he go home.

Simone, whose default is more results driven, was in stress herself, so her balance tipped into an immature type of ferocity with no filter. Simone was trying to look after her staff member but doing it in a fearsome way. She wanted him to go home, do no work and look after himself. Unfortunately, he thought he was being fired. Simone's concern for him came out as attack. Her emotional intelligence skills of self-awareness, self-regulation and empathy were not engaged.

Our insight becomes myopic when we are in ferocious stress. We focus on the outcome we're seeking and believe that our way to fix it is the only way.

THE FEARSOME LEADER CAN INFLICT TRAUMA

When this is the default style, the fearsome leader rules through fear. They are closed to ideation with their teams or senior leaders. There is a lack of psychological safety for those they lead, with people not willing to take any interpersonal risks for fear of retribution. They are the archetypal extreme authoritarian leader – my way or the highway. At its worse, the fearsome leader inflicts trauma on those they lead. Their focus is on being right. Their style of feedback is based on harsh criticism rather than growth. Forward momentum is difficult as people are not working at their best. Toxic behaviour is either brewing or in evidence when transformation is demanded and delivered as an ultimatum and through compliance. People do not buy into change due to a feeling of powerlessness.

Trust is very low and people are fearful. Self-preservation becomes the driving reaction.

Conversations are persecuting and seek to highlight what's wrong.

Impact is trauma. People exposed to this type of leadership over time can suffer wellbeing issues. Staff turnover can be high. Staff morale and other student and community indicators are low.

THE ENMESHED LEADER

When I was a young teacher I was on staff with Darren. He was a gregarious and personable team leader. People were drawn to his good nature and humour. If you were in Darren's clique, life was good. He would say the right things to make you feel better about the establishment, throwing shade at the bureaucracy and feeding the 'we're alright Jack' approach to maintain the status quo. Darren was charismatic and drew people to him with ease. People shared confidences with him, because they felt safe. Unfortunately, he would also get boozy at drinks with his mates and spill people's stories. As one of these 'chosen' few I became privy to information about others that I should not have known. The discussion would then dissect the revelations and gossip about that person. It felt very wrong to me, but as a new teacher, the need to belong and be part of the 'cool crowd' overwhelmed my integrity. It also made me very wary of sharing anything important with Darren.

Challenges started to appear for Darren's leadership when external measures on outcomes and a principal with transparent expectations started increasing the pressure on performance. Darren's connections to those he led had become firmly entrenched in 'mate'. When the need for open feedback and shift in practice became necessary, many of us looked at Darren like a mate down the footy club or at a barbecue, rather than a leader, as he never inspired us to lift.

Deep down Darren had an overwhelming need to be liked and be the centre of attention. He used other people's life challenges to raise his importance in the group. He also led a resistance to change in the school due in no small part to not stepping up in his leadership role. Later, he became a principal of a small and struggling school. As the new leader he could have helped to turn the school into an amazing place for the students. Unfortunately, the opposite happened. Enrolments dropped. The last conversation I had with Darren was him blaming the department for the lack of support for his school. Of course, none of it was his fault.

THE ENMESHED LEADER CAN INFLICT DRAMA

The enmeshed leader unconsciously wants to be the centre of emotional attention within the culture. While supporting their teams, their relationships are unhealthy and drama-filled. This leader is deeply concerned about people not liking them and shies away from making decisions that might create disharmony. They deny, blame and justify when things are not going the way they want. They seek out the drama within conflict and add fuel to situations through a lack of clarity and objectivity. Often displaying rescuer behaviour, the enmeshed leader feeds a need to protect and be needed emotionally. They can create drama by getting too involved in people's emotional lives. Gaining momentum for change is difficult amid a lack of clarity of strategic direction and where people's work fits into the big picture. Harder decisions are avoided to keep the peace.

Trust is of a wary nature – we don't fully commit to a relationship with an enmeshed leader as their emotional response to open and honest discussion about the important things is inconsistent.

Conversations are rescuing in nature, stifling growth and autonomy in others.

Impact is drama. People walk on eggshells not wanting to offend. Bad behaviour runs rampant because the more important and clear conversations are avoided.

Both extremes – fearsome and enmeshed – keep others in victim roles, either feeling persecuted or expecting to be rescued.

RESCUER AND PERSECUTOR

The Karpman[38] drama triangle is a well-known mental model that helps unpack this. It identifies when we can be caught in a cycle of victim, rescuer or persecutor. Each of us can bounce around the triangle and go into all three positions, depending on the context and the relationship.

Victim: The victim is 'done to' by a persecutor and needs to be 'saved' by a rescuer.

Rescuer: The rescuer 'needs to be needed' by the victim and has a pattern of saving them from the persecutor.

Persecutor: Pays out on the victim and sees the rescuer as weak.

This model is all about patterns of behaviour. Habits that we can go into with certain people in our lives. While this framework is mostly used in family and partner dynamics, in many professional groups I work with there will be a number of people who can identify this dynamic is playing out. The Ferocious Warmth work endeavours to turn this relationship triangle into functional interactions.

But first we need to discover what pushes us out of balance towards the extreme realms in the first place. These steps can be confronting, but give us insights and self-awareness to regain equilibrium.

chapter six

UNCOVERING OUR UNMET NEEDS

The Guest House

This being human is a guest house.
Every morning a new arrival.

A joy, a depression, a meanness,
some momentary awareness comes
as an unexpected visitor.

Welcome and entertain them all!
Even if they're a crowd of sorrows,
who violently sweep your house
empty of its furniture,
still treat each guest honourably.
He may be clearing you out
for some new delight.

The dark thought, the shame, the malice,
Meet them at the door laughing
and invite them in.

> Be grateful for whoever comes,
> because each has been sent
> as a guide from beyond.

I love this poem by Rumi.[39] It honours our messy humanness and acknowledges that all of our feelings have a place; that we should honour and heed them instead of pushing them down or away. How often as leaders do we give ourselves the space to own and honour how we feel? Sometimes the most extreme life stories teach us that doing so helps us step into our humanness even more.

Long periods of stress stretch us thin. Most of the leaders I have worked with or known are high-functioning achievers. Usually this means they push themselves far beyond what many others would do, sometimes to the detriment of their overall health. As they push through and push on, without dealing with the stress, they become either a volcano waiting to explode or a balloon slowly deflating. In 2015, I learnt this the hard way, as a result of what I now know to be one of the most extreme and traumatic experiences of my life.

My husband, Justin, and I were on a motorbike trip with two other couples, all of us close friends. Justin had a Harley and we loved riding through the mountains on road trips. We would ride all day and then stay at country pubs overnight. The evenings were full of laughter, good food, wine and company, the days full of the joy of the ride. Then the next day we'd do it all again.

I loved being on the back of the bike. There is nothing like the rush of going around winding mountain roads. As a pillion I got to look around and see the beautiful countryside, hugged in tight behind Justin.

Our trip over the long weekend in March 2015 was to go along the Great Alpine Road in Victoria, from Bairnsdale up to Bright. All six of us were excited about exploring a road we'd wanted to for a long time. We'd attempted it the year before but it'd been closed due to bushfires.

We set off from Bairnsdale on the Saturday morning. I remember the first part of the day clearly. Two of our friends were well out in front and the other couple were slightly ahead of us. As usual, before we started, we arranged our next stop and everyone rode at their own pace, which would differ every time, depending on how the boys felt like riding. The morning was clear and crisp. I remember riding along the river, reminding myself to take in every moment. To be present.

About an hour into our ride, I noticed a plume of smoke ahead over the top of a ridge. I tapped Justin's leg, but didn't know if he'd seen it. A sense of foreboding settled in my stomach as we continued. Around a corner someone stood on the side of the road waving their arms for us to slow down. As we did, we went over a bump. Justin concentrated on keeping the bike steady as I let out a scream. I could see our two friends lying on the ground, their bike on fire.

The intense and tragic details that followed are not for this book. What's relevant is that I went into action. I felt numb, but part of my brain switched to making sense of the carnage and trying to help our friends. I did what I could, but it was too late. That day 'up on the mountain', as the four of us have referred to it since, significantly altered our lives, the trauma affecting all of us in different ways.

During the weeks after, our home became the central house for people who loved our friends to come together to grieve. I took two weeks off as we tried to not only deal with our own grief, but support our friends' children and families. We had two funerals to attend, with my girlfriend and I speaking at one, the boys speaking at the other. People wanted to talk with us and share their grief, as we were the people who'd been with their loved ones at the end. They wanted reassurance and some sense of closure. We were the closest of friends before the accident, but that experience 'up on the mountain' has bonded us for the rest of our lives.

As the main income earner in our home I went back to running my business. Occasionally, we talked about what had happened, but both Justin and I tried to get back on with life. I just kept on going. My work has always been important to me, as has being a good mum, so my head went down and I worked hard. I now know that I disconnected from what had happened. I pushed it down and looked straight ahead. I needed to be the 'strong one', the provider and the fixer.

One night a few months later I had to head down to the same part of the state to present at a conference. I was already feeling sick about it and, as fate would have it, another accident had happened and I had to go through a police road block past an overturned truck. Luckily, no-one was badly injured. After this, I pulled over and breathed deeply for a long time before I could drive on. I then got up in the morning and went on working with a room full of school leaders, who would never have known anything was wrong.

THE AFTERMATH OF NOT DEALING WITH EMOTIONS

It wasn't until three-and-a-half years later, as my marriage broke down and everything crumbled around me, that I realised how out of balance I was. I was angry and resentful in my relationships. All the best parts of me I gave to my clients, not my family. Two unconscious things were going on for me: a huge need to be in control, but, also, deep down I was crying out for someone else to take care of me. Yet I'd disconnected from those who loved me and was showing my care through action (must keep going, must keep going), not through loving presence and emotional connection. The irony of it all? I was doing the opposite of what I would encourage my clients to do – show self-compassion, pay attention to what was going on underneath, and breathe.

'The irony is that we attempt to disown our difficult stories to appear more whole or more acceptable, but our wholeness, even our wholeheartedness, actually depends on the integration of all of our experiences.'

Brené Brown, *Rising Strong*[40]

I wanted to be seen as the strong, capable woman, able to pick myself up and dust myself down. A few years later, I was diagnosed with PTSD in among a separation and becoming a single parent.

Brené Brown calls this the Reckoning: understanding where you are at so you can find yourself a new course. Her book, *Rising Strong*, was a gift, allowing me to work through the stories I was telling myself as my life became more rocky. I used her process of an SFD, 'Shitty First Draft', to write down what I was thinking, something I had never wanted to do in my life before. I didn't need to read these again. The writing got the stories out of my head. I learnt about a whole range of things I'd been doing to numb the hurt and confusion going on deep down. I recognised that I'd been 'chandeliering' – pushing down emotions to appear stoic and fabulous out in the world, and then harsh and critical with those I loved the most, up on the ceiling, hanging on tight to the chandelier.

I also learnt about what we do to form an armour. We either over function, which is my particular poison – 'I don't feel, I do. I don't need help, I help.' Or we under function – 'I won't function, I will fall apart. I can't help, I need help.' As a chronic over-functioner, sitting in my feelings and just letting them be, not trying to 'do things' is something I find hard, but am slowly getting better at. As I work with many leaders about what their inner voice is saying to them, their 'story', we often end up in the same place – the limiting belief of 'I'm not good enough' is holding us all back unless we own it. Then, as Brené Brown, author of one of the best leadership books that deals with these real situations, *Dare to Lead*[41], says, 'rumble with it and see where it comes from'.

In 2019, I saw Brené Brown speak in Melbourne and unearthed that when I work outside of my values, I experience not only resentment but go into victimhood. Everything went 'clunk' when Brown asked, 'What do you do when you are working outside of your values?' Boom! I saw my less-than-useful behaviours clearly linked to a lack of alignment with how I really wanted to work in the world when my two highest values are integrity and compassion. I realised that instead of showing compassion to those closest to me, I was resentful towards them for the smallest of things. This resentment turned into strong feelings of 'poor me'. All of this work was painful and enlightening. Thankfully, I'm continuing to embrace this aspect of my experience to bring the whole me to my children, my family and friends, and my clients. I look after myself and my needs better. I deliberately seek joy in my life and am surrounded by loving friends and family. I love my work and my clients. Gratitude has helped me get through some of the most challenging times in my life with as much compassion and grace as I can manage. Far from perfect, but a work in progress.

DOING THE INNER WORK

Are you thinking as you read this: 'Why is this story in a book about educational leadership? This is too much personal information!'

Because it's life. And I don't think we talk it about these things enough. It does affect how we lead, no question. It's the messiness of life that every one of us goes through. We have our own stories and journeys and every school leader has a life outside work. Joy, tragedy, elation, trauma. They all form the weave and weft of who we are. They affect our ability to bring our full-hearted self to the important work of educating students and leading communities. Knowing ourselves better allows us to understand how to get back to the balanced centre. We are more capable of blending ferocity and warmth and more in control of standing strong at the intersection of both. This is part of the reason I run small group mentoring programs for leaders. We can discuss the impact of life in general and unearth how it helps, or hinders, our leadership.

This inner work is important. Great schools see curriculum and wellbeing as intertwined and dependent for positive student outcomes. Similarly, great leadership development sees that wellbeing and emotional health is an everyday part of leadership work, not an add on. Leader wellbeing is a vexed and challenging issue. During COVID-19, I asked many school leaders how well they were looking after themselves so they could look after others. The answer was: not well enough.

The Principal Wellbeing report, compiled by Associate Professor Phil Riley of Deakin University and Professor Herb Marsh from the Australian Catholic University, has a 50% response rate from Australia's 10,000 principals. It shows a disturbing trend for school leaders:

'For health and wellbeing, school leaders reported very high levels of burnout, sleeping troubles, and stress compared to the general population. These factors, which are a risk to school leaders' long-term health and even their life expectancy, are not isolated to school sector, school type, socioeconomic background or geolocation, only the degree of occurrence differs.'

Dr Theresa Dicke, Institute for Positive Psychology and Education (IPPE) Research Fellow, Australian Catholic University[42]

As leaders in the community, school leaders need to be open about what they need to thrive in the complexity of the work, and our systems support their fulfilment. Our system, community and media need to understand the pressures of leading schools and treat educators with more respect than evidenced at the moment. Professor Riley is hopeful that the positive impact of the leadership response to the 2020 pandemic will translate to greater understanding of the stressors and challenges facing school leadership.

But the first person we need to be open with and support fully is ourselves. The alternative is out-of-balance leadership and living. When we don't fulfil our nourishing needs, the fearsome or enmeshed leaders take over, using control or manipulation to get their less than useful unconscious needs met.

UNMET NEED

Do you know if you move towards the fearsome leader or the enmeshed leader when you are out of balance? Do some of the following statements resonate for you when you sit in the discomfort of examining instances of less-than-brilliant behaviour? Remember, the fearsome leader can inflict trauma and the enmeshed leader can create drama. With self-awareness we observe our impact on others and ourselves. These are some of the needs that might be driving behaviour if they're not being met:

EXAMPLES OF FEROCITY'S NEEDS

- To be right
- To be in control
- To achieve high status
- To be seen as credible
- For wisdom to be acknowledged
- To be 'good enough'.

EXAMPLES OF WARMTH'S NEEDS

- To be useful
- To be confided in
- To be liked
- To be irreplaceable
- To belong
- To solve others' problems
- To rescue others
- To be accepted
- To be 'good enough'.

AN EXAMPLE IN ACTION: THE NEED FOR IT TO BE SOMEONE ELSE'S FAULT

The meeting was an important one, but disorganised and running rampant. In the room was a principal, assistant principal, leading teacher and a student's parent. Emotions were high and no one was listening to the others. The relationship between the principal and the parent was historically not great. The parent looked to the leading teacher and said, 'I've always been able to talk with you'.

'Yes,' replied the teacher, 'I know we've always been able to talk about things.'

At this point, the principal sat back, folded her arms and withdrew from participating. We could equate this with 'spitting the dummy'. Both the principal and teacher had a sleepless night over the disastrous interactions. The next day, the principal, assistant principal and the teacher met to discuss the fallout. The teacher was relieved they were debriefing and looking forward to seeing what they could learn from the whole experience and what they needed to do next. How wrong she was. It turned into a beratement of the teacher over the statement about having a good relationship with the parent. The principal had felt undermined and was determined to let the teacher know her mind. Fearsome. She refused to own any of the responsibility for the debacle, the disorganisation, the lack of deep dialogue that had people talking at rather than with each other, instead focussing purely on the teacher and her 'lack of support' for the principal.

This is a classic case of inflicting trauma through unmet need. The senior person in the room was not willing to take stock and reflect on all the elements that led to the negative outcome. She was overcome with a need to be in control and the one in the right. We could say she had a self-righteous need to be the victim, which was one of the reasons the meeting did not go well. This is not to say that responsibility should not have been shared. Perhaps the teacher inflamed things by saying what was said. Perhaps the assistant principal hadn't planned the discussion with the correct reports or clarified the purpose at the beginning? Maybe. The critical part is that the conversation exploring this could not be had because of the unprofessional and cutting way the feedback was given to the teacher, and the lack of reflection and willingness to take responsibility shown by the principal. With the teacher in tears, the only thing that occurred in that meeting was a scar in the relationship that would take a long time to heal, if at all. With courage, the teacher stood up to the vicious scolding, took a deep breath and said, 'The whole meeting was terrible. Disorganised, not prepared for, adversarial. We did not do a good job of it at all. And you are trying to blame the whole thing on me and my comment.'

TAKE ANOTHER DOOR

Any time we feel the need to blame, stop. Breathe. Pause. What is this all about? Is there something I could have done differently? Until we can acknowledge and articulate at least one thing, don't put any blame on anyone else. When we reflect on similar situations, step into self-compassion. We can be blindsided when we have a strong unmet need that surges up. What do you notice in yourself when you reflect on these types of interactions? Be kind, and learn.

When we're imbalanced, one of these unsaid needs has not been met. This doesn't mean it should be met, but that the need for it is outweighing our ability to work from a place of centredness. The principal in this story had a driving need for being right, for status and credibility, which she thought had been undermined by the teacher. This led to damaged trust. The other complexity was that the teacher's default towards relationships had become a red rag to the principal and seen as a weakness, which had coloured many of their interactions. Their baggage was determining the outcome.

A measured, Ferocious Warmth response could have been to understand the hijacking of our own emotions (emotional intelligence), objectively identify the lack of structure and purpose (strategic intelligence) and hold a debrief that set about exploring the learning, not who was to blame (learning intelligence). This process would have led to them all learning what they could have done differently.

WHO'S DRIVING THE BUS?

When unmet need is driving the bus, we can lack a conscious focus on either results or relationships. One goes by the wayside. We become victim to the voices in our head telling us that we need more control, more action, better standards, that people's work is not good enough! Or that it's not our fault, that people won't like us if we tell them the truth, or don't do what they want. These inner voices keep us small thus we unconsciously act in ways that are either unhealthy or don't get the best outcomes for a strong culture. These voices are also habitual, stepping in when we are stressed, tired, anxious or simply unaware of their power. We head towards the extremes of leadership – fearsome (far too ferocious) or enmeshed (far too warm).

Here's an example. There's a report due in which I've found errors. My unmet need for perfection and control over the quality of work I'm associated with sends me into less-than-useful behaviours. I slam out an email to others in the team, liberally peppering my email with fault finding, blaming and shaming. No winners there. I lurch into too much ferocity.

Another example. There's a big event coming up. Instead of letting my team get on with the work, my inner voice is hyper-alert to all the dangers that could ruin it, so I micro-manage everything, getting very picky over the smallest things, and frustrated to the detriment of the quality of output and enjoyment of all involved.

While exploring these unmet needs, I was introduced to the work of Shirzad Chamine, author and Stanford lecturer. Chamine wrote *Positive Intelligence*[43] and it is a beauty. His Saboteur test has been taken by over 500,000 people worldwide.

According to Chamine, Saboteurs are a universal phenomenon, formed in our early childhood that keep our minds busy. They start off as our guardians to help us survive the real and imagined threats to our physical and emotional safety. But as we get older, and don't need them as much, our habitual ways of thinking keep them in employment. His approach is to invoke the Sage. The Sage is the wise thinker, able to reframe our less-than-useful beliefs. The challenge, as always, is about being aware of them in the first place! I call the Sage my Ninja.

Our inner Saboteurs can come from a number of types:

- **Judge** – constantly finding fault with self, others, circumstances, conditions. Chamine calls the Judge the Master Saboteur. We all have it at various times leading our thinking and feeling,

The 'Accomplice' Saboteurs:

- **Pleaser** – wants us to gain acceptance and affection by helping, pleasing, rescuing, etc. Our real needs become secondary and then we become resentful.
- **Controller** – wants us to take charge, get others to do what we want, and then gets highly anxious and impatient when that doesn't happen.
- **Hyper-Achiever** – must perform, must achieve, must be the best. Workaholic tendencies and a disconnection from deeper emotions and relationship needs.
- **Avoider** – avoids unpleasant and difficult tasks by being positive and pleasant in an extreme way. Procrastinates, puts things off until things fester or explode.

- **Hyper-Vigilant** – highly anxious that things around us could go wrong and the danger we may be in. Wears us down and blows things out of proportion.
- **Restless** – continuously on the lookout for greater excitement. Always busy. Highly distractible.
- **Stickler** – needs perfection, order and high levels of organisation. Causes anxiety and stress for ourselves and those around us.
- **Victim** – wants us to feel emotional and temperamental as a way of getting attention and affection. A big focus on internal feelings. Martyr behaviours can come up.
- **Hyper-Rational** – wants us to process everything from a rational viewpoint, including relationships. Causes us to be impatient with other people's emotions.

I find this explains many of our voices! And, of course, from a Ferocious Warmth perspective, some are more attached to the fearsome extreme (Hyper-Achiever, Hyper-Rational, Controller) and others to the enmeshed extreme (Pleaser, Victim, Avoider). Others can apply easily to either end.

When I coach and mentor leaders and teams, we often investigate the beliefs sitting underneath our thinking. The Saboteur is a rich and useful framework to help explore the unmet needs and behaviour drivers. The Sage or Ninja approach is one of the best ways to centre into Ferocious Warmth.

IS YOUR SAGE DRIVING THE BUS OR YOUR SABOTEURS?

Many of you would be familiar with Professor Carol Dweck's growth mindset work.[44] The saboteur approach is similar to Professor Dweck's way of identifying and working with fixed mindset personas. I had the privilege of working with Professor Dweck at a conference a few years ago, where she gave us a flamboyant experience of her 'Madame Perfect', whom she imagined dressed up in a red crinoline dress. Madame Perfect was the voice in her head that stopped her from sharing her book manuscript with colleagues for feedback. Oh, the irony – the book was on growth mindset! One of the biggest characteristics of growth mindset? Being open to feedback. This is of course not lost on Dweck, and the delicious paradox of this gave us not only a good laugh, but insight into looking at our own ironies.

Saboteurs, fixed mindset personas, we all have them.

Reflecting on my own saboteurs, I know that both my Hyper-Achiever and Restless voices were big in my head for a number of years. I know them well now. When they raise their heads, I hear them and see them in action. I name my personas. Two of them are Veronica Victim and Megalomaniac Marie. You might notice one is enmeshed; one is fearsome. I acknowledge them when they turn up. Now I'm armed to negotiate with them and dilute their potency by invoking my inner Ninja!

chapter seven

LACK OF CONNECTION

Along with unmet needs, the other context that can dislocate us from our centre space is lack of connection. This connection can be to ourselves, as we explored with the unmet needs of our inner voice. It can also be disconnection to the people we lead or to our purpose.

LOSING CONNECTION TO PURPOSE

Principal Paul had lost his connection to what inspired him most. He was trying to keep his head above water and lead his school out of a lengthy time in the doldrums, academically and culturally. Paul was a lovely man, a generous spirit who saw the very best in people. Unfortunately, he had a hard time holding people to account and creating an environment of transforming teaching and learning through collective efficacy.

The day I met Paul I sat down with him in his office. He closed the door and put a copy of my book *The Buzz* on the desk, full of colourful post-it notes. It always gives me a thrill to see that the thinking in my books is useful to people and so I clapped and took a photo (of course!) Paul looked serious and began. 'Tracey, I want to thank you for this book. I have been down in a great big rut for quite a while now. I go home and sit on the couch unsure what I'm going to do to change anything here or in my life. Then I started reading your book and I realise I can do something. It's inspired me again and given me the reason to get up in the morning.'

The thinking in that particular book at that particular time helped re-ignite Paul's connection to his moral purpose. He'd suffered from burn out and mental-health challenges and needed something to open up his thinking and his heart to why he became an educator in the first place. He started to bring the joy back into the school and his own life. He stepped into more courageous conversations with his team and co-creating the vision they wanted for their students.

I started working with this school just as they had received their four-year evaluation. For the third cycle (eight years) the results had stagnated at the same level. We began using a multi-pronged approach to transformation, building their professional collaborative learning culture (The Buzz). Paul and his team worked closely with their senior advisor to create a solid action plan to transform teaching and learning. They were building their pedagogical capacity through strategic professional learning and peer observation. As we worked on the new plan for the school, we shared the story of the school. During this process, we map the journey visually for everyone to discuss and contribute to. At the end of the story, one of the more established teachers commented on how sad it was that the message was the same as it had been eight years ago and that they still needed to shift. It was now obvious to her that they hadn't listened back then. 'We need to do something to shift!' she said. Paul and I looked at each other in secret glee. His refreshed approach had helped move some previously immovable hurdles. People were becoming more aware of the status quo and their complacent environment. The work had begun!

Paul was building strengths previously not utilised. His default was more relationship driven, warm, and clear expectations and standards were not so easy for him. As stress increased, his need to be liked in the midst of hard decisions made him move towards too much warmth. He avoided the trickier conversations, which caused a lack of connection to purpose. As he connected to this purpose, his resolve and courage increased.

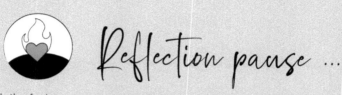

Reflection pause ...

Let's refresh our previous thinking on strengths and shadows. If your shadow is showing up instead of its strength, what could you pull from the other side to help centre? Which strength have you disconnected from?

For example, if my high expectations (head strength) are causing me to challenge people harshly and with judgement (head shadows), I might pause and step into compassion and empathy (heart strengths) to guide the discussion. This would help me have an open dialogue to find out what's happening for 'the others' rather than jumping to assumptions. It helps me challenge with curiosity rather than judgement.

But if I'm out of balance and disconnected, the shadow is let loose. I might feel better, but will the other person? Maybe, through fear. But it will be short lived. Fear shuts down thinking, collaboration and wellbeing. Not a great cocktail.

Figure 9. Strength and Shadow

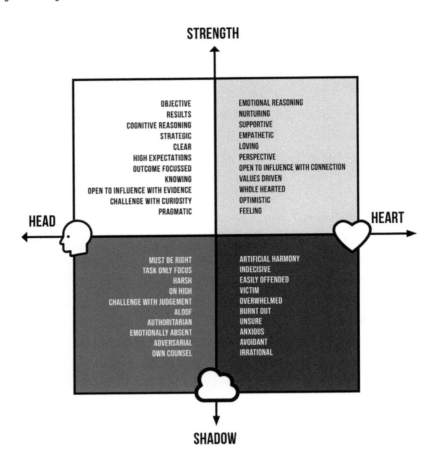

chapter eight

RECALIBRATION — BACK IN BALANCE

BEATING YOURSELF UP BEATS YOU DOWN

The metaphor of the dance of Ferocious Warmth came up in my discussion with Dr Briony Scott, Principal of Wenona School. In discussing the tension of staying in balance, Briony sees that we need to hold things lightly, as if moving backwards and forwards.

'You're constantly recalibrating. It's like being in a boat. You're never going to be stable, never going to be in that centre period for long. The challenge is how not to beat yourself up when you come away from the centre, just recalibrate and get back.'

By nature, we judge ourselves harshly. The judge in our head tells us we're not good enough when we slip, that we should have known better. When we recognise this, it's best to stop and appreciate the learning we've just been given. If we see it as learning, it's a gift not a tragedy. This self-reflection allows us to be better armed for the messiness of leadership. We then recalibrate and add to the way we work because of that messiness. As Briony shared: 'When you're in leadership where it's messy and you can't control people, it's because they're people, not factory parts. They're people and they're complex. If you can get 80% of your people doing 80% of what they're meant to do 80% of the time, it's a brilliant day!'

Here's a 'zone check' to help you assess the messiness, whether it's optimal, frayed or fragile...

OPTIMAL ZONE

The Ferocious Warmth zone – dancing the duality of both sides. Not always getting it right, but consciously getting insights, perspectives and behaviours that come from both sides of ferocity and warmth, head and heart.

FRAYED ZONE

When we're feeling frayed, we default to either results or relationships, a bit more head or a bit more heart. This sends us out of balance. Can you feel tension rising in yourself when starting to lean too much to the ferocious side or too much to the warmth side, without the tempering of the other to stay balanced? I asked one of my principal clients to explain how she might do both 'hand in glove'. She's an insightful and aware principal, who likes to push for excellence and sees herself as more to the ferocious side of the model. She knows she allows one of her leadership team to push her work-ethic buttons, judging the other as 'lazy' or 'full of excuses'. She realised that her unsaid expectations of this person were subjective and her empathy was in short supply. She pulled from the warmth side to bring her back to balance before she had further conversations about expectations.

FRAGILE ZONE

This occurs when we burst out of balance into extreme behaviour. It's a warning flare of what might happen if we don't take some quick measures to recalibrate to centre. For others, stress and rigid ways of working mean this is where we hang out most of the time without even realising it. It's where the fearsome or enmeshed behaviours rear their heads.

Some might not equate fragility with those at the more fearsome end as it tends to be about power *over* another, but I believe that whenever someone is behaving at the extremes, there is fragility, perhaps trauma and definitely high stress. If the extremes are a strong default position, narcissism can be at play. Narcissistic behaviours include an inflated sense of self-importance and entitlement. These types of leaders need constant praise and admiration and often come from an 'I' position. They are masters at exploitation and manipulation without guilt or shame. This is the world of the true bully, one that intimidates and demeans others as a matter of course – a true 'fearsome' leader. Research by Professor Charles O'Reilly, Professor Jennifer Chatman and Bernadette Doerr[45], focussed on the impact of narcissistic leadership on collaboration and integrity. Their results found that more narcissistic people are less likely to demonstrate collaboration and these leaders prefer to lead organisational cultures that are less collaborative and place less emphasis on integrity.

Sitting for prolonged periods in the fragile extremities of Ferocious Warmth can be evidence of low self-awareness. Korn Ferry Hay Group research[46] found that among leaders with multiple strengths in emotional self-awareness, 92% had teams with high energy and high performance. Great leaders create a positive emotional climate that encourages motivation and extra effort, and they're the ones with good emotional self-awareness. In sharp contrast, leaders low in emotional self-awareness created negative climates 78% of the time. Too much head, logic, ferocity results in low empathy. Too much heart, emotion, warmth results in increased anxiety and worry.

GETTING BACK INTO BALANCE

Charlie, a leader I had for a few years, sent grenades every weekend in the form of emails that would greet us on Monday morning. He would sit at home, red wine in hand, and come up with all the reasons we weren't living up to his standards. He was highly stressed and dealt with this by trying to be in control. He had very little self-regulation and did little self-care, more self-medicating. He'd kick the filing cabinet if he had a bad phone call. It was all sorts of ridiculous. And, of course, we just had to duck out the way. His self-regulation was low and affected the standard to which we could do our work.

Emotional self-regulation is one of the skills of emotional intelligence. It provides us with the skills to deal with high-stress situations. It puts us in touch with what's happening cognitively and emotionally. Self-regulation increases our ability to manage situations and reframe them to something more useful. When we focus on self-regulation, self-care is one of the best ways to 'lengthen our fuse'.

SELF-CARE

Often leaders leave self-care on the bottom of the list. Yet we know that self-care is vital to our wellbeing and ability to fulfil our role. Without looking after our own wellbeing, we hold to the frayed and fragile zone more easily and frequently. Knowing what brings about calm and centredness for ourselves and investing in those activities, whether physical, mental, emotional or spiritual, increases centredness.

There are many ways to show self-compassion and self-care when we start to tip out of balance. Often, we know what keeps us centred, we just forget to use them or they slip right down the 'to do' list. There are many brilliant books and courses on such things as mindfulness and resilience that can help you if this is an area you know needs attention. More education systems are supporting school leaders through coaching and supervision, as a result of the stress of 2020. I hope this resourcing continues and becomes an accepted part of leadership support.

Here though, are some relatively easy ways to recalibrate:

JUST BE

Sometimes we just need to sit with our feelings when we're faced with difficult times and not staying as centred as we'd like. I remember lying on my couch after the devastating Victorian Black Saturday fires in 2009. I watched Paul Kelly sing 'How to Make Gravy' at the Sound Relief concert held at the Melbourne Cricket Ground raising funds for those who'd suffered during the fires, and balled my eyes out. It's a song that always gives me a tear. This time, it helped me let it all out. Sometimes we need to sit with being sad or angry or lonely. Just feel it. And that's OK. And then if you want to shift, it's great to put on pumping music, be silly, sing out loud and dance in the garden – or whatever takes your fancy!

BREATHE

When Justin and I and my friends experienced the trauma of losing our friends in the motorbike accident, our adrenalin and cortisol was sky high. One of the first people I called was my oldest friend, Ree. She's a therapist and counsellor. We've known each other since I was eighteen months old. All I needed to say to her was 'I need you here' and she was on the doorstep thirty minutes later. Over the next three days, Ree spent time being present. She is a beautiful soul who has lived a life of huge challenge herself, yet manages to be the life of the party. Her laugh is infectious and everyone loves her. So much so that when she needed a hip replacement at the age of 41, all her work mates donated their sick leave so she could undertake the operation, even only being at the organisation for a short time. That is the type of impact Ree has on the world.

But this time Ree quietly took each person aside and let them talk. She taught us all, including the children, to square breathe. In for four with the nose. Hold for four. Out for four with the mouth. Hold for four. Repeat. Sometimes we would all do it together to settle ourselves and come together. I also use this in workshops to settle us down if the discussion is red hot or people are 'brain scattered' before they walk in. It's a calming, gentle way to recalibrate.

DO A WONDER WALK

Take time to walk around your school, specifically to observe and relish in things that are wonderful. So many awesome things go on in schools every moment of the day. Make a note in a journal about them, mention them to others, show gratitude, acknowledge them. Give your head and your heart a moment to acknowledge all the good going on, and your contribution to these.

TAP INTO JOY

For many school leaders the biggest joy bubble comes from hanging out with students. Primary school leaders talk about sitting in with the Foundation classes enjoying that energy and curiosity again. Secondary leaders tell me one of their week's highlights is teaching their favourite subject. Connecting to purpose yet again. I've seen Professor John Hattie walk through schools. He seems to spend a good chunk of time talking with students. While I am sure he's asking them about their learning, a part of me wonders if this is a bit of a joy bubble for him as well – connecting to the people at the core of the work.

MOVE

One of the easiest things to do is shift from where you are and move. Walk, dance, just move rooms. These shift energy.

CREATE SQUADS WHO HAVE YOUR BACK

Sometimes leaders are surrounded by people, but still feel alone. We don't always want to share work issues and challenges at home with those we're closest too. Our collegiate connections become more and more important as the world becomes more complex.

I have a few 'squads'. Different pods of close friends and colleagues who help me recalibrate when I get off kilter. These people love me for and despite of all my flaws and help to make me a better person.

When COVID-19 hit and my business calendar become blank for months ahead, Donna, Lynne and Maree became my strongest safety net. As the sole income earner in my family (well, to be perfectly honest, at that stage my son who works for McDonald's was way ahead), I really needed a plan!

Donna, Lynne, Maree and I have been friends for over a decade. Meeting through our professional networks we've learnt and laughed together through professional development, many meals and think-tank weekends where we go away to hatch some new thinking. We're lucky that our relationships straddle professional and personal. We don't work in each other's businesses. In a sense we're in competition, but we all have unique intellectual property that means we often refer our own clients to others in the group, due to the clarity of our particular message.

The four of us were all in the same boat of consulting practices – speaking, educating and facilitating. We usually work with groups or speak at conferences, which all came to a standstill in March 2020. It could have been a very scary and anxious time, and it was to a certain extent, but we put in strategies straight away to support each other.

Our WhatsApp group worked overtime. There were quick comments, early morning hellos to get us up and out of bed and dodgy memes sent for a laugh. We celebrated the smallest wins with silly bitmojis and virtual high fives. Most of all we made sure we caught up frequently online. For a number of years, we've enjoyed virtual Friday night drinks, as we don't live close, but this was a virtual support group on steroids!

At first we caught up every couple of days. Some days we were exhausted from the pressure of working out what to do. On those days we'd just let it all hang out, sharing our feelings and fears. Usually, by the end of the time we'd also had a good laugh as well. Other times we were deliberately strategising, throwing audacious ideas around about how we could support our clients, as well as survive ourselves.

The interesting thing was that all of us had made shifts in between our frequent chats. We experimented and then shared our findings. As soon as someone had more information or insight, it was passed on. Those connecting times gave us the strength of resolve and conviction to keep going. After a few weeks the frequency of catching up lowered, as we got our heads into the tasks at hand.

Working with a number of principal networks during COVID-19, I asked them to share what was helping them stay centred and supported in trying times. Many principals shared that the support within the network had reached new levels of collegiate and generosity. New principals to the networks mentioned that they felt more connection in those first few weeks than they had previously in the group. Collegiate groups make all the difference to keeping our heads up.

But I have a few caveats.

STUCK IN THE VORTEX OF DESPAIR

Collegiate groups that keep us thinking the same way are not very useful. Debriefing and support are important, but if the responses keep us stuck or in a downward spiral, time to re-think. When one person's emotional state grabs us and we disappear into the vortex of despair, we all feel far worse.

CHALLENGE AND SUPPORT

Conversations that challenge our current perspectives and expand our thinking is what I gain from this particular squad of peeps. If these people can't challenge my thinking, who can? I also find support when I'm finding things tough.

ELEVATE OTHERS

Our purpose is to elevate each other whenever we can. I have a friend who disengaged from a group he was a part of because it started to become passive-aggressive when he experienced big wins in his professional life. Jealousy reared its head and came out as snide comments, sarcasm and lack of celebration. He realised that the people in the group were getting together through habit, not through a particularly deep connection. Realising that the people we're with are making us feel guilty for achieving, or not, is a good step in releasing the power their opinions might have over us.

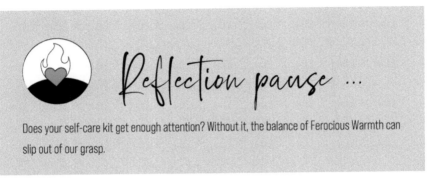

Does your self-care kit get enough attention? Without it, the balance of Ferocious Warmth can slip out of our grasp.

Write down your top eight favourite balancing activities and track how often you do them. Is it enough?

Now for the Elements of Ferocious Warmth, the foundational attributes of Ferocious Warmth leaders, and to meet some exemplars. When we're centred, these elements: Expansive, Connected, Courageous and Authentic encompass our leadership. They bring together both sides of ferocity and warmth, hand in glove.

THE FEROCIOUS WARMTH

Elements

Expansive

Connected

Courageous

Authentic

expansive

chapter nine

EXPANDING SELF

'We keep moving forward, opening new doors, and doing new things, because we are curious and curiosity keeps leading us down new paths.

Walt Disney[47]

Have you ever felt stuck in a rut with your wheels spinning in mud? Doing the same thing the same way, day in day out, not moving forward? Fortunately, humans are designed to evolve, so sooner or later we choose to step out of the rut, or the universe conspires to do it for us! The context becomes unworkable, or our environment deteriorates to a state where we say 'enough is enough'. We seek to expand the way we work in the world. Expansion is the continual growth beyond our current mental and emotional state. For many it also includes spiritual growth. Being expansive is a way of being for Ferocious Warmth leaders. It moves us from 'I' to a 'we'.

Do we ever stop learning? Sometimes we might need a few failed attempts before we learn the lessons, but we're adaptive and responsive to what works and what doesn't work. The best entrepreneurs in the world see failure as opportunity. Learning our craft expands our toolkit, our approaches and our beliefs. Whether in the classroom or leading the school, the learning never stops. When my second child was just about to be born, I was sharing with a friend that I wondered if you love the next child as much as the first? As the father of two beautiful babies, my friend said, 'Having a second child simply expands your love. Love continues to grow and expands as your family grows.' Learning is the same. There is no end.

BE EXPANSIVE IN YOUR LEARNING

What are you reading and listening to at the moment to expand your world view and your mental models? What podcasts pique your interest and help you think in different ways? There is no better time to be pushing into expansion of thinking. The podcast world is exploding with entrepreneurial thinking in business, life and education. Blogs and books abound with thinking that shakes the way we see the world, in a good way. In some schools there seems to be a famine when it comes to reading articles or books that expand thinking. It is seen as something 'extra' rather than a professional responsibility. As leaders the best way to shift this is to model it. A colleague I've worked with for many years is head of campus in a large school and runs a journal club that no one is expected to come to, yet all are invited. Jane flags the articles or chapters coming up then simply turns up and opens the space. The momentum of this 'no pressure' approach has normalised discussion and expansion. It is now an accepted item on their professional development menu.

ARE YOU CURIOUS ABOUT YOURSELF?

I run a group mentoring program for Ferocious Warmth Women in Leadership. Eight professional senior leaders come together regularly to reflect on themselves as professionals, but first and foremost as human beings. Their reasons for joining this group are varied, but the most common one is to take the time to reflect on themselves – what they believe and what they stand for. The other is the opportunity to expand (that word again!) their network and learn from people outside their orbit. All of them do a huge amount of professional development for their craft of school leadership, but this program is about the being of leadership. This work takes courage and a willingness to explore those things about yourself that might be hidden, but it is fulfilling and rewarding. This deep dive requires us to peel our layers like an onion and examine the thinking and feeling beneath. We look at the unmet needs and lack of connection that might be separating us from our purpose and our values. We explore the triggers that move us out of balance and from our strengths to our shadow. We explore these things through the four elements in this part of the book. Are you up for it? It's the journey to become the calm, balanced Ferocious Warmth leader.

SELF-AWARENESS

The first skill of emotional intelligence is emotional self-awareness. The first step in the Ferocious Warmth journey is understanding what we feel. We hold so much of our past history in our current behaviours. As we have explored previously, many of our behaviours are unconscious. They are responses not so much to the situation in front of us, but the trigger it sets off and attaches to a situation from the past. How many times have you responded to a small situation with a large over-reaction? Emotional literacy is the first step in this journey. Did I stop to acknowledge how I was feeling and what might have triggered this reaction? What pushed me out of being firmly balanced in the moment? Was it the call of the past or the fear of the future? What can I learn about myself from what just happened? The difference between this last question and one around what the other person should have done can be life-changing. Reflecting on our strengths and shadows and re-calibrating when we're out of balance is self-expansion at work.

NOTICE WHEN YOU SQUIRM

I always know when I'm in for a big dose of learning, something that really expands my thinking and will push me further. I get uncomfortable. It makes me squirm a bit as I see how it fits my own thinking and feeling about the world, my own mental models. Sometimes it's a simple question from a coach or colleague that stops me in my tracks and I sit there with my brain exploding. I'm a bit of a sucker for this type of learning now as I know this is where expansion happens.

Some reading this book may squirm or push away as we discuss the emotional side of leadership. Perhaps they don't see much value in this as getting things done. 'Seriously, life would be easier if everyone just drank a cup of concrete and got on with things. I don't have time for this stuff'.

My experience is that leaders drawn more to 'warm' seek out leadership development that helps them build more conviction and 'ferocity' because they are already very reflective and seek to build their less-developed side. They tend to have high levels of self-awareness and understand the impact they're having in the negative. They recognise their tendency to go too far to the relationship side and want to learn how to stay steady when the need for hard decisions or a stronger stance is in front of them. I find people with very developed ferocious or results-oriented sides and not so developed in emotional intelligence skills resist this type of work for longer. It gets labelled 'fluffy' and not as important. I was surprised when I first started doing leadership work in corporate settings to find that they labelled professional learning in skills such as leading difficult conversations, emotional intelligence and culture as 'soft' skills. Yet they are the hardest to do.

This paradox tells us something about the bias set up in the world of work about emotions and leadership. The concepts of belonging, love, compassion and self-care can scare some people off and be seen as non-essential. Yet these are the essence of leadership. This is not a judgement on people drawn more naturally to the logical lens. This is my reflection on observations over many years working in this space. I find people drawn to connection and emotions step towards it and are passionate about it, those drawn to task, measurement, structure and certainty find it more of a challenge.

Of course, the shift to the balance of Ferocious Warmth is learnable from both preferences. We can learn emotional intelligence and the ability to build more logically based thinking. Ferocious Warmth is also not about leaving behind our essence. This work brings them together. It's important to build our skills in managing the emotional side of ourselves and the people we lead, whether students, staff or community. So is stepping into the tough decisions required to lift education to a new level.

BE THE LEADER — THE OPEN EXPANSION OF SELF

Professor Michael Fullan, global educational leader in collaborative cultures for deep learning, found in his team's research that leaders who also lead the team learning get better results. In his words, 'We have found that leaders must lead and learn in equal measure.' [48] He coined the term 'lead learner', which is another one of his 'sticky messages', built on from the findings of Professor Viviane Robinson that effective school leadership not only promotes, but directly participates with teachers in formal or informal professional learning. [49]

Leaders in learning institutions have a responsibility to be the lead learner. A leader who doesn't sit back when people are investigating the why and how of their work. One that doesn't ride in on a white horse to save the day with the answer to everyone's problems. A lead learner steps into the learning arena with their team and pulls the issue apart as a partner. Curiosity and wonderings fuel the conversations, rather than judgement and black-and-white thinking, right or wrong. They create systems and structures for the learning to occur. Teams who learn from each other as part of the way they work shift the fear of 'stuffing up' into an opportunity for collaborative inquiry and exploration. Leaders who model this approach help to cultivate a culture of trust, collaboration and support, rather than one of competition and judgement.

BE A LEADER THAT IS LEARNING, NOT ONE THAT HAS LEARNT

Do you know people who see themselves as an expert and are closed to thinking differently? They have learnt, but are not learning. In this dynamic environment of change and revolution, an expert who has mastered their area and then stopped learning quickly ceases to be relevant. Slowly, we're breaking down the old, hierarchical thinking that leaders must know the answers to be good at their jobs. Great leaders help their teams find even better solutions. Leaders who let their teams innovate with a reasonable amount of autonomy through the 'COVID-19 experiment of 2020' made the shift far more quickly. Leaders who learn with their teams not only create a culture of learning, but say to their teams: I am open to learning, too. One of my favourite photos of a workshop is one of three schools together learning about the 'HITS' initiative of the Victorian Department of Education[50], a useful document guiding teachers in high impact teaching strategies. We designed a thorough dive into all ten of the strategies and there was deep learning and sharing throughout the day. Not once could you see or hear dominant voices from the leaders nor did you see the leaders standing at the back watching everyone else learn. They were in there up to their elbows, learning deeply with their teams at the tables. How many workshops related to critical paths the school is taking have you taken without the senior leadership present? To be honest, I just don't get that. Symbolically, it doesn't look the best, and strategically it's gravely flawed to miss the opportunity of vital learning with our teams.

> THE EXPERTS OF THE 21ST CENTURY ARE THOSE THAT ARE LEARNING, NOT THOSE WHO HAVE LEARNT.

ARE YOU AN EXPERT WHO HAS LEARNT OR ARE YOU STILL LEARNING?

Dr Victor Ottati of Loyola University, Chicago has researched what he coined 'Earned Dogmatism Effect'.[51] Ottati's hypothesis states that social norms dictate that experts often adapt a 'dogmatic closed-minded orientation'. When experts feel like experts, they are less likely to admit they're wrong or say they don't know something. Across six different experiments, they found that experts will act like experts even if they are wrong, because they feel they're expected to have dogmatic opinions. This pulls us back to the concept of duality and paradox. Being a learner should not mean you leave your knowledge and expertise behind. It does mean, however, that we're open to not knowing, and that others can bring things to the table that we may not have seen or known before. Knee deep in the information explosion how can we expect to know it all?

STEP INTO CURIOSITY, NOT JUDGEMENT

A Ferocious Warmth response when our assumptions are challenged is to pause and reflect. It may be about recoding responses. Defensiveness, judgement and discomfort are significant signs that there is some juicy learning to step into. Asking questions rather than defending our position creates an inquiry mindset.

The need for shift in education challenges us to rethink the way we have always done things. If we increase curiosity about our own and other's thinking when faced with a new challenge, our learning turns on. Arming ourselves with questions that seek to understand, rather than invalidate another's position, is a powerful skill to develop. A useful mental model for this is the Ladder of Inference by Chris Argyris.[52] The Ladder of Inference highlights that we leap up the ladder of inference via our bias and assumptions made on a sliver of data. If we can accept that many of our beliefs are based on erroneous assumptions, then we are more able to test and challenge our thinking. We seek more information, knowledge and data to base our beliefs on. I expand on this model in my first book *The Buzz* as a way for teams to unpack their beliefs and misunderstandings. Viviane Robinson of Auckland University uses this model and Argyris' double loop learning model as the critical part of the Open to Learning™ methodology.[53] This methodology provides a rigorous framework for discussions that promote understanding and learning.

KEYS TO GROWTH — MISTAKES AND FAILURES

Own your 'stuff ups'. Nothing drops more trust points than when we don't admit when we've experienced failure. It creates a sense that mistakes are not tolerated. Our default is that we brush them under the carpet. Impressed into our psyche is that making mistakes is a weakness. Yet a learning culture creates space for learning from mistakes. I left an organisation because the leader not only failed to take responsibility for a serious issue that was definitely his doing, but also pinned it onto two of his senior team. Our trust for him as a leader went down the drain as we saw him bluff and bluster, spraying excuses and accusations at everyone else. All that was needed was for him to say, 'Wow, sorry, I made the wrong decision there, team. Let's look at what we need to do to fix it.' We could have approached the issue as a group, discovering how we might mitigate the problem and make different decisions in the future. Breaking this habit of not owning failures and mistakes occurs when we're willing to wrestle with the muckiness of learning and become aware of the musings of that unhelpful little voice in our heads.

DROP THE NEED TO BE RIGHT

The need to be right drives distrust in teams. When people feel we're not open to influence, the chance for collaboration and exploring options dives. Our brains get a dopamine hit when we're right, but if we continually seek to be right over others, we increase their cortisol and their resistance increases. For some of us, the need for that dopamine hit drives us to make others wrong and ourselves right. Believing ourselves to be 'right' shuts down our thinking's 'peripheral vision'. We fail to see what falls outside our view of the world. Peripheral vision has been found to decrease significantly when we're highly stressed, causing tunnel vision. The same can be said when we feel the driving need to right. Our focus becomes myopic, based on what we think, rather than what others think. What if we weren't right? Even holding that thought as we walk into any conversation will hold us in the centred Ferocious Warmth position.

As we expand ourselves, our outward attention focusses on creating a culture that supports our students, teachers and support staff to expand their own capacity and capability. One links to the other. Without growth in self, it's difficult to encourage growth in others. Yet growing and expanding others is the essence of a leader's job.

chapter ten

BUILDING COLLECTIVE CAPACITY

'Most maddening or exciting for Musk's employees, depending on which one you ask, is the time scale on which he often expects work to be done. For example, one Friday when I was visiting, a few SpaceX staff members were frantically rushing back and forth from the office to the parking lot across the street. It turns out that during a meeting, he asked them how long it would take to remove staff cars from the lot and start digging the first hole for the Boring Company tunnel. The answer: two weeks. Musk asked why, and when he gathered the necessary information, he concluded, "Let's get started today and see what's the biggest hole we can dig between now and Sunday afternoon, running 24 hours a day." Within three hours, the cars were gone and there was a hole in the ground.'

Elon Musk: 'The Architect of Tomorrow', *Rolling Stone*[54]

March 2020 was education's SpaceX hole in the ground. Schools and their communities moved whole systems to an online learning model in a matter of days!

Before COVID-19, when working with people on thriving in the learning zone and not getting stuck in the comfort zone, I shared stories from Christchurch not long after the earthquakes in 2010/2011. I was working with community and health agencies to create technology strategies that linked authentically to their purpose and organisational goals. One of my major insights was our adaptability in a crisis. Christchurch leaders told of aged care nurses and others, historically labelled as 'hard to shift' around technology, moving to case notes recorded on tablets and held in cloud storage in a remarkably short time. Their original case notes? Buried in sludge and debris in the centre of town. The motivation for change couldn't be ignored – care for their patients.

Now we've experienced our own version of this throughout the world. As a profession, educators have been at the front of the 'pivot' to a new way of working. (I wanted to land that word at least once, just to make a few readers wince at the sound of the most used word in Australia during the pandemic!) In working with many hundreds of leaders and teachers during lockdown and remote learning, I found that schools already firmly in a learning culture, with high collective efficacy, sustained their energy with a 'we can do it' approach. Their forward momentum through continued focus on growth stood them in great stead. Collaboration, trialling and a culture of learning from successes and failures were critical to success. For those whose default is the comfort zone of 'same' and certainty, the energy and stress around shifting was undoubtably higher. Many of us crave certainty, reliability and lack of ambiguity, and the pressure of not having them to fall back onto took its toll on many.

Within a culture of 'we never arrive', during COVID-19 we experienced an opportunity for transformation and renewal. To go back to Nassim Taleb's antifragile approach: 'The resilient resists shocks and stays the same; the antifragile gets better.'

This shift out of our comfort zone expands us – our thinking, our skills, our attitudes and beliefs. Our role as Ferocious Warmth leaders is to create the culture for expansion to thrive.

CREATING A CULTURE OF 'WE NEVER ARRIVE'

Several years ago, as I searched for Ferocious Warmth leaders outside my orbit, I was introduced (via the global next-door chat that is Twitter) to a wonderful exemplar of the whole Ferocious Warmth concept. Sarah Martin, Principal of Stonefields Primary School in Auckland, portrays all the attributes of Ferocious Warmth. She is warm, yet ferocious about her students, her team and her community, and consistently contributes to the New Zealand dialogue on education. She speaks internationally at conferences and is committed to increasing excellence in education through leadership and capacity building. Sarah fulfils every Ferocious Warmth characteristic and brings to her leadership entrepreneurial thinking that guides Stonefields through a constant cycle of learning, improvement and innovation.

I met Sarah one afternoon in the Stonefields' staff room, a welcoming and homely retreat. She was elbow-deep in marinade. With a parent information evening that night, Sarah was cooking the lamb for the shared staff meal before the evening's business. This symbolic element of Sarah's leadership screams of connection and humility in one action. Food is one of the great connectors. When it has the authentic hand of a leader involved in its creation, there is a humility of service and appreciation that is unsaid, yet felt in the act.

A few more things stand out for me as the 'beyond leadership 101' behaviours of any leader into real expansion:

- Sarah is fiercely committed to building the capacity of all her team.
- The whole school has a relentless focus on creating learning for their students and each other with a stated purpose to 'cause learning'.
- Sarah has a beautiful connection to her students. The day I visited was sunny. Rather than getting on the speaker and telling the kids 'no hat, no play', she was singing a song to remind them. Smiling, the kids scampered off to get their hats.
- In Sarah's classroom wanders, she is deeply connected with the students in their learning and the teachers in their pedagogy.
- Sarah is savvy about sticky messages. Using a graphic designer, Sarah had the mascots and the school values made into relevant little 'stone people', who are recognised by every student and family.
- Anyone can download the school's approach to teaching and learning. It outlines their values and acknowledges the evidence base underpinning their approach.
- Sarah draws from beyond education to test and expand her thinking. She is what Jim Knight, educational coach expert, would call a 'radical' learner.[55]

- With her community, Sarah revisits the essence and purpose of the school to ensure it reflects their diverse and changing population.
- Sarah shares an office with her leadership team, where they often work at a round table in the middle of the room, symbolically shouting 'we collaborate!'.
- Stonefields has developed many of their own methodologies and frameworks, and regularly share these with others.
- Sarah and her team constantly check in with their teachers, aiming to balance collaborative work and cognitive load.
- Sarah encourages her staff, students and parents to talk openly when things are tough.
- Whenever Sarah is questioned, she comes at her answers like a learner, curious and seeking to understand more, rather than an expert.

Sarah's expansion approach extends further, but you get the idea! Ferocious Warmth!

Sarah and her team fiercely commit to the concept of 'we never arrive'. They have carefully curated this culture since the school opened. It is overt and discussed often. They recruit provocative leaders and educators. This advertisement for a Deputy Principal at Stonefields a few years ago clearly articulates the hunt for a change agent and learner:

Are you comfortable being uncomfortable?
Do you enjoy being challenged and imagining
possibilities to best serve learners?
Are you a learner and able to be a mindset provocateur
to grow capacity in oneself and colleagues?

Continuously iterating our teaching practice can challenge educators who haven't experienced an overt learning culture within the staff. For Ferocious Warmth leaders, it's an embedded part of the discussions. Recruiting for mindset leads to growing collective capacity in our teams, which sets the environment for learning and growth. The work is creating a thriving learning culture that says 'we never arrive'.

CULTURE AND STRATEGY

After a decade of working with teams on how to work better together, it was clear to me that schools making the most difference to their students were those blending strategy and culture, collaborating together to create change in teaching and learning. At the same time, the evidence base was mounting that collective efficacy dramatically affects student outcomes. In 2015 I created a model for collaborative learning cultures and published *The Buzz*.

In 2016, Professor John Hattie and the Visible Learning Research ranked collective efficacy as having the greatest effect size affecting student achievement.[56] Jenni Donohoo's book *Collective Efficacy* is a thorough and brilliant exploration of this approach. Her definition is worth noting as part of the Expansive skills of a Ferocious Warmth leader.

Collective efficacy is evident when teachers see themselves as part of a team working for their students. When educators believe in their collective ability to lead the improvement of student outcomes, higher levels of achievement result.[57]

This work in professional learning culture is now well underway in most schools across Australia and New Zealand, led by global experts such as Michael Fullan, Viviane Robinson, Mary Jean Gallagher, Dr Lyn Sharratt, Beate Planche and others. For some schools it is a profound shift. Over 7800 educators and 270 schools have taken part in my Buzz diagnostic. This data provides me and the schools insight into the building of The Buzz collaborative culture: growth and learning mindset, a compelling environment for learning and authentic dialogue. Learning cultures require the draw from ferocity to lift standards and the warmth to create an environment of safety to learn.

A strong expanding learning culture draws from another duality: culture and strategy. Of course, this is most effective when the strategy is created by and for the whole school community. Examples like the Northern Territory of Australia lead the way in student-voice involvement with strategy. Student Learning Ambassadors discuss, dissect and address data and pose solutions to the department for future strategic direction. With the important issues of engagement, wellbeing and motivation of both students and teachers impacting on organisational success, culture is the critical component that brings strategy to life. It builds the social capital that enables people to do great things together. If we work on cocreating the strategy of the organisation we can affect culture, because we tap into a vital way to strengthen people's engagement and sense of purpose: increased voice and recognition of their value.

If we insist on strategy only being developed and shaped by leaders, or the 'school improvement team', with no input from the people doing the work, we end up with words on a page that no one pays any attention to. Strategy created by a few people in a closed room won't create the momentum we need for success. But collaboration builds professional trust. Trust builds as we engage in greater discussion. Schools that made big leaps in creating professional learning cultures now never create a strategy without rigorous exploration of the current state. All of the voices at the table must explore scan, then focus on the priority areas of need. This is emotional and strategic intelligence in concert together.

At a very basic level, collaboration avoids people whinging about edicts from above and changes for no good reason. In this environment, everyone should feel heard and have the opportunity to share ideas in robust discussion. The evidence base is clear that the effect on students is far greater when education staff work together as collective change agents, rather than as individuals.

"BRINGING STRATEGY AND CULTURE TOGETHER IS ABOUT CULTIVATING CONVERSATIONS THAT CONNECT PEOPLE TO PURPOSE AND PEOPLE TO PEOPLE."

COLLABORATION IS LEARNING OUT LOUD

Collaboration is all about learning deeply together. When we come together as professionals seeking to improve our impact, we share our thinking and approaches, challenges and strengths. It's about building our leadership and teaching toolkits to shape teaching and learning. The dialogue is critical, as is the trust and purpose behind working together.

LEADING THE LEARNING

While some schools are only just starting to get out of classroom silos, many have been on the path of collaborative professional learning for a number of years. In 2006, Michael Fullan wrote:

'Collaborative cultures are ones that focus on building the capacity for continuous improvement and are intended to be a new way of working and learning. They are meant to be enduring capacities, not just another program innovation.' [58]

Schools with these capacities cannot imagine going back to an individualistic approach to the classroom. Whole school improvement, innovative practice, transformation of teaching and learning, inter-disciplinary approaches – none of these can be achieved without collaboration at their foundation.

Collaboration encourages deep dialogue about our own beliefs, our teaching and learning strategies and, for leaders, our leadership strategies. Unfortunately, my findings in The Buzz diagnostic of over 7800 educators indicates we have a way to go. The statements that trend downward, no matter the level of collaborative culture, are:

1. 'I am confident to speak up when I see behaviour eroding our school's professional culture.'
2. 'I trust my colleagues' intentions.'
3. 'As a school we actively seek to challenge each other's teaching and learning strategies using evidence to inform our dialogue.'

The lowest response across all respondents?

4. 'We actively encourage pedagogical debate in our meetings.'

Collaboration is about transforming and expanding teaching and learning, yet many schools' teams simply cooperate. They have trouble lifting beyond sharing resources and getting to the space of 'learning out loud' with each other.

BEYOND COOPERATION

The Collaboration Continuum is useful to reflect on where the work in any particular school or system is needed. We're aiming for the top two levels: co-creation and collective capacity.

Figure 10. Collaboration Continuum, Tracey Ezard, 2015

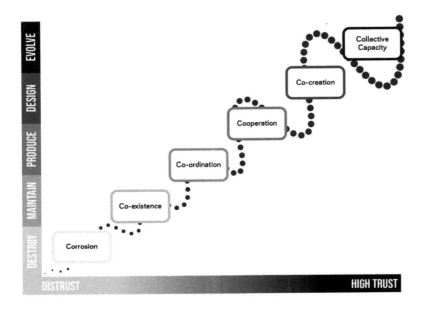

Here's an overview of the levels, starting at the dreaded bottom.

CORROSION

It's a pity we need this level at all, but unfortunately corrosive environments exist. When this happens at a leadership level, the whole school is in intense pain with powerplays and egos running rampant, creating havoc on any plans to work together – too much ferocity and not enough warmth. Opportunities to collaborate are derailed by lack of trust and poor behaviour.

My niece was on the receiving end of this corrosion. A Year 12 English internal assessment, set by one English teacher, was on completely different topics to that which the other English class had been studying for. The reason: lack of any sort of professional communication or relationship between the teachers. In the words of a furious 17-year-old, 'We know they hate each other.' How's that for an example of toxic interpersonal relationships affecting student futures?

CO-EXISTENCE

At this level there's little or no interaction between colleagues beyond being part of a group that co-exist in the same space or content. Co-existence still happens in many schools. The Year 8 science teacher sits next to another Year 8 science teacher in a staff room, yet they never discuss how they teach concepts and differentiate, or share strategies that help students engage. The reasons? Some of it is simply historical – 'we don't do that around here'. Or perhaps their relationship doesn't extend beyond civility. They don't know each other and don't seek to find out. At the other end of the spectrum, but with the same impact, they're good friends and don't go near the teaching and learning discussion. So, they simply bob along in their comfort zone, not realising that gold is uncovered when we can learn from each other.

COOPERATION AND CO-ORDINATION

When organisations say they're collaborating, cooperation and co-ordination is what they're up to. While these two levels are important, they're only an immature version of collaboration. Transactional rather than transformative, knowledge and information is shared and discussed. Work tasks, such as planning, are divided between members to use time more effectively and build consistency. Duplication of thinking and delivery moves toward collective and integrated approaches. Information is disseminated and discussed for co-ordination and management purposes. Interaction is about smooth processes and organisational issues.

CO-CREATION — TOGETHER YOU AND I CREATE BETTER

Discussion and activity are centred on working and learning together to create more effective and targeted ways of working, resulting in more effective outcomes. This is collaboration. Teaching teams dive into pedagogical discussions to improve student learning, using evidence to guide the conversation. Psychological safety is critical for all members to have a voice.

COLLECTIVE CAPACITY — LEARNING FROM OUR COLLECTIVE WISDOM

At this top level, we build our own and each other's capacity. We actively seek to learn from each other and test our thinking and judgement. We test new ways of working and support each other to try new ways of teaching, assessing impact on learning. We are actively modelling a collective growth mindset. The work evolves and transforms. This is the true nature of a collaborative culture – we're all seeking continuous improvement and growth, together.

Where does your team sit? Your whole school? Where is co-creation critical? How could you lead this work by modelling growth in your sphere of influence?

chapter eleven

WHAT STOPS US LEARNING TOGETHER?

In my work with schools and systems, I have found that the biggest barrier to us working more collaboratively is our mindset and the environment. As educators, we pride ourselves on knowing our 'stuff' and work hard at providing the best possible learning for our students. Yet when we first start learning more deeply as a collective, we can experience interesting internal dialogue. Using stronger evidence as a basis for discussion and action can be confronting. 'Is what I'm doing good enough?' 'Is what I've been doing all these years right?' 'I feel very uncomfortable with this level of discussion on my professional judgement.'

Professor Dylan Wiliam, Emeritus Professor of Educational Assessment, University College London, puts this into a powerful statement that emphasises key cultural and leadership work:

'If we create a culture where every teacher believes they need to improve, not because they are not good enough but because they can be even better, there is no limit to what we can achieve.' [59]

From talking with thousands of educators I know there is truth in this statement. Collaborative cultures are born here. And it's where the learning intelligence of Ferocious Warmth leaders comes into sharp focus. This is The Buzz.

Figure 11. Elements of a Thriving Learning Culture, Tracey Ezard, 2015

WHERE SHOULD WE FOCUS?

During my fifteen years of observing this work in action plus data from The Buzz diagnostic and other evidence-based research, I discovered three pillars are the foundation for a thriving collaborative culture:

1. A collective growth mindset that expands our thinking individually and collectively.

2. A compelling environment in which we are drawn to learning together, due to the processes, protocols and energy we bring to the table.

3. Authentic dialogue where we focus on discussing the things that help us expand our impact on student learning.

When these three come together, we create psychological safety for learning, focus on the right things and build forward momentum.

PSYCHOLOGICAL SAFETY

At the intersection of a growth mindset and a compelling environment sits psychological safety. Any dialogue is influenced by the mindset with which we enter it. Our mindset can be affected by the environment we are a part of.

Have you ever been engaged in an interesting, open discussion with a group of people, only for the environment to totally change when one person walked in the room? When we make it safe to contribute and create processes for learning, psychological safety begins and cultures of toxicity, avoidance and blame weaken.

Fortunately, the psychological safety is now coming into consciousness. Ample media, articles and references from Google's Project Aristotle research on high-performing teams and Professor Amy Edmondson's research and writing on psychological safety prove what we know intuitively as classroom educators. We feel safe to speak and make mistakes when we're able to bring our authentic self to the table. Professor Amy Edmondson, Novartis Professor of Leadership and Management at Harvard Business School, is a leading researcher and expert in psychological safety, high performance teams and learning cultures. Her definition of psychological safety is: 'A climate where people feel safe enough to take interpersonal risks by speaking up and sharing concerns, questions, or ideas.' [60]

Easy to say, perhaps harder to do.

EXPANDING PSYCHOLOGICAL SAFETY

The whole leadership team needs to be able to create safety for deep discussion. Team leaders are the shapers of this environment, yet many are not sure how to facilitate conversations that are open and robust. Professional learning cultures end up looking like one person telling people what to do with others either nodding compliantly or silently resisting. True collaborative cultures provide opportunity for voice and input, query and exploration.

Robust ideological debate stems directly from psychological safety and helps us develop antifragility. Yet The Buzz diagnostic shows that the statements, 'As a school we actively seek to challenge each other's teaching and learning strategies using evidence to inform our dialogue' and 'as a school we encourage pedagogical debate' receive the lowest overall scores. If these shape and shift classroom practice, then our ability to create this challenge space is crucial.

Timothy R. Clark's book, *The 4 Stages of Psychological Safety*[61], outlines the levels we move through as a culture of safety matures. As you read Clark's levels and my link to collaborative work, you might like to consider three circles of culture. Your school culture (focussed on student/student and student/ teacher relationships), your staff learning culture (collegiate culture) and your community culture.

STAGE 1: INCLUSIVE SAFETY

'The need to feel accepted precedes the need to be heard.'

When people feel they cannot get approval from others, they seek attention, even through destructive means. This correlates to the corrosion level at the very bottom end of the Collaboration Continuum.

STAGE 2: LEARNER SAFETY

'When the environment belittles, demeans or harshly corrects people in the learning process, learner safety is destroyed.'

When school staff start working with The Buzz, we collectively investigate and identify the safety nets that need to be in place for learner safety. One of the biggest shifts is the quality of the conversations people undertake. Is there personal responsibility, accountability and engagement? Or is the environment full of the DBJs – denies, blames and justifications? Here, the work for most schools is to enable the safety of every learner – student and adult. Tragically, there are far too many students who do not feel learner safety, fearing being made to look stupid, thus not engaging in learning.

STAGE 3: CONTRIBUTOR SAFETY

'As the individual demonstrates competence, the organisation normally grants more autonomy to contribute.'

This is an interesting space for schools. In my experience, it's dependent on two main factors:

1. How strongly a school is tied to a hierarchy. For example, a head of faculty's contribution to a discussion may be more valued than a classroom teacher.
2. The cultural hierarchy, such as the cool kids in the staff room, the more 'academic' subject experts, the vocal, having more influence.

By the time we've developed the first two stages of inclusive and learner safety, we can assume that cultural hierarchy has flattened such that collaborative discourse, shared learning and exploration start to fly.

Without contributor safety, our inner voice of 'not good enough' can run rampant. I asked the teachers at a school with a strong professional learning culture to open up their inner voice to each other in a visual process. They generously shared the voices in their heads that stopped them from contributing:

- What if I look stupid?
- What if I'm wrong?
- My ideas aren't good enough.
- Is anyone even listening?
- Everyone else is much more of an expert.

The list goes on. Not only do we need to change the voices in our heads about our worth, but also the way we treat others.

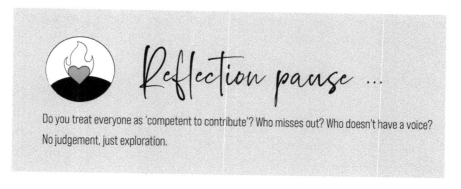

Reflection pause ...

Do you treat everyone as 'competent to contribute'? Who misses out? Who doesn't have a voice? No judgement, just exploration.

Authentic student voice and agency approaches also challenge the long-held beliefs about who is 'competent' to contribute. Schools are changing their conversations with students, valuing their input authentically and openly.

STAGE 4: CHALLENGER SAFETY

'Permission to challenge the status quo.'

I call this the ability to have 'robust ideological debate' [62] that challenges thinking and beliefs. Clark says this stage is best built in at the beginning of a team's formation. My own research concurs. The lack of these behaviours reflect the two lowest scores of over 270 schools in the diagnostic: 'As a school we actively seek to challenge each other's teaching and learning strategies using evidence to inform our dialogue' and 'as a school we encourage pedagogical debate'.

CHALLENGING THINKING

When we've achieved psychological safety we authentically step into co-creation as a team. Real collaboration that challenges current paradigms intentionally looks to evolve the current situation. It comes to life in a rich learning environment, where failure and mistakes are critical parts of the journey. Challenging our assumptions, beliefs, frameworks and processes is important in a robust learning culture.

How do we stop the habitual dynamics?

Here we are, wanting to challenge status quo thinking that's outdated or could do with a good 'looking at'. But we're wary – we don't want to create World War III or have people think we're 'having a go' at them. We need good robust debate without the baggage! If we've already created safety for people's voices then shifting our habits requires just two tweaks:

TAKE AN EXPLICIT GROUP CHALLENGER STANCE

As a group, articulate that you're creating a challenge space, where challenging the norm is invited. Ensure the group decides the most effective way to act and react in this space. Make sure everyone has said what they need to safely voice their thoughts and feelings.

DROP ONE LITTLE LETTER

This is the big shortcut to getting everyone involved. When you're tossing things around and want to increase the group's perspective, unearth assumptions or pull things apart, just drop one little letter. Too often we challenge thinking by coming from an 'I' position, saying: 'I'd like to challenge your thinking.' There's a pesky 'y'. Unless you've worked hard at setting up psychological safety for challenge, often division, expectation of criticism and fear of judgement raise their ugly heads.

Change the statement to: 'I'd like to challenge our thinking' and the world shifts from judgement to wondering and curiosity. Our willingness to challenge our own thinking models the debate and deep-dialogue space we often desperately seek from our teams. Be prepared for the microscope to turn on ourselves along with everyone else. It creates partnership and exploration, not conflict and defensiveness.

Shifting language from you to our, I to we, me to we, changes culture and enables collaboration. Ferocious Warmth leaders continually challenge their own thinking first, not other people's.

Surely it can't be that simple?

Often it is. Sometimes it's the simplest things that make the biggest impact.

I have found that Ferocious Warmth leaders create this psychological safety and a culture of The Buzz through the lens of mindset, environment and dialogue. More than behaviours, it's a vibration. They're able to discuss with their teams what does and doesn't create safety for people, and ferociously protect it when it's threatened. Warmth encourages everyone to voice their ideas without fear of retribution or ridicule. Ferocity steps in when people fall below that line. It does not step over or ignore behaviour that should be dealt with. General Morrison's famous quote of 'The standard you walk past is the standard you accept' is a mantra that holds Ferocious Warmth leaders steady in the face of difficult conversations. Similarly, Brené Brown's 'What stands in the way becomes the way' [63] encourages us to stand by the behaviours we want as the norm. Ferocious Warmth leaders lift the bar and support people to reach for it.

NORMS THAT STICK

One of my favourite Ferocious Warmth leaders, Anthony Simone at Harvest Home Primary School in Epping, Victoria, co-created professional learning principles and protocols with his team when the school was set up four years ago. Harvest Home's five values of achievement, cooperation, acceptance, responsibility and integrity were created with the community, and represent the foundations of a thriving and dynamic school. The principles and protocols are based on their five values and, as a Ferocious Warmth teaching and leadership team, they speak these values regularly. The results from Harvest Home in The Buzz diagnostic puts them on the highest rung of the culture ladder – Committed Collaboration – one of only a handful of many schools surveyed. The staff see evidence of high results in all three areas of The Buzz: a collective growth mindset, a compelling environment for learning, and authentic and student-focussed dialogue.

Sometimes I see teams use protocols and norms in a way that makes me feel a bit cynical, mainly because I see many struggling to speak up in meetings. They're information downloads, not collaboration. The statements become not worth the paper they're printed on. No one looks at them beyond checking off the list of 'things good teams do at the start of the year'. But the Harvest Home statements have a lot of heart, are discussed regularly, visually accessible all around the school, and used to assess and keep themselves accountable. Importantly, they continue to sharpen review and are tweaked to respond to the needs of the staff and the students. Through collaborative reviews, the statements morph every year using surveys to keep tabs on how the Professional Learning Communities are meeting these.

Harvest Home teams live their 'way we work' statements. You can feel it, hear it, see it as they work together.

Do your 'norms' or 'team agreements' mean anything?

When you participate in a meeting of these teams, do you see them in action?

If not, how will you tackle this? What ferocity or warmth will you bring in to help your teams live their norms and pursue them, not just write it down?

I see teams make huge breakthroughs when they concentrate on the quality of their team culture. When we explore what's happening in our brains, when we are in a state of learning and openness compared to fear and shut down, we discover how we should do the what of our work.

It's about trust, connection and lifting expectations with one another. It's about honest reflections and candour. It expands us as a collective.

The extraordinary work of creating amazing results follows.

EXPANDING LEADERSHIP CAPACITY IN OTHERS

Ferocious Warmth leaders build capacity in leadership. They also inspire people to want to become leaders. In some schools, people see leadership as a burden, something so hard and challenging that only a sadist would do it. In some places there is also a level of competition between the leaders, which creates a lack of trust and openness.

> FEROCIOUS WARMTH LEADERS BUILD MORE LEADERS.

Some wise words from Piet Langstraat, Former Superintendent of Red Deer, Alberta and Victoria, British Columbia:

'Every time I've entered a position, my primary responsibility is to grow the people around me, so that I have 25 people who can replace me. So the first piece is that my job is to grow people around me. The second piece is that unless you are modelling it, living it, it simply doesn't work. There's a phrase I use to set the scene for us to learn together, "I'm not interested in sitting around in a senior leadership meeting and have everybody look at their feet. If we're going to do that, then you are all redundant and I don't need you." We all come from different backgrounds, we have diverse thoughts, and we are far stronger as a whole than as individuals. Thirdly, people have professional responsibility for personal growth. I've never asked people to do things I wouldn't do for myself. I explicitly stand up and say: here are the things I'm struggling with, here are the things I need to get better at, here are some areas I know I'm weak in, and here is what I'm doing about that as a professional. My expectation is that you are also growing as a professional, whatever that means for you.'

Piet goes on to tell the story of staff members entering his office with their heads down, saying, 'I really screwed up.' And all Piet would ask was: Were any children hurt? Did you learn something? Do you think you'll do it again? If the answers were: no, yes, no, in order, he left it at that.

Leaders are not perfect. Showing vulnerability by sharing what we are learning shows that we are willing to expand the way we lead.

Piet again: 'Safety comes from the culture of contribution. How do you get people to contribute? By showing vulnerability, allowing people to make mistakes, by valuing different perspectives, by supporting growth. And you have to model it.'

HOW DO YOU BUILD YOUR LEADERSHIP TEAM'S CAPACITY?

Anthony Simone and Sarah Martin also seek to build other leaders, as well as teacher capacity. One of the leaders in Anthony's school, Stacey Lawler, has worked with Anthony in two schools. Stacey is an insightful and skilled leader herself. She is also a continual learner. She observes leadership patterns that make positive impacts in others, and supports her colleagues to build their skills. She offers this insight into how she interprets Anthony's focus on building leadership capability. He:

- leads to empower and grow leaders
- captures and articulates leader strengths
- optimises their craft at the school, network and community level
- challenges areas for improvement through thought-provoking reflection questions and conversations in safe environments
- provides opportunities to improve
- models continuous learning through leadership meetings
- models and references the importance of trust in a team as this underpins true authentic growth
- is strategic and innovative in his planning and the opportunities he provides to align with the bigger picture
- shows compassion, connects personally with each staff member, recalls details about a person and their personal and professional interests
- provides opportunities to celebrate successes while maintaining high expectations of all staff.

Anthony also provides vital opportunities for growth. He highlights his belief in people's capability, but still requires the leader's willingness to take those opportunities. Supportively, he provokes to connect how this builds the individual's craft, behaviour and responses with student learning.

Do you expect the same rigour of learning in your leadership team that you do in teacher's examining their pedagogical practices? Sometimes we don't, because this means we need to examine our own, and that might be scary.

When I ask this question in leadership programs, the schools that reply in the affirmative are generally led by a Ferocious Warmth leader. The duality of high challenge, high support is evident. Why would we expect our teachers to uncover how to transform their teaching for more impact, if we don't do this ourselves in our area of responsibility – leadership?

Reflection pause ...

One of my mentors, Linda Hutchings, a leadership consultant in New Zealand refers to leadership for education and health professions as our 'second profession'. To my mind this is a perfect way to look at it. If leadership is our second profession, how much time does your team invest in expanding your skills as a collegiate group?

chapter twelve

OWNING OUR IGNORANT TRUTH

'Ignorance is something cannot change as long as I am blind to it.'

Byron Katie[64]

'The whole problem with the world is that fools and fanatics are so certain of themselves, but wiser people so full of doubt.'

The Triumph of Stupidity Bertrand Russell[65]

At the time of writing, the world is in a world of pain. Often the pain felt in countries less privileged than Australia is held at arms' length. Wars, famine, genocide, poverty can seem far away. Yet many Australian educators see first-hand the impact of poverty, addiction, family violence and other social disadvantage. Some schools have refugee families who've seen horrors and trauma in their countries of origin that we can never fully understand. Our First Nation children come into school holding ancestral scars of oppression and vilification. They begin the education journey from a position of severe disadvantage on all of our societal measures, despite years of 'Closing the Gap' initiatives. The COVID-19 pandemic is also currently sweeping the planet. My home town is in its second lock down with a curfew – something I have never experienced. The streets are quiet. When outside, everyone wears a mask. Countries all over the world are battling with an unseen enemy. In some countries deaths have reached the hundreds of thousands.

In among this pandemic, protests over police brutality and deaths in custody have encouraged momentum around the Black Lives Matter movement in cities globally. We're divided into clear camps. Social media algorithms skew what we see and read. The ability to vilify others with different opinions to ourselves is as easy as a tap on a smartphone. Leading in the middle of this is stressful and challenging. Keeping ourselves protected, yet open to different perspectives on the world is not easy in this context.

How do we make sure we do not fall victim to closing down our own minds to other perspectives?

OWNING OUR IGNORANT TRUTH

Our ignorant truth is what we think we know to be true. It brings together our knowledge, assumptions, values, biases; our thinking and feeling. But we only really know a sliver of anything. A miniscule portion of the whole picture. Our personal map of the world. Scientist and philosopher, Alfred Korzybski, wrote: 'The map is not the territory.' [66] Like a map, our interpretation and understanding of any situation can be outdated quickly, only have certain information present, or only show one perspective.

What we think we know is simply an abstraction or a reaction, not the thing itself. And then we take a little sliver of something – a fact, an opinion, some data – and pass it through many levels of distortion. The discussion we had with some colleagues yesterday, the article we read online, the way we were brought up, the education we received, the values we hold. These levels of distortion morph the original intent or information into something quite different, perhaps, from what was intended. Our children, as we as ourselves, are absorbing fake news all the time. We have a running joke in our home when my teenagers bring up something that seems ridiculous: 'Did you get that from Buzz Feed?'

These distortions become our model of the world. Unless we are very careful, we start to see the world through a very small window.

Our ignorant truth sits outside the way we currently see the world. It is all the things we don't know. While Ferocious Warmth leaders have conviction about their knowledge, they're also very mindful of the number of things they don't know. I was in a meeting recently where a senior leader called some of the more vocal opponents of traditional schooling 'nut cases'. This is an example of someone not owning their ignorant truth. Instead of exploring the differing views, and provoking their own conviction about schooling, this leader simply discarded the other as 'crazy'. Ignorant truth is not about whether we agree or not, it's about whether we're willing and able to hold an intelligent, cogent discussion to explore possibilities in the realm outside of our 'knowing'. Testing our ignorant truth means we step into a conversation to learn more rather than step away. Being curious about how others see things is the first step in opening up our ignorant truth.

> THERE IS HUMILITY IN OWNING OUR IGNORANT TRUTH. WE SEEK TO DISCOVER MORE, RATHER THAN HOLDING ON FIERCELY TO OUR BELIEFS.

I have a friend, David, who I've known for many years. We don't see each other often any more, but social media gives us the platform to keep in touch with our lives. Over the last couple of years, it's become apparent that David sees the world very differently to me – politically, spiritually, mentally. I am so tempted to block him as his posts make my blood boil. They are not offensive, racist or sexist (then I would block him!) but they do trigger my buttons and threaten me right out of balance.

My solution? Keep reading his posts. Keep looking at the sources and pushing myself to understand his perspective more. Own my ignorant truth, and examine the biases, beliefs and attitudes that form the way I currently see the world. I also hope he owns his, because then we could have a conversation listening deeply to each other, expanding our understanding of the world. If I blocked him, or threw shade at his comments, we would likely spiral down into a slanging match.

The world of 2020 has been a bubble of its own. Within this, one of the biggest strides forward has been the racial justice movement. In Australia, it's been heartening to hear more open discussion of the tragedy of inequity, wrongs and historical prejudice that our indigenous people have suffered for over 200 years. Even more importantly, Aboriginal voices are being heard and life experiences acknowledged, sometimes for the first time in that person's life. Generational trauma will not be undone, yet I hope with all my heart that we can move to a place where, as a society, we deeply listen to the people who've suffered the most and seek to do better in the future. Owning our ignorant truth is a start.

'Do the best you can until you know better, then when you know better, do better.'

Maya Angelou[67]

I am no expert in this space whatsoever. Yet I'm hoping to be someone who owns my ignorant truth, always keen to learn more. I'm hoping to seek to understand and be humble where all I have is the sum of my own experience and learning. Our alternative is to fall prey to surrounding ourselves with the sameness of thinking that's causing division throughout the world. This approach of truth is something one of my mentors, Matt Church, has been thinking and writing about for a number of years.

Identity politics are responses to the fear that people feel in this decade of disruption and century of transformation. The generalised fear and anxiety are causing people to cluster around "like" and this, as history has shown, is a recipe for disaster. For a society to evolve, for a culture you lead to future-proof itself, you must drive a diversity and inclusiveness agenda.'

Matt Church, *Rise Up, An Evolution in Leadership*[68]

Great leadership creates psychological safety where we can test our own ignorant truth and expand our world. High quality collaboration does this out loud. Owning our ignorant truth requires us to drop the need to be right. That's when we get to the great outcomes Have you been in an organisation where there could only be a couple of people who were right and everyone else was wrong? When we're open to learning, people aren't so scared of hierarchy. We flatten the status of everyone around the table, so that everyone has a voice.

Does your presence allow for voices to be heard?

> HOLD WHAT YOU KNOW LIGHTLY. LISTEN DEEPLY AND NEVER ASSUME YOU'RE RIGHT.

Figure 12. Ignorant Truth – Expanding our Model of the World, Tracey Ezard, 2019

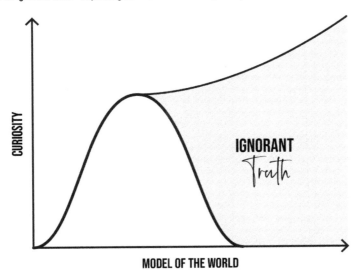

HOW BIG IS YOUR MODEL OF THE WORLD?

One of the earliest influences on my work and thinking about leadership was Thomas Sergiovanni in his book *Strengthening the Heartbeat*. Around this time, Sergiovanni's leadership domains were used for a number of years in the Victorian education system (Australia) as the foundation for leadership development. Sergiovanni was one of the first education experts to draw our attention to the critical element of human leadership, through his cultural and symbolic domains. These stood with just as much importance as technical leadership. Like Peter Senge's mental models, Sergiovanni gave us insight into the warp our mind can have in the way we see the world.

'Mindscapes operate a lot like maps. They shape our perceptions and we see what we expect to see. Mindscapes also have a stealth quality to them. Unnoticed, they frame the way we think and then provide us with a rationale for legitimising our thoughts and actions. They work unknowingly and are difficult to escape from. Figuring out ways to help leaders break out is an important step in bringing about change. By paying attention to mindscapes and by knowing the outside better we can free ourselves from their influence, thus seeing reality for what it really is.' [69]

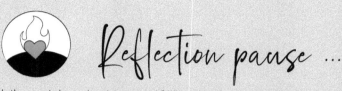

Is there a mindscape keeping you stuck? Where can you loosen the way you see the world, expand and step into the freedom of owning your ignorant truth?

TESTING OUR MODEL OF THE WORLD

I love the Balcony and Dancefloor concept of Ron Heifetz and Marty Linsky from Harvard Business School.[70] It has revolutionised many a leader's approach to leading and is used in development programs all around the world. The metaphor reminds us to either get out of the reactive and focussed nature of the dancefloor to take in a broader perspective or, conversely, ensure we're not making decisions from a far off and disconnected balcony.

In complex organisations, where there's often a lack of understanding about what's happening on the floor, it's the staircase between the balcony and dancefloor that needs the work. The quality of the conversations when we come down from the balcony enables strong connection to the people dancing (doing the work). We need to meet in the middle.

Collaboration, co-creation and co-design sit firmly on the staircase. Design thinking works when the perspectives of strategic, long-range and big-picture (balcony) thinking join together with those dealing with the day-to-day delivery of the work (dancefloor), and the end user's perspective. All are important – not one more than the other. The staircase in action is those conversations that explore and ideate these perspectives and ideas, then synthesise them into solutions.

This is where the Ferocious Warmth leader thrives. They understand their responsibility to ensure the environment is safe for deeper dialogue, sharing concerns, ideas, challenges and humour – often all in the one discussion.

> ON THE STAIRCASE WE CO-CREATE SOLUTIONS FROM BOTH PERSPECTIVES. LISTENING DEEPLY, ASKING CURIOUS QUESTIONS AND LETTING GO OF THE HIERARCHY OF WHO'S RIGHT IN ORDER TO MAKE BETTER DECISIONS.

The staircase discussions require skill and a new way of interacting in organisations. It's collaboration in action. It requires leaders to let go of the need to be right and creates lateral learning.

Having the students on the staircase moves student agency to a higher level. This is the real test of owning our ignorant truth. What do our students really think and feel? What are their ideas, perspectives and hopes? What can they teach us? What unknown perspective have they bought to us?

When the staircase is activated:

- **Hierarchy fades** – positional power is put to the side to enable open and transparent discussion.
- **Curiosity leads** – our questions about how we might do things differently create a space of exploration rather than judgement.
- **Listening deepens** – we seek to understand perspectives and insights at a much deeper and informed level.
- **Trust and connection emerge** – our understanding leads to seeing the situation with both empathy and a clearer lens. Relationships strengthen.
- **Possibility appears** – we can make decisions about future steps from a much richer and informed platform.

As with any workplace conversation, tone and mindset are vital. When discussing perspectives from the balcony view and those on the dancefloor, does your curiosity sound like wondering or judgement? Judging people's responses leads to shut down and low-level, transactional conversations. But when we activate deep listening and ask questions that expand our understanding, we're well on the way to a robust, insightful and useful staircase conversation. How strong is your school's staircase? Does it expand your model of the world?

REAL-LIFE EXAMPLES OF THE SYSTEM STAIRCASE AT WORK

There are real and valid concerns raised by school leaders when central offices set policies from the balcony without any input from the dancefloor of schools.

This happens more often that it should, as policy people in some systems come in and out of roles in the bureaucracy with little or no education experience, their job a stepping-stone up the public-service career path. The voices of school leaders, teachers and students are not given the professional respect they deserve. In too many cases, it seems that the wisdom and experience of educators is dismissed by policy makers who see 'stakeholder engagement' as a tick box rather than a rigorous process of listening and deep dialogue. Oh, for the enlightened system that creates a process where all policy makers have to spend a certain percent of time on the ground in the places where their policies will be enacted!

Fortunately, there are signs of a shift in the silos of the balcony and the dancefloor. At the end of Term 3, 2019 I worked with all the educational system leaders in Tasmania at a conference with early learning leaders, school leaders, adult learning leaders and department leaders. A real meeting of collaboration and learning. We investigated the ways they could increase the collective mindset for deeper efficacy in their own settings and across the system. There was a definite buzz in the room with people listening and sharing to work out ways forward together.

In another state system, central leaders in policy met with a group of school leaders funded to investigate inclusive practice in schools in the US and Canada. Policy changes and initiatives in this key direction were in the planning stages. The principal associations who'd overseen the project were keen for policy to be informed by the experts on the ground – the principals and their teams. The workshop to share their findings was deliberately designed for discussion using a World Café facilitation approach. People from the central office listened deeply to the school leaders in small groups. They probed, asked questions and were curious. It turned the table on previous workshops, where conversations were didactic and one way, rather than exploratory. In the next round of discussions, the whole group explored scalability from the perspective of both the balcony of the system and dancefloor of the schools. This work then informed the development of further inclusive practice initiatives.

Three things need to be in place for this to work:

1. Open and learning mindset.
2. Compelling, well-designed collaborative environment.
3. Two-way, exploratory, authentic discussion around the findings.

Let's hope central systems continue to shift approaches to create authentic connection to the real-life, on-the-ground work. There is light at the end of the tunnel!

'We are at our best when the table is long, all voices are valued, and we stay curious as both teachers and learners.'
Brené Brown[71]

DOES YOUR PRESENCE ALLOW VOICE?

For perspectives to be heard and authentic discussion had, the one thing we need is voice from all levels. I'm challenged by the number of middle leaders and team members I work with who've said that their senior leaders don't 'allow' voice.

Do you allow, invite, enable and enact voice?

Projects, initiatives, working as a team – voice is vital in all of these. We embrace contribution and co-creation when we encourage people's input. We move from a permission, compliance and control environment. We drop the mindset of 'only leadership knows what to do' or the habit of 'I know better than you so you have no say'. More voices mean better ideas, more perspectives. Discussions become partnership-focussed rather than leader-led. We test our ignorant truth.

Voice enables autonomy and wellbeing. Authentic voice creates a culture where people felt heard, seen and valued for their skills, expertise and perspectives. The more we encourage voice and contribution, the more connected we are. The less people feel a part of that, the more distance between us.

US AND THEM VERSUS WE

Power distance is a term from the research of Geert Hofstede, a Dutch social psychologist.[72] Hofstede studies the cultures across nations. Autocratic and paternalistic power relations characterise high power distance. Participatory, consultative and democratic power relationships characterise low power distance. While Hofstede applies this term to research between nation cultures, and their interplay, it also guides us as to where we might sit in creating open environments for voice. If we seek greater involvement, collaboration and innovation in our teams, we need to lower the power gap between 'them and us' and move to a 'we'.

Are you seeking more voice from students? Teachers? Support staff?

Parents? As always, the first step when building voice in your school is to examine our own behaviours to see what needs to shift. Here is an easy framework to identify where you might sit. Are you still at the 'allowing' stage? Or have you moved beyond that and now want to develop the skills to enable effective voices? What needs to be in place to move up a stage?

Reflection pause ...

Level 1: ALLOW VOICE – Let go of having to have all the answers

Does my behaviour give the space for voice? Do people need explicit permission from me to share their thoughts, opinions, knowledge?

If so:

- drop the need to be right
- acknowledge the importance of other opinions
- assume you may not have the right answer
- talk less, listen more.

Level 2: INVITE VOICE – Open up the energy for discussion

Do my actions create an inviting environment for contribution?

To do so:

- be explicit about inviting contribution
- welcome contribution
- be present
- ask specific questions rather than broad closed questions or making statements
- listen more, seek to understand
- show genuine warmth and interest.

Level 3: ENABLE VOICE – Set up structures and prompts

Do the questions I ask and processes we use in meetings provide a framework for purposeful dialogue to grow?

To do so:

- explore the topic through curious and open questions. Use protocols for discussion when unpacking difficult topics
- sense-make the discussion. Frame the purpose and outcomes
- ask clarifying questions to deepen the dialogue
- acknowledge and synthesise contribution
- move beyond status updates to co-creating and exploring issues.

Level 4: ENACT VOICE – Co-create solutions from contribution

Are contributions authentically heard and incorporated into our work?

- If not:
- abandon meetings that simply rubber-stamp decisions already made
- validate and acknowledge contribution
- identify next steps
- explore ideas
- co-create new ways of solving problems through piloting, trialling, taking action and discussing impact.

Testing our ignorant truth expands the way we see the world and the way we think. Lead learners should continually seeking to expand. This enables and empowers transformation.

chapter thirteen

CO-CREATING POSSIBILITY

Vision without action is merely a dream. Action without vision just passes the time. Vision with action can change the world.

Joel Arthur Barker, American futurist[73]

Like a well-oiled wheel, creating momentum for change and transformation needs the lubricant of commitment. How many initiatives have died in schools and systems because the people implementing it were not included in the planning stages, thus major obstacles not recognised until too late? Often new initiatives make compliance the only measure of success. This works for only so long, before the wheels fall off. Without creating a strong engagement in the purpose behind the transformation, we move back into our comfortable old ways. Without clear actions to create the transformation, we don't move anywhere. To avoid this, we need to meet on the staircase for robust, dynamic conversations between leaders and people on the ground. We need to co-create a vision, and a plan.

Recently retired Chief Executive of the Northern Territory Department of Education, Vicki Baylis, led a fierce strategic and collaborative approach to lifting education standards, quality and resourcing over the last five years. Vicki is one of those very senior leaders who make you feel at ease straight away, yet she's well aware of the tough job ahead, and ready and willing to buckle down and work as a collective to do it. This, plus Vicki's passion and vision, encouraged those around her to invest in the work. She balanced the dance of being the most senior executive in education in the Northern Territory with the approachability of a kind and compassionate human being.

The Northern Territory has one of the most challenging contexts in Australian education. Schools range from large and well-resourced in the main cities and towns through to the most remote in the country. The Index of Community Socio-Educational Advantage (ICSEA) of Northern Territory schools has an average of under 1000[74], 1000 being the average across all Australian schools. The system provides for a large indigenous population with schools ranging from 8% to 98% indigenous students. Historically, Aboriginal and Torres Strait Islanders have not thrived in mainstream education. Consequently, the system is charged with ensuring these students get quality access. The best outcome would of course be a system that enables the First Nations people to thrive as well as learn their culture and language, and provide an education that engages all students in a way that helps them achieve and succeed in society. A complex and difficult vision.

As an education system, the data indicated that the whole system was making incremental shift, but it was quite slow paced and not sustained across the whole of the Territory. It seemed to be dependent on the individual person and their commitment, not so much the system.

In 2018, the Territory went about building a new strategy. As a Ferocious Warmth leader, Vicki was determined to have good robust debate and input with the key stakeholders. Previously, they had a very traditional structure, with the corporate arm of the education system writing strategy and policy. But this was continuing to get the same low results. A small number of principals raised the issue of the overwhelming number of strategies they were already using and the confusion they were experiencing.

Vicki asked them to step into being influencers in the system, rather than sitting on the side lines waiting for the next strategy to come out.

In her own ferocious words: 'I need you to have the courage of your own convictions to stand in front of me and the executive board of this agency and challenge us around the system lift that you want and what you want to see.

'My invitation is for you to address the Executive Board that make the decisions around the way the world operates in this agency and you need to provide sufficient provocation and challenge. Are you up for that? You will have my backing. I will do the introduction and you will have my support.

'In the unwritten conversation that was, "Will we be safe?" I said, "If we do this we're not about to go and do something that's going to place us in a position where we won't be supported. You know you've got my backing, you know you'll have the Deputy Chief Executive's backing, but you need to put forward a cogent argument." The team of principals went away and put together their 'pitch' to the Executive Board, after undertaking international and national research and linking it with practice based knowledge.

Vicki continues: 'They stepped into the space with dignity and respect to the way it had been done before. They were analytical about what they were experiencing in terms of the myriad strategies and the confusion it was creating. They were quite clear that they wanted something that was simple. And they had looked internationally and nationally at improving systems, provided us with a couple of provocations and then they left.'

I reflect on the courage of those principals to take up and step into that challenge. The fourth stage of psychological safety – the challenger stage – requires both courage to step up and the trust that the executive do indeed 'have your back'.

TRYING SOMETHING NEW

Vicki says: 'I went to my strategic policy area and said, "Well, we've been challenged. How are we going to do it?" So they started to have meetings…. and more meetings. "No. I'm not doing any more meetings. Meetings have got us to where we are. We have to try something else." The policy unit became the facilitators of the work. We asked for volunteers who were not normally part of the strategic policy unit. The Deputy Chief Executive and I became part of a team of five school leaders, five corporate leaders and five people from our executive corporate team who provided support. Through plane visits, boat rides and many road trips, we hit thousands of people in every part of the Northern Territory.

'We had three questions:

- What's working now?
- What would make it better?
- If we were going to stop, what should we stop?

'It's not rocket science. They're just good common-sense questions. When you ask your parents, when you ask your students, school leaders and educators, all your stakeholder groups, they all have a view. And they all get a voice. From the gift of all of that information, the themes started to emerge. A lot related to stopping writing strategies about measures. Attendance is a measure, but it's not a strategy in itself. We need to get the kids to learn and getting them to school is a big part of that. But when you just measure kids' learning through an attendance measure, that's not sufficient.'

Vicki reported that the students were very clear: '"I come to school when somebody knows and cares about me and I come to school when my learning is something that I can take home and my family is proud of me." That's now where our strategy goes. It's about engagement. It's about growth and it's about achievement. It's pretty simple.'

LISTENING TO THE STUDENTS

Increasing the student and teacher input into this strategy was pivotal to its development. As Vicki says, 'It was the children who wrote the strategy for the Northern Territory. It was their voice and their agency, but it was also amazing educators and incredibly talented leaders, both within our corporate sector and in our schools, who facilitated that agency. From the grassroots. It has to start with committed people wanting to learn and that starts with your educators and your school leaders. But, importantly, they know the primary group they work with. We've been able to connect young people into a legitimate, known and trusted process where they are scaffolded and supported to grow their capability for genuine voice. You start by giving them a voice, but you build it into agency to influence. You get them into collaboration and cocreation and they are partners in whatever the work is that you're on about. That's where you get the real momentum. It's not a top-down thing. But as a leader, you need to be open to sponsoring this, you need to create the space and the enablers to let that happen.

'You also need the goodwill of intelligent, decent people. They don't have to be teachers, but they need to be intelligent, decent people who value a future and see that young people are part of that. They know more about the service they want, whether it's in a classroom or whether it's a mental health service or whether it's access to a sporting service. They absolutely have a deep understanding about how the world could be better and how they could contribute to that in a process that starts at the grassroots and then you create the broader opportunities to influence politically.'

The Northern Territory Department of Education's Learning Commissioner program is a perfect example of this grassroots approach to student agency and influence. The concept started in Katherine schools. It's now an ongoing program in the Northern Territory across sixteen schools from Katherine to Darwin, which sees students from upper primary and middle school engage in long-term analysis of school data and provides recommendations built into the school and system strategy. This work is led on the adult side for the Department of Education by John Cleary, former Casuarina PS principal and now General Manager, School and System Improvement, in conjunction with Dr Tanya Vaughan, Evidence for Learning, Summer Howarth, Founder and Learning Designer at The Eventful Learning Co., and Helen Butler, Education Services Australia.

'The student, teacher and leader commissioners meet as part of the Learning Commission to discuss, analyse and set direction for the school year informed by whole school data sets. Based on their school data student, teacher and school leader commissioners set goals, design evidence gathering processes, sample sizes for inclusion and identify how they will measure the impact of their school-based research.'
Vaughan et al.[75]

DOING THINGS DIFFERENTLY

The combination of co-creating the initial plan and ongoing support of the Learning Commissioner's approach demonstrates how Vicki and her team were determined to not do things the way they'd always been done. Not only did she want to provide provocation for the schools and the system, but for herself and her executive team. Their new strategy, released in 2018, was clear, actionable and resourced. Their journey, based on three clear goals of Engage, Grow, Achieve and four strategy areas of Quality Teaching, Data and Accountability, Community Engagement, and Differentiated Support for Schools, is making major inroads. The Northern Territory was the most improved system in the 2019 school year. Shift and growth are visible. Most importantly, the system is moving as a whole. They are working together to transform education.

Vicki is a fine exemplar of Ferocious Warmth. She set the tone for raising the bar to achieve transformation and providing the safety and support for the people she led to co-create, take risks and work together.

chapter fourteen

LEADING TRANSFORMATION

'We've got two constructs in the world. It's love and fear. Which one do you want to choose? Do you want to wake up and chase your dreams? Or do you just want to wake up and simply exist? Your choice.

'The only risk I see in education is schools, school leaders and systems who continue to be wedded to the one-size-fits-all industrial delivery model. They are risking young people's holistic growth and achievement and perhaps even their future, in this new world environment we all find ourselves in.'

Adriano Di Prato, Entrepreneurial Educator[76]

WHAT WOULD YOU DO IN YOUR SCHOOL IF YOU WERE BOLDER?

I asked you to consider this at the beginning of this book. It is one of my favourite questions to ask of leaders. I think we should be pushing ourselves with this question on a regular basis. Usually fear keeps us thinking small. Fear of failure, fear of how the community will react, fear of push back from teachers and students.

Tracey Breese is the dynamic secondary school principal of Kurri Kurri High School (KKHS) in NSW. I first met Tracey when I was presenting at a NSW Secondary Principal's Conference. Talking with her immediately had my Ferocious Warmth radar tingling. I could hear her ferocity about the moral purpose as well as her humour, love of her students and staff. Tracey is all about her team and what they have done together. It's a definite 'we' and 'innovation' culture, but it wasn't always so. The change began with her maintaining a ferocious stance on changing the status quo.

When I last spoke in depth with Tracey about the journey at Kurri Kurri, they were three years into shifting from the uncomfortable space of innovation being scary and very new towards it being embedded in the way they work. Kurri Kurri uses a hub-based approach to Year 7 schooling, with the curriculum taught through real projects. Learning pathways follow that allow for students to choose a Big Picture[77] studio school path or a more mainstream one. Both pathways have a focus on individualised and engaged learning, with an emphasis on real experiences.

Tracey speaks with conviction in videos on the school's website, clearly articulating the vision of the school: 'Our vision for teaching and learning is to produce knowledgeable, creative, collaborative students of the future, who are well balanced citizens, walking out into the world knowing their skill base.'

When Tracey came to KKHS in 2016, every person in the school was working hard, but she could see they were heading for the wrong set of goalposts. There were old mechanisms in place with a strong focus on behaviour and little on learning. Tracey's belief is that when you focus only on behaviour, you're not actually focussing on wellbeing. KKHS in an area where 85% of the students are in the lowest two quartiles of socio-economic disadvantage so wellbeing really matters.

UNDERSTANDING EXPERIENCE

One of the first things Tracey did was spend a day in the life of a Year 8 student. 'I wandered around as a Year 8 student for the whole day. And it was the most boring day of my life. I think I would have rather eaten cardboard. So, that really shifted what I was thinking about. I started reflecting and asking questions "What are these kids doing all day? Six-and-a-quarter hours we've got them." And pretty much what I saw was that we were taking them away from a life outside of school, putting them in prison for six hours, putting the moat down in the afternoon and letting them go back to life. I started to reflect on the question: "Did we have the capacity to shift?"'

Tracey 'lurked with intent' in corridors, looking and listening to what was happening in the classrooms. What was the teacher-talk like? How did they interact with the students? How were they framing the lessons and work? She saw patterns and habits of working that she knew needed to shift. And if she saw one more death by PowerPoint, she wanted to scream!

The second thing Tracey did was survey how many assessments the Year 7s were doing. They were doing 75 per year! She started to realise why so many students were disenfranchised by the time they reached their last year of school. It was a great example of the over-schooled and under-educated mantle that is often used when referring to Australian education.

It also highlights the piece of work that sits side by side with any transformation needed in a school – a collaborative learning culture in the staff. Strong communication and a collective approach were not in place.

At Kurri Kurri, Tracey began speaking to the staff, especially middle management, around the provocation: 'If we've got these kids for all of this time, why are they not leaving with better outcomes?'

They began working on the premise of three driving principles:
1. No child in conflict can learn.
2. Maslow's before Bloom's.
3. Schools need to be places where students are no longer learning to work, but learning to live.

The Ferocious Warmth leader understands the need for conviction and clear statements that people can grab, those 'sticky messages'. They hold our beliefs in 'bumper stickers' that become embedded in culture. These three distinct, memorable headlines gave Kurri Kurri solid direction.

Tracey is sure of her moral purpose and her ability to bring people along the way. To get the three vision statements moving, Tracey knew she needed to control the narrative and lead the change. 'When things did start changing with their wellbeing and teaching and learning, some teachers worried that the students would not be able to do the work. People would come up to me saying, "Kids in Year 11 can't do this." I replied, "Well, that's our fault. We've had them for four years."'

Ferocious – yes – in a good way. It started people thinking differently to get a shift.

I also see in Tracey the paradox of yet. For change to happen she needed to be the visionary and also be on the ground helping add oxygen to the flame. Visionary yet grounded.

Kurri Kurri High School is now firmly learning and innovating, and a lighthouse school for the New South Wales system and beyond. In response to queries about introducing their project-based model in Year 7 rather than the 'traditional' Year 9, Tracey replies: 'Why would you introduce something to the most disengaged kids in your school? They're already cranky, often already indoctrinated against learning and school. Why would you start with failure? In 2016 the Year 7 data on high efficacy and high expectations was 32%. Basically, is there someone who loves me (that word again!) that I can trust and are there high expectations around my learning? In 2018, the data was up to 61%. Shifting both the work of the teachers and the work of the students.'

JOLT THINKING

We won't re-set entrenched thinking if we don't jolt it. John Kotter, the guru of large transformation change, designates creating a sense of urgency as his first step in *The 8-Step Process for Leading Change.*[78] As we know, urgency was high during COVID-19. Agility and flexibility abounded as schools wrestled with the challenge of providing quality education remotely, while maintaining strong connection and compassion for vulnerability and anxiety. Our challenge is to keep that learning, and agility into the future.

Ferocious Warmth leaders post COVID-19 are not prepared to let the status quo creep back in. They're maintaining inquiry, challenge and curiosity. They're tapping into the innovators and early adopters, and retaining their voice. To take from Tracey's view of the world: if we go back to the way it once was, we've let that happen.

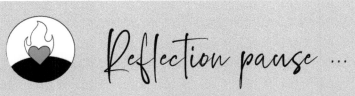

Reflection pause ...

How does the teaching and learning look different in your school from two, three, ten years ago? What does it need to look like in the years ahead?

SEIZE THE DISRUPTION

Let's seize this disruption to help us transform the way education is provided in our schools. It's expansion at work – evolving what we have into something more fit for purpose in this complex world.

Charlene Li, author of *The Disruption Mindset*[79], shares these three elements of disruptive transformation:

1. **Strategy inspired by future customers to make 'big gulp' decisions.** Consider the unmet, unexpressed needs of people you'll serve in the future.

2. **Leadership that creates a movement of disruptors.** A special kind of leadership is needed to inspire followers to build a coalition of key people who will help make change happen.

3. **Culture that thrives with disruption.** Openness, agency and action transform cultures from 'stuck' to 'flux' – able to thrive in disruption.

All three are pertinent to education right now and support the Ferocious Warmth approaches to leadership. Here I expand Li's elements to make them even more relevant to education leaders:

1. STRATEGY THAT KEEPS EYES FIRMLY ON THE STUDENT (THE CUSTOMER)

Educators all went into the 'big gulp' of remote learning in 2020. What unmet and unexpressed needs did you discover about your students and families that this context actually fulfilled for them? How has that changed the way your school provides education? My home state of Victoria, Australia, experienced two lockdowns and remote-learning stretches. The second stretch allowed schools to apply the learning from the first. Many schools found that students who were historically disengaged in the classroom engaged in the online school environment. For an alarming percentage of students, the classroom environment simply does not work. Too noisy, too much distraction, fears of comparison and judgment, not being good enough, lack of psychological or cultural safety. All sorts of needs that, in reality, schools might not be fulfilling.

How have you interrogated your own and your team's thinking about this? Stephen Kendall Jones and the staff at Albany Junior High School in Auckland, New Zealand, went into a design-thinking cycle while they were still in lockdown. At the time of writing, they were fullsteam innovating around an opt-in online stream, perhaps two days face to face, three days online. The aim is to fulfil the needs of students with mental health challenges or learning preferences, and to open up opportunities for geography not to be a barrier to learning at the school. This work in progress is considering partnerships with other schools, so as not to impact negatively on local school enrolments and to create a positive outcome across the whole of the system.

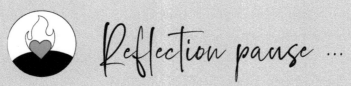

Reflection pause …

How many schools have jumped on the chance to really transform via the learnings of the remote phase of COVID-19? How many have simply 'snapped back' into the way we've always done it? Where are you on this scale?

Whether we face COVID-19, or some other future global upheaval, the premise remains the same: Ferocious Warmth leaders step into disruption and claim the opportunities rather than shutting them down.

2. A MOVEMENT OF DISRUPTORS

Tracey's team is a perfect example of creating a collective approach. To begin the transformation, Tracey knew she needed an 'A' team who were ready to innovate and lead the shift. She also made it clear to her middle leaders that they needed to be in on the innovation. In fact, leading innovation and change was a criteria for their achieving their positions. (There's the ferocity.) These leaders then ran an expression of interest within their faculties to apply for the lead role. Others were not ready to jump in. They needed to observe, to gain confidence to give it a go and be OK with failure if it didn't work straight away. When people were concerned and not ready to be a part of it, Tracey gave them the space they needed to be on the periphery and watch before they jumped in. (There's the warmth.)

3. A CULTURE THAT THRIVES WITH DISRUPTION

Ferocious Warmth education leaders know that intense learning creates disruption. Charlene calls this working in the space of 'flux'. It's also The Buzz. In a thriving collaborative learning culture, we're not surprised by change, disruption and transformation. It's the space we seek to create every day for each other and our students. The learning zone should be one of energy, innovation and excitement: Antifragile.

If we create an environment where responsive teaching is based on feedback then we should be in a constant state of minor disruption, always tweaking and shifting our approach to achieve the intended impact. However, meeting the needs of every student in this complex world requires major disruption.

GET MORE IDEAS

The global design company IDEO found that many people stop at three ideas when iterating and finding solutions to problems, yet those who go for at least five iterations or ideas are 50% more likely to launch successfully.[80]

One of my mentors, Kieran Flanagan, Chief Creative Officer for The Impossible Institute and author, says, as she delivers her keynote speeches to conferences full of people eager to be more innovative, 'I'm not more creative than you – I just work harder.' Kieran and her business partner Dan Gregory create a huge number of ideas individually first around a concept or problem, before they join together on them. I'm not talking ten ideas, I mean 50 to 100! What they co-create when they bring these ideas together is quite often mind-blowing!

'Creativity is an ability to think, to solve problems in ways we haven't seen before. It is innovation, flexibility, agility, ingenuity and mental fluidity. All things that will be incredibly useful for our ongoing success, no matter what the future brings. In our experience, creativity is more discipline than talent. It is something we can practise and improve on, which makes it very much a skill, and vital one at that.'

Kieran Flanagan and Dan Gregory, *Forever Skills* [81]

Reflection pause ...

How do you tap into the ideation of your teams?

Is there a wonder and excitement to the environment you create?

Is there psychological safety to challenge own thinking?

IDEO's findings show that the chances of a failed launch decreased by 16.67% when team members felt comfortable to challenge the status quo. Through The Buzz diagnostic, I've also found this applicable to school teams. For example, 'I feel confident to challenge our assumptions and beliefs' sits on the bottom of the rankings of 'very like us' as a team, creating a challenge space is high performance work.

How often do we code new things as a huge change rather than simply responding to learning – what's working and what is not? What needs a nudge and what needs a rewrite? What needs revolution, what needs evolution? What just needs some new thinking?

GET OUT OF BINARY

As we've discussed, the very nature of Ferocious Warmth is the tension and duality that pulls from both sides of the concept. Yet often when we're trying to solve problems, we approach things from an 'either/or' rather than an 'and'.

Peter Hutton, former principal of Templestowe College and now convenor of the Future Schools Alliance, is a prime example of someone pushing strongly against the status quo. He questions why we've always done things this way, and ruffles feathers by fearlessly asking provocative questions to get people thinking differently.

Peter would unashamedly say he's pushing for revolution, not evolution. His twitter tag is @Edrev and his views are sought from educators all over the world. As is often the case, the biggest push back on Peter's views can come from educators in his own back yard.

Under Peter's leadership, Templestowe College (TC) completely transformed the way it ran and grew from 286 students to over 1000 in seven years. The school has its foundations in strong student agency and subject choice, and does not run on the structure of traditional age year levels.

Peter and the TC team's work took a number of assumptions and turned them on their head, such as:

- Subject choice should be limited and follow strict rules.
- Students take six years to move through the curriculum properly.
- Students cannot make choices about their subjects except from a narrowly defined list, made up by adults.
- Students should be sorted by age.
- Individual learning plans are only for specific students, not all.

SATISFICING

Herbert Simon, an American economist, political scientist and cognitive psychologist, developed theories and undertook research about decision-making. His theory of 'bounded rationalism' [82] explains some of our reticence to change approaches we're comfortable with. These become habits and assumptions that we no longer challenge. Simon's bounded rationality states that people are 'bounded' by the:

- information they have
- cognitive limitations of their mind
- finite amount of time they have to make a decision.

This leads to 'satisficing'. We make decisions that shortcut deep deliberation, but that 'satisfy' and will 'suffice'. Think of all the things going on schools every day that are simply 'satisficing'!

This is why we need people like Peter Hutton to prickle us. To make us examine our assumptions and decisions that are just 'satisfactory' or easier for us.

I asked Peter if he could unpack his approach to testing assumptions and challenging the 'norm'. He believes it's influenced by his dyslexia.

Peter understood by about Grade 2 that his literacy skills were not up to his cognitive ability. He soon learnt to change the system that sought to put him into the bottom category through negative results that didn't accurately represent his ability. As a student of the seventies, his story of cheating at the reading comprehension cards had me in hysterics! Peter found that his dyslexia forged two reactions when confronted with a problem – go around it or be crushed by it.

Getting around the system was something Peter learnt early. Interestingly, dyslexia affects 10% of the population and is highly represented in both prison populations and entrepreneurs. Many teachers are never taught how to deal with dyslexia in the classroom, yet the diagnosis requires specific pedagogy to help students learn to read. Templestowe was one of the first schools to bring in dyslexia testing for all students.

When coming out of the remote-learning phase in 2020, I was fascinated to hear some school leaders concerned that nothing would change because the system would not let them, while other leaders who I knew to embed innovation in the way their school worked were excited by the huge variety of changes they'd seize from the time. Innovators and early adopters versus the late majority, perhaps? Will you go around the system or be crushed by it?

Templestowe College is in an area surrounded by high-performing state and independent schools. When the team at TC were looking at growing the school population, they found out quickly that, for the demographic around them, high academic results would be the only way people would even entertain sending their children to the school. Tricky to provide the proof of something before it's begun! At this stage, the college had 286 students and was struggling in all measures used to identify high performance.

THINKING DIFFERENTLY

So, they thought differently. Like Tracey Breese of Kurri Kurri, Peter 'jolted' thinking to test assumptions. He developed a methodology to test thinking. In any area of schooling, teachers asked:

- What if we did five times as much of it?
- What if we did a fifth of it?
- What would the costs and benefits be?

For example: take the approach to welfare in any school.

If we did it five times as much – what might the down side be? What might work better?

If we did no welfare, what would the negatives be? The positives?

What do we not know that we need to find out in order to test our assumptions rigorously?

Every time they challenged an assumption, they opened up new thinking, strategies and approaches. It also helped the staff understand that nothing is black and white.

One red flag for Peter, which is a good lesson for all of us, is polarity. As soon as only two options are put to Peter, he challenges the thinking – either internally or out loud. When polarity is questioned, it brings in the grey, the ambiguity and the uncertainty we need to purge structures and assumptions that no longer serve us. Simply asking: does it have to be either/or? Can it be and? Or flagging another option completely can create a bubble of thinking beyond the ordinary.

Peter is comfortable making others uncomfortable. He chooses deliberate language that prods and prickles, such as 'emancipating the young'. This provocation comes from a strong conviction of a better world, through the power of a different paradigm of education.

The Future Schools Alliance that Peter convenes brings together schools from all over Australia who want to expose themselves to better thinking, innovation and shaking the norms that education has set in concert over time. Does this work make some in the establishment annoyed? Probably. Is it trying to question the status quo and create a better education for students?

Absolutely.

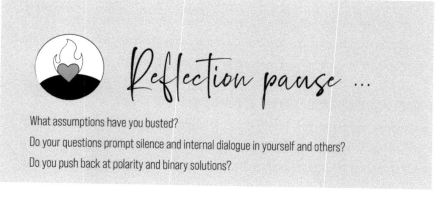

What assumptions have you busted?

Do your questions prompt silence and internal dialogue in yourself and others?

Do you push back at polarity and binary solutions?

A FEROCIOUS WARMTH APPROACH TO INNOVATION

How do you approach innovation and transformation in your school? This framework can assist putting your strategy to work. It combines both action and mindset work.

Figure 13. Ferocious Warmth Innovation Framework

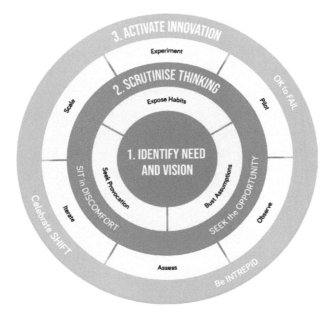

Both shaded rings in this Ferocious Warmth Innovation Framework contain a way of 'being' when leading or incubating an innovation culture.

As the framework suggests, we need to start with vision and evidence of the driving need for change. We continue by scrutinising thinking, sitting in discomfort and seeking the opportunities, then we activate innovation. Here's how.

1. START WITH VISION AND EVIDENCE OF DRIVING NEED FOR CHANGE

Didn't the whole experiment that was 2020 show us how we can be compelled to act when the need for change is critical to the ongoing wellbeing and learning of our students? Prior to this, generally the reason for change in our systems was often limited to the very dreary, 'to improve student outcomes'. Let's not pretend that's a vision. That's an outcome. So many educators turn off every time that term was used as a reason for change. We know it's an outcome we're after, but it bureacratises what we're all about. Let's be more inspiring and ferocious in our visions, and use warmth and connection to bring people along with us. Link what is being done to an inspiring purpose and big why.

2. SCRUTINISE THINKING, SIT IN DISCOMFORT, SEEK THE OPPORTUNITIES
CREATE A CATALYST FOR THE DISCUSSION

A few years ago I worked with a very established, high-performance school in Sydney, Australia. They were led by a Ferocious Warmth leader who, with her leadership team, wanted to help the whole staff step into a space of innovation for the future. Uncomfortable with their more traditional style of working, which they felt was not arming their students for the complexity of the world, they wanted to explore possibilities and bust some of the school's cultural assumptions around what education should provide.

We designed a day where over one hundred staff gathered in the school hall to scrutinise thinking, sit in discomfort and seek the opportunities. Diverse groupings identified the different skills students currently use and those they'll need when entering the workforce that are different to the skills we needed when we left school. This type of discussion puts a couple of key Ferocious Warmth things in place. It creates connection between people beyond their usual teams and this personal interaction connects the school. It also links each person intimately to the discussion at hand, as everyone reflects on 'the world as it was for me'. This individual connection with the inquiry is critical to buy in and 'cracking the thinking'. The discussion also creates an environment of expansion and learning. Active curiosity, listening and wondering is the premise, rather than sitting and consuming what someone is spouting out the front.

We watched the Prince Ea YouTube video 'I Just Sued the School System'.[83] Prince Ea is an American rapper, spoken-word artist and human rights activist. The premise of this emotive video is that education as it currently stands in most schools is a system built for the industrial era, which has caused millions of students to disengage and be judged against arbitrary measures that are not fit for today's world. The challenging premise and delivery can cause discomfort. The discomfort is a perfect provocation for discussion. It is important to give 'permission' for people to discuss their discomfort. What they agree with, what they don't. If you're thinking of using provocations to 'jolt' thinking, whatever you may use, having empathy for those people is Ferocious Warmth in action. Be armed with questions that open up the space. For example, 'There is so much in this video. Some of it you may reject and some may be right on the mark for you. It makes me uncomfortable in places, but it also encourages me to check in on my defensiveness. In your teams, would you discuss how this video made you feel? What prickled? What hurt? What made sense? What excited you?'

After unpacking this video, provocation from closer to home was provided in the form of a video created prior to the day. This video contained vox pops from a variety of school parents in their professional roles, as well as former school students, who came from a range of industries and startup businesses. They gave insight into the skills they and their employees need to thrive in business. The former students gave insights as to the grounding the school had given them, as well as their wish for other approaches that would also have helped them further. For many in the room, this video was a useful 'conscious convincer' for both the need for this work and the opportunity before them.

SEE THE OPPORTUNITIES

Framing the mindset for a day like this is critical, so the discussions can be open and curious, rather than fearful and judging. We looked at the neuroscience foundation of the learning zone, psychological safety and curiosity (The Buzz). This allowed people to step into a place of wonder for the future and possibility. The most important feature of this discussion was the connection to 'we'. Educators in this together, not separate. Collective efficacy.

Our afternoon was spent visioning the future, using an impactful visual activity I learnt from Grove Consulting in California called Cover Story Vision.[84] The finished product is an education-magazine article curated by the 'editorial team', with headlines, stories and images are all about the school and the dynamic, rich education provided in the future. The whole school split into smaller, mixed teams of about eight people to envisage the school in ten years' time. The provocations and discussions from the morning uppermost in their minds, they wandered through the school, discussing what could be in place by then, adding their thoughts to large visioning sheets. The groups returned to chart their imaginings on the large template provided. I've used this process in a number of schools to encourage bigger picture thinking for the future. I've also had groups deliver Ted-type talks. All create an energy of possibility and opportunity.

The ideas created during this type of activity are quite surprising, such as gallery walks and funneling processes to identify themes and 'big ideas'. The synergy between the groups astounds people. Teams identified key insights, plans for the future and next steps.

HEAD AND HEART

Can you feel the connection of head and heart? More often than not, these groups are so mixed that people are working with others they've never spoken to about hopes and fears for the future. This process provides a deeper connection than any 'stick post-it notes on the flipchart' activity. It creates a momentum and excitement about the future. The provocation for shift is accepted, acknowledged and then the whole staff look at what it means in context.

Days like these never work in isolation. Hopefully we gave up long ago the idea that a day of professional learning and discussion will fix all challenges. (Though some leaders still assume this should be the case, with no change in behaviour or thinking from themselves.) As a very high performing school, much was at stake for them, based on the system and their community's measures of success. Fortunately for this school, the leadership team guided the significant shift from a very traditional, content-driven and teacher-focussed curriculum to a more individual, exploratory approach that embedded 21st century skills and student agency. This was possible through a well-crafted strategy that contained high support and high challenge over the following years. The school continues to achieve high results and it's a lighthouse school for innovation.

3. ACTIVATE INNOVATION

The Kurri Kurri High School innovation journey is a wonderful example of mindset activating innovation. Innovation is not about having a solution, it's about trying things until you find the right one for the context. It's about being at ease with not knowing the answers. The leader's learning mindset sets the tone for this to work. Any learning culture will be comfortable with 'not always knowing'. It flows from our 'challenge with curiosity, not judgement' approach. For some of us, the fear of being out of control or not knowing what to do next can stifle our ability to step straight into innovation. Yet others thrive on the thrill.

Everett Rogers' Diffusion of Innovation Curve[85] is a model I find useful to reflect on people's readiness when creating a movement for innovation. The model was created to reflect the uptake of technology, but serves as an effective lens to use on any innovation. Topic and context affects interest and uptake, so Ferocious Warmth leaders plan how they connect people to the initiative. The opportunity lies in our viewing new approaches, products and ways of working through different lenses.

Figure 14. Diffusion of Innovation Curve, Everett Rogers

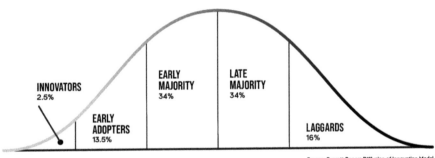

Source: Everett Rogers Diffusion of Innovation Model

Here are the Innovation Curve groupings and the application within an innovation education culture:

THE INNOVATORS

People with seemingly harebrained ideas who are willing to give them a try. Experts at failing more than succeeding. These people are our entrepreneurs. We owe so much of our growth and development to them taking the risks they do. They're only a tiny percentage of any group. Be careful: to your detriment, the culture may not allow them any air time.

THE EARLY ADOPTERS

They love the bright, shiny new objects and want to play with them straight away. These people are the lynchpins of getting innovation and shift off the ground, often sitting there itching to get creative and out of the straitjacket of 'we don't do things like that around here'. They are OK to fail and thrive on experimentation. Many early adopters stepped forward during the remote learning shift of 2020 and held the light up for others to follow.

Language to use: the opportunity, excitement, coolness of an idea. Cutting edge, leading the way, making a difference.

THE EARLY MAJORITY

This crew watches the early adopters with interest and is willing to trial things that they're playing around with and support the investigation. Open to learning, they make a great support crew to pilot new approaches. They see the impact and positive outcomes of the innovation and take it up. As more people join the early majority, we climb towards the top of the bell curve and a tipping point occurs. This is a sure sign you are on the way to adopting a new way of working.

Language to use: practical, shifting outcomes, evolving practice, making a difference.

THE LATE MAJORITY

More cautious, needing more support and reassurance, this group makes up the bulk of the remainder. They want to see clear evidence that this initiative will work or make their lives easier or deliver far better than the status quo.

Language to use: well-tested, positive impact, safe, supported.

THE LAGGARDS

Only on board because there is no choice. It's now part of policy, compliance or the only way to do the work. My experience is that laggards hold a far louder voice in many schools than they should. Many leaders try to shift these people first, rather than beginning at the other end. The language of change becomes bogged down trying to shift the thinking of a few, rather than exciting those early adopters and majority, who will provide momentum and shift.

Tracey Breese's pilot approach discussed earlier is a living example of the Innovation Curve. Now it's an accepted way of working at the school. Tracey and Kurri Kurri's mantra? 'Don't hold too fast to change, because it will change again.'

BE OK TO FAIL — CREATE A STUFF-UP ZONE

As previously discussed, owning that we don't need to get it right all the time is one of the hallmarks of a strong learning culture. Our articulation and modelling of this makes a big difference in people's mindsets.

As a profession, we are generally risk averse. Our systems are built on consistency and certainty, which can create status quo. Often people are looking for permission to innovate. This seems counterintuitive, yet in education 'permission' is still something sought. This permission becomes a safety net we can give to both teachers and students. While we would hope that all good teaching allows for innovation, the strong drive for consistent, evidence-based-only approaches has taken us too far. This encourages us all to stay well within our lanes: safe.

> FEROCIOUS WARMTH LEADERS ARE EXPLICIT ABOUT CHANGE. INNOVATION AND A WILLINGNESS TO FAIL. THEY CREATE A SAFE PLACE FOR PEOPLE TO SHARE THEIR BIGGEST STUFF- UPS AND WHAT CAME OUT OF THEM.

As we move further into the development of authentic student agency, project-based learning and divergent thinking skills, permitting teachers to experiment in partnership with students will help shape a new way of working in many schools. I encourage you to give people the structure, the instructional model, the frameworks, the evidence base, and the respect to innovate and create new ways of getting the outcomes you're all after. Without practice-based experimentation, no evidence base would appear. Expansion requires risk taking.

Reflection pause ...

Where are your opportunities to be expansive? Is it more self-reflection and stretch of your own self-awareness and growth? Is it expanding the leadership capability of the people you lead? Or perhaps you're ready to be bold and lead some serious transformation in your school through expanding collaborative culture.

Whichever it may be, remember the connection between Ferocity and Warmth creates a place where people feel safe to expand their thinking, their learning, their risk taking. High challenge. High support.

connected

chapter fifteen

LOOKING TO THE SELF

Connection is predominantly a feeling-focussed element. When we feel connected, we're strengthened in our emotional and mental wellbeing. Research indicates that connectedness is also critical for our cognitive health. Better thinking comes from connecting ideas, connecting to each other and connecting to our purpose. Connection and belonging in both our personal and professional life are the strongest drivers for our behaviours.

The stories throughout this book demonstrate leaders who connect people to purpose; leaders who connect strategy to action, innovation to outcomes, learning to improvement, the why to the what. Ferocious Warmth leaders' strengths lie in their ability to do three things not readily seen in out-of-balance leaders.

Ferocious Warmth leaders:

- connect deeply to self
- hold love for and belief in others
- connect the head and the heart.

> PROFESSIONAL INTIMACY – VALUING EACH OTHER'S PROFESSIONALISM AND HUMANNESS.

In the leadership context, connection is a form of professional intimacy. Our world is crying out for more empathy and purpose, more deep wisdom and willingness to continue learning. It needs leaders who can be ferocious and warm in harmony, not in competition. People are seeking more open discussion and deeper listening. When we achieve professional intimacy the people we lead feel both seen and heard. Ferocious Warmth leaders are present with whomever they're with at the time. Not disrupted by phones, emails dinging or looking over the shoulder for a better option. Connecting not just through conversation, but through focussed, compassionate presence.

The word intimacy is a provocation here. Can we pair the word 'professional' and the word 'intimacy' together? Why not? Connection requires us to know the people we lead. Ferocious Warmth connects people to us both as humans on a journey together, and professionals aiming to create extraordinary things together. This flies in the face of the 'us and them' that is often felt within cultures where trust is low. But before we can connect authentically with others, we need to connect to ourselves.

CONNECTING TO SELF

The Ferocious Warmth approach to connection starts with connecting in. Connecting to self gives us insights that can help us grow, in turn connecting more with others in a useful and functional way. I asked Julie Kennedy, a Ferocious Warmth school leader I've known for many years, how important it is to understand and know her emotions and drivers as a leader.

'I believe there is great value in making what I stand for visible to others. That makes it important for me to be able to understand and articulate my beliefs, motivations and influences. It might be a natural assumption to think that we know ourselves well, but the longer I am in this job, the more I realise how important it is to continually ask myself questions. Why did I jump to that conclusion? Why am I feeling this way? What made me do that? I often get more value out of asking the right questions than necessarily having the answers to those questions. All of us have a blind and unknown self, and asking questions helps me to bring more of myself into my known side. I believe that leaders, teachers and students have to go hand in hand as learners or they don't go at all. So, as a learner, what I know and understand about myself changes as I have new experiences and develop new skills and knowledge. Understanding myself helps me to be more persistent, undertake more difficult tasks and be less emotional when I fail at things. Knowing what drives me as a leader helps me make strategic decisions about where to put my time and energy.'

PROVOKING CONNECTION AND INSIGHT THROUGH QUESTIONS

This insight into Julie's thinking shows not only her connection to herself, but also the element of expansion and learning deeply embedded into her practice. How true is it that sometimes the biggest insights can come simply by asking ourselves questions, rather than knowing the answer? A truly provoking question can unearth some massive 'aha' moments that shift our thinking with one short sentence. One of the principals I work with journals constantly. He is an insightful leader who is constantly curious about himself and the world. Occasionally he'll send me an email with some context, simply asking: 'Can you ask me a question to ponder that will help me get unstuck?' That's all I need to do – the rest is his work to delve beneath that.

STOP IN YOUR TRACKS QUESTIONS

I love questions that create a bit of a 'brain fry', leading to a type of circuit breaker in our heads and hearts. They make a space in our thinking for reset and recalibration.

One of the most potent questions we can ask ourselves when we're stuck, whether in our own thinking or in a group, is: 'For what purpose?' This steers us towards the real issue and closer to the key outcome rather than getting caught up in our own 'stuff'. If we're well aware of our inner-voice saboteurs we can realise that the rabbit hole we're going down into is more about baggage, perhaps self-worth, than the actual issue at hand. A whole lot of heightened emotional interactions could be avoided if we stopped, paused and thought to ourselves: 'For what purpose am I doing this in this way?'

Other useful connecting-to-self questions:

'What advice would I give to a colleague or friend?'

This helps you step out of your own shoes and into a more meta position.

'What am I feeling right now?'

Labelling emotions reduces their potency.

'What assumptions am I making?'

This makes us explore the gaps in our thinking or knowledge.

'Am I showing integrity right now?'

This one jolts us back to our values.

'What is this really all about?'

Encourages us to see beyond the surface of the situation.

And one that hits at the heart of connecting to the unsaid parts of ourselves:

'What am I not willing to admit?'

Boom! And Ouch!

Juicy and fascinating.

Other questions help us get into the shoes of those we lead:

- 'What is it like to be on the other side of me?'
- 'How would I describe my behaviour if I saw it in others?'
- 'Where can my strengths be my shadow?'

This work is confronting yet transformative if we're willing to step into the challenge. Just as important as asking the questions is giving ourselves permission to reflect on them.

SELF COMPASSION

WHAT'S THE QUALITY OF YOUR INNER VOICE?

The inner judge pops up and berates you for not being good enough, wise enough, fast enough. We look at the things 'undone' rather than the things we've done. We seek out the mistakes, rather than the wonderful work. We go into analysis-paralysis, turning ourselves inside out, instead of calming and accepting that where we are is exactly where we should be. Whatever is happening is a learning or an adventure. Or we lash out at others, letting our shadows out to play. What if we treated ourselves with kindness and compassion instead? Show gratitude for what we have achieved. Acknowledge all the bits that others see in us. Breathe. Take some time for ourselves – probably the least used self-compassion strategy in the school leader bag of tricks. And after we've calmed and looked after ourselves – what's the next step?

chapter sixteen

THAT WORD ...

LOVE

*'The mark of a wild heart is living out the paradox of love in our lives.
It's the ability to be tough and tender, excited and scared, brave and afraid –
all in the same moment. It's showing up in our vulnerability and our courage,
being both fierce and kind.'*

Brené Brown[86]

Ferocious Warmth leaders speak kindly about people – educators, students, parents, and this can be felt even during emotionally-charged conversations. However, leadership legends often come from military stories of the hero's journey, fearlessly leading the troops through deft pivots, death-defying moments and brilliant strategy. The DNA of leadership, built into leadership theories, programs and archetypes, is essentially one of capabilities and attributes seen as more masculine. Yet more research is being undertaken that points to a more heart-centred approach getting better outcomes. With research from such places as Gallup[87] showing levels of disengagement in many organisations, mental ill-health on the rise, and the top reason people leave their jobs being related to their manager, a stronger focus on humans rather than results is long overdue.

For Ferocious Warmth leaders, this focus on connection to people is one of their most important tenets. For many, the word love is woven through their conversations without conscious thought. Love and belief in the Ferocious Warmth approach are a component of the connection element. And one that challenges many!

In all my interviews with leaders who've transformed their schools or systems through the balance of ferocity and warmth, results and relationships, deep love for others is evident. It's demonstrated through kindness and compassion and a strong believe in people's positive intent. Let's explore it further.

LEADING WITH LOVE

Ferocious Warmth Leaders lead with love. They love their people and the work. When I shared this observation at one of my first leadership workshops on Ferocious Warmth, a school leader said, 'I have a real problem with the word love in the context of leadership.' Unfortunately, in the context of the horrible findings of the Royal Commission into Institutional Responses to Child Abuse[88], some people's reaction to words like love in the professional sense has been coloured. For others, the idea of 'loving' those we work with does not correlate to their concept of love.

> SO, LET ME BE CLEAR ON WHAT I MEAN BY THE TERM LOVE. LEADERS WHO LOVE THEIR PEOPLE LOVE THEIR HUMANITY. THE CONNECTION IS DEEPER THAN SIMPLY A TRANSACTIONAL INTERACTION. THEIR CARE AND EMPATHY FOR OTHERS IS AT THE CORE OF THEIR BEING AND ACTIONS.

C.S. Lewis in *The Four Loves*[89] describes the original Greek versions of love:
- Storge – Empathy bond. The love for family or others bonded by chance.
- Philia – Friend bond. The love between friends as close as siblings, between people who share common values, interests or activities.
- Agape – Unconditional love. The love that exists regardless of changing circumstances. Lewis recognised this as the greatest of all loves.
- Eros – The sense of 'being in love' or 'loving' someone.

The love I have seen described by Ferocious Warmth leaders is both 'agape' and 'philia' love. A deep unconditional love for people no matter their context. Dr Briony Scott agrees that her relationships with students is 'agape' loving. 'I've never met a kid I haven't thought was absolutely wonderful – and I mean that genuinely. So, it's of no consequence to me if a student misbehaves. I'll still engage in tough love with them in terms of rules, but I've never met a child whose story is not amazing.' So many students have had their lives enriched by teachers and leaders showing this love. For some, this connection is the only positive constant in their lives.

Steve Farber, author of: *Love is Just Damn Good Business: Do What You Love in the Service of People Who Love What You Do*[90] has a great formula: Kindness + High Standards = Love at Work. That's Ferocious Warmth right there. Farber comes from a strong corporate environment where the concept of love in whatever form is foreign. His premise is: first, do what you love, then do it in the service of people, not in spite of them.

DO WHAT YOU DO WITH LOVE

Dr Lindsa McIntyre, former principal of Jeremiah E. Burke School, calls 'love' her soapbox. She and her team shifted a 'turn around' underperforming school in Boston. The school was full of disengaged, disadvantaged students who hated school. High levels of poverty, trauma and generational distrust of education meant that Lindsa's first work was in connections, trust and relationships. Lindsa turned up at every family's home, connecting with them on their terms, bringing her authentic self to where they felt comfortable. She made relationships with families and students one of her highest priorities, helping them feel hope in a school where their children would be in good hands. She led this through a message of love, creating a strong collaborative learning community and personalised learning. Graduation levels increased, as well as achievement, attendance and connectedness. She passionately believes that all educators should love students and that all students deserve to be treated as if they are family. Lindsa is now a school superintendent. If you ever have the opportunity to hear her speak, take it up. She is down-to-earth, funny and inspirational.

This 'agape' love is even for the educators and students who confound you. In fact, don't the most difficult to lead teach us the most about leading? 'Agape' is the love that we bring in when people are not doing the right thing or challenging us in a less-than-useful way.

THOSE WHO CHALLLENGE US MOST NEED OUR LOVE THE MOST

Former Superintendent of Red Deer, Alberta and Victoria, British Columbia, Piet Langstraat's perspective centres our thinking around those who challenge us most: 'I always thought that my mark as a teacher was how I treat my most troublesome students when no one is looking. I carried that into leadership. So how I treat the most abrasive, stubborn, stuck-in-their-ways antagonist person in my organisation is my mark as a leader.'

Piet helped transform two very different school districts with remarkable increases in results and graduation rates, especially in First Nations students, by treating people with respect and as adults. I discussed with Piet the irony of the way adults can be treated in education systems. In some schools there seems to be leadership mistrust in staff professionalism. One of the main messages out of our remote learning of 2020 was how many people flourish when leadership place more trust in their professional abilities.

Piet again: 'I see people treating staff and whole school boards like they're a bunch of automatons, and it's a very top-down, restrictive approach. It's such an irony in the environment of educating students to think for themselves.

'We need to forget about the numbers for a minute. When you focus on treating adults with respect, focus on equity, letting people have personal exploration of their own goals, taking their own paths, allowing people to seek out the learning they require, the irony is the numbers improve.'

'It's not some theoretical construct I've come up with. I have lived this in two very different provinces in Canada and two very different school districts as superintendent.

'In both places, I never sat down with anybody and said, "Here's the test scores, or here's the graduation rates. I always talked with the adults about meaningful contribution. Common understandings, common ethics that we hold dear, things like equity and opportunity, valuing people's individual journeys and contributions. By focusing on those things in both places, there was a remarkable increase in test scores, in English, in mathematics, in sciences. There was an increase in graduation rates. But I never once talked about those things. Putting it simply, if you love the adults as much as you love the children, things just look after themselves.

'I would stand up in a crowd of people, a grizzled old superintendent, and talk about loving your people, and people would look at me as if to say, "We weren't expecting that out of your mouth!". You have to truly, in your heart of hearts, love the people for whom you are responsible.'

I asked another Ferocious Warmth principal, Justine Mackay, where her ability to stay centred for difficult conversations in tough times came from: 'It absolutely comes from a place of love. I love the kids and I love the people I work with and that's why I get up every day. Sometimes I hear leaders bag out their staff, and while my people are far from perfect, I am so grateful for everything that they do.'

> HOW LEADERS SPEAK ABOUT THOSE THEY LEAD SPEAKS VOLUMES.
> HOW EDUCATORS SPEAK ABOUT STUDENTS THEY TEACH SPEAKS VOLUMES.

WORDS CREATE WORLDS

I always wonder when I hear teachers and leaders talking down the parents and students. Connectedness and genuine love for the people they serve seems to be sadly lacking. Empathy and understanding are restricted to supporting each other to deal with the 'hopeless parents' in their community. The culture is 'us' and 'them'. Often there's a link to their student- and parent-satisfaction data being below average. How do your teachers talk about the community generally? Is there empathy and understanding? Good qualities acknowledged? Even with challenging behaviours, can they see the positive intentions behind the behaviour? We create culture through our language and the world that our students learn in.

'The way you see people is the way you treat them, and the way you treat them is what they become.'
Goethe[91]

A SHINING EXAMPLE OF LOVE IN ACTION

A wonderful example of love and connection in a Ferocious Warmth leader is Claudine Moncur-White, former Principal of Rasmussen State School in Townsville. Sadly, Claudine passed away in September 2020. Right to the end of her life her intention was to lift others up. I met Claudine in 2016 when I presented some workshops for the Queensland Association of State School Principals. Deeply interested in people when she was talking with you, you felt you were the only one in her orbit at that time.

I worked with her school leaders on The Buzz, creating a collaborative learning culture. They were well on the way to this already, through Claudine's thoughtful leadership. 'Rassy' as it's affectionately known, was a school with major challenges when Claudine started. They'd endured seven principals in nine years prior to Claudine joining. Low achievement rates, low attendance. Low trust in leadership, community disengagement. You get the picture. When I worked with Claudine and her team, they were already well on the way to shift and transformation for their students.

Visitors to Rassy now see classrooms (both inside and outside) full of students engaged in learning and seeing themselves as learners. The learning is deep and rich, and the pedagogy focussed and responsive. The culture is warm and connected. The staff work with purpose and passion. People know one other and genuinely care about bringing out the best in themselves and each other. Over a number of years, the impact on student learning, attendance and love of school has been huge. Rassy has seen a 347% decrease in major school behaviour incidents since 2014, an 8.7% increase in indigenous attendance (the school has an indigenous population of 62%) and a 365% increase in Prep to 2 achieving regional reading benchmarks. Enrolments rose from 403 in 2017 to 501 in 2018. There was a 23% increase in students achieving C and above, from 48% to 80%. As well, staff morale increased from 51% to 87%.

Rassy's vision and the targets they're aiming for covered one wall of Claudine's office, ensuring these were front and centre. While this might seem cold, it was the opposite, brought to life by Claudine's stories about students and educators. As I walked around the school, students and teachers told stories linking relationships and results, their students' learning with their own love of learning.

Rassy was achieving balance between driving clear vision and strategy with building trust and connectedness across the whole community to reach that vision. They balanced achieving purpose with love of people. Claudine connected to the children and staff as we walked around the school. I could feel the collective energy as well as the heart-warming pride she had for students, staff and community. The smiles and joy in the students as they engaged in learning was such a joy bubble. The last time I visited Rassy in 2019, Claudine excitedly showed me their new staffroom, designed to create connection and enjoyment when staff come together to relax. Their professional learning room is constantly evolving, showing the focus on the students and their growth, academically, socially and emotionally. It also reflects where they draw their inspiration from. Rita Pierson is one example, her TED Talk 'Every kid needs a champion' reaffirmed their approach to student-teacher relationships. Rasmussen is truly a place with a buzz!

If you happened to be looking for Claudine between 8am and 9am, you'd find her at the school's front gate, welcoming each and every student and their carer as they come into school.

Our world is a better place for Claudine's presence. She brought magic to those she connected with.

The synergy between achieving purpose and love of people does create a magic. There are so many passionate educators around Australia doing this work every day. Who's influenced your leadership in this way?

WHO COULD DO WITH YOUR LOVE AND CONNECTION?

Are there people in your school or team who could do with a bit more belief that you love them?

I once asked a principal who was having challenges building trust with her school team whether she loved, liked and trusted her people. She answered that she always focussed on undertaking trusting behaviours so they liked and trusted her. I mentioned that wasn't what I asked her and repeated the question. She was silent. She hadn't reflected on it. If we don't 'like' the people we lead, not as friends but as human beings with their own story, then trust and collaboration will be hard.

LOVING THE JOB

I asked Pitsa Binion, Principal of McKinnon Secondary College in Melbourne, about the importance of love for her students and staff. Her first point? You have to love what you do. When you love your work, your students and staff, the work becomes a joy. As a principal of one of Victoria's biggest and highest achieving state schools, Pitsa is a busy leader, as is all of her leadership team. But they stand by their mantras of connection and relationships.

Pitsa says, 'Every child matters. You don't know what's going on in their lives. Our job is to bring some joy to them, to help them achieve, to help them learn, to help them succeed.' Pitsa is out talking with her students every day, seeing how they are, what they need, what's happening for them. The leadership team is in the staff rooms every day, connecting with the teachers and support staff.

Reflection pause ...

If staff morale is an issue, student connectedness or pedagogical transformation is slow or student numbers declining, could you examine how to display more love for and belief in your staff, so that they can rise to the transformation ahead?

BEING SEEN

Being 'seen' and belonging are fundamental human needs. Being seen helps us feel that our contribution matters. Some like to be acknowledged and valued through big accolades, others prefer a quiet conversation that shows that you've 'seen' them or a reprieve from yard duty.

WHO DO YOU NOTICE?

Does the principal of a sports-oriented school interact only with the louder, more active and gregarious sporty types? Or also acknowledge the quieter student industrious in the corner? Do the leadership team know the names of the students in the library, the breezeway or at the edge of the oval? This is a priority for Ferocious Warmth leaders. One of the reasons we, and many other parents, chose a particular primary school was the interaction with and mindfulness of the principal towards all of the students. He didn't let the size of the school get in the way of knowing everyone's name. He was immensely proud of both his students and team and it showed in the way he spoke. His name was Hans Kueffer and I am honoured to have known him. In 2009, we lost Hans to depression. This book is dedicated to him.

ACKNOWLEDGING THE QUIET ACHIEVERS

I was reminded of these quiet achievers when shopping at my local food market where Rose runs a magnificent gozleme kitchen. Every day, Rose is there flipping and twirling dough as she creates the lightest filo pastry and fillings. I love that Rose doesn't hide away in some back room of the shop. There she is out and proud for everyone to see in her beautiful, signature red headdress. The same colour every day, the same smile, the same delectable, reliable food. She hardly speaks, yet you know she's the glue of the place.

Who are the Roses in your school? The quiet and unassuming heroes. Without them there, the foundations would crumble. They work quietly. They work with a beautiful disposition and they're fulfilled when serving others without fanfare.

The Ferocious Warmth leader notices them, these quiet, industrious people, the glue of our culture and our services. The Ferocious Warmth leader understands that the way they deeply value people shifts depending on the person.

The best way to acknowledge our Roses? I think the language they love is quiet service and quality interactions with you. I'm betting that taking the time to pop down to their usual haunt in the place, sitting down and yarning over a cup of coffee, would make their day. Discussing the ins and outs of the last few months, chewing over their insights and sharing yours. Much more than a thank you in the newsletter or at the team meeting.

BEING SEEN CREATES BELONGING

I have worked in schools who've had a shift in trust that surprised everyone when a new leader began. In a number of cases, the leader 'saw' people who'd been forgotten. Their opinion had not been sought, their work not valued. The people in the wing furthest away from the office were never visited, as the leadership team didn't stray too far from their desks. Meagan Cook, who we met in Chapter 2, is a perfect example of the principal seeing staff, students and parents thus creating loyalty and trust in a short space of time.

Contrast this with a secondary school bleeding enrolments and staff. Walking around that school with the principal I noticed he only gave eye contact and acknowledgement to the teachers, never the students, even when they were trying to catch his eye. Adult-to-adult conversation and joking was going on with some staff, excluding the students in the classrooms. He seemed not to know many students' names, even though the population was small. Symbolically, these actions indicate who was 'seen' in that culture.

I have stood in the foyer of a school for a solid five minutes as a mother and her child stood at the desk waiting to be 'seen' by the office people in discussion with a school leader. No acknowledgement, no comments, no, 'Hi Jo, I'll be with you in a second.' I assumed they were serial latecomers and were unfortunately put into the 'not important' bucket. The office staff couldn't see me as I was around the corner, waiting and observing. Sadly, I was acknowledged as soon as I moved into view. Was this symbolic of who or what mattered most in that school? Yes. Strong hierarchy, lack of connectedness, and students and parents who didn't feel seen.

As the principal of a school of over 2000 students, what's Pitsa Binion's perspective on this? 'Am I busy? Too bloody right I'm busy. And could I do other things? Absolutely, but there's nothing more important than my connection to my students, staff and families.'

Ferocious Warmth.

BE THE SPACE. HOLD THE SPACE

Discussing love, kindness and compassion in the context of principalship, Judy, a principal in Queensland, shared with me a poignant example of love in action. A little boy at the school appeared to have hearing problems. The child's mother was very hesitant to come into the school so Judy visited the mother at home to discuss the issue and ensure the boy got to the audiology appointment. The mother didn't want to go to the specialist by herself, so Judy offered to come by taxi, pick them up and take them.

At the appointment the mother didn't want to fill in the forms, because she was embarrassed about her level of literacy. Judy gently asked, 'Would you like me to fill them in?' With relief the mum passed over the forms and Judy began to fill them out.

'Is there anything you'd like me to put down about your medical history?'

'Well you know I am a drug addict, don't you?'

'OK, are you OK for me to write down what you're addicted to?'

'Valium. And I self-harm.'

'Are you OK for me to put that down?'

'Yes.'

The child got his hearing aids. That support for his learning and the conversation would never have happened without Judy visiting the mum personally, asking if she could help. This situation required Judy's compassion, not pity. She gave kindness, not judgement. Both had love for the child. And Judy stepped into Ferocious Warmth to push where she needed to push, and hold the space for the mum to feel safe to be vulnerable.

Kindness: loaning someone your strength, instead of reminding them of their weakness.

Unknown

chapter seventeen

PROFESSIONAL INTIMACY

Have you ever found that you can work with someone for many years yet not really know them? Then you meet another person and feel an almost instant connection with them? They let you see the whole of them straight away, and they see the whole of you. The connection is easy, warm and deeply fulfilling. This is a hallmark of Ferocious Warmth leaders.

CONNECTION BEFORE CONTENT

Connection before content is the mantra guiding Ferocious Warmth leaders, no matter the context. Professional intimacy is the platform for deeper and more connected relationships that encourage people to take risks, innovate and transform.

Prahran High School in Melbourne, Australia, is a young school building a culture of connection and professional intimacy from the beginning. Founding principal Nathan Chisholm came from successful schools, full of great students. Yet he felt they were in essence being dutiful and passive. This led to him create a vision with his new school community based on creativity and curiosity, envisaging students asking questions and wondering, rather than sitting and consuming. Nathan says, 'Sir Ken Robinson's Ted Talk[92] always spoke to me. This is strong language, but in some ways schools are killing creativity. There are many things in school that seem to work against learning, not for learning, barriers and boundaries rather than opportunities to flourish.

'Transformation is urgent and important. We really need to push people, but I genuinely believe that we can't do anything unless we prioritise relationships. I also believe you can't lead people who you don't care about.'

Prahran High has cocreated a 'Connecting Us' framework to build the skills required for a culture of relationships. It's designed to support adults to grow their skills in connection to students. They've also developed a continuum that takes the development of the five skills (listed below) from foundation to extension. A perfect example of professional intimacy.

'Knowing and connecting with students is at the heart of teaching. It is through our relationships with them that we teach, and also learn ourselves. We teach students first and foremost, and curriculum second. We form relationships with students through giving parts of ourselves, and through this we all grow together. At PHS, we build constructive, deep relationships with our students and each other through the development of five skills – co-regulation, forgiveness, positive language and interactions, boundaries and consistency, and genuineness.'

This explicit framework ensures professional intimacy and connection are critical to school culture. Their criteria for the five skills speaks volumes about quality relationships. The inclusion of forgiveness shows just how evolved this connection framework is. Imagine what more forgiveness between teachers, students, leaders and families would do for our community.

INCREASING CONNECTION IN THE DIGITAL WORLD

The use of cameras and virtual meetings is a fascinating opportunity to explore professional intimacy. In many cases, remote learning increased the professional intimacy between leaders and teachers, school and community. Leaders who mastered the craft of leading through a lens noticed increased connection with those they led. When I say mastering the craft, I mean looking into the camera, having good lighting and bringing the authentic 'you' to the camera. All of a sudden the English teacher, usually up the back of the meeting avoiding going anywhere near you, is right on the other end of the camera. One to one, even in a meeting of many, often leaders seized the opportunity to speak with authenticity and openness in these forums, allowing people to hear them, see them and understand them more. Communities who watched live streams or videos of the teachers and school leaders built a stronger understanding of what was going on in the school.

For others, especially those out of senior leadership, professional intimacy became harder during the time out of school working remotely. I ran a leadership program for school middle leaders during remote teaching. Their feedback showed that while connection between teams increased, some felt disconnected from important decisions. More casual conversations usually held in the corridor or resource room, informally becoming abreast of the leadership team's thoughts, were no longer possible. In some instances, this meant that leadership decisions were made in a vacuum. These were replaced by formalised online meetings that, unless carefully designed, became one-way downloads. Some leaders approached this challenge by holding regular, informal times online, open to anyone joining the virtual space to connect and ask questions. These types of connections build trust and clearly show openness and accessibility. Some people may not agree that relationships can be strengthened by camera, but for many teachers and leaders, they were.

chapter eighteen

STORIES CONNECT THE HEAD AND THE HEART

'The longest journey you will ever take is the 18 inches from your head to your heart.'

Unknown

Have you listened to an experienced storyteller and felt connected immediately to the picture they're painting with their words? Stories are one of the quickest ways to connect our emotions and our thinking. People often remember these stories for years after the event. Skilled leaders use stories to rewire disconnection between the head and the heart, bringing people together quickly through the common experience of a story that connects the work to purpose.

If you live in Australia you will be familiar with the Welcome to Country or Acknowledgement of Country. This is an important ritual held at the beginning of many official meetings to pay respects to the traditional owners of the land, their elders past, present and emerging, and other Aboriginal and Torres Strait Islanders present. A Welcome to Country is held when a traditional owner starts a conference or important meeting by welcoming everyone to their land. These Welcome ceremonies are done in different ways, depending on the Aunty or Uncle leading, perhaps with a yarning story, a song or music on the didgeridoo. These wise elders always connect a strong tie between the yarn and the reason for the gathering. One powerful experience for me was when I heard an Uncle entreating us as non-first-nation people to see this country as part of us as well and to work together to look after it.

As the new Area Executive Director in the Central Highlands of Victoria, Jen McCrabb brought this ritual to life at a whole staff meeting. This was the first time Jen and the whole staff were together for a planning day. After her Acknowledgement of the traditional owners and other elders present, Jen put up a photo and asked people to reflect on how the picture made them feel.

It was a lone tree in the middle of a paddock. You could tell it was in Australia by the type of tree, the yellow-brown colour of the paddock and the intense blue of the sky.

After some reflection, everyone shared the feelings evoked by the photo with their colleagues at the table. I personally found it peaceful. My table partner felt expansive.

This was Jen's view when she looked outside her window as she was growing up. She shared her connection to that land and other special spots that evoked strong feelings of connection to community, such as the place on the river where picnics and gatherings were held regularly by the families in the town. She shared parts of her life through this storytelling and it felt like a special gift – poignant and open. Then we all shared special places that connected us deeply to country. The professional intimacy in the room was palpable.

For me, it was also a profound example of a Ferocious Warmth leader standing strong in her conviction to create a culture of connection and purpose. This simple yet powerful 15 minutes did more for the culture and connection of that large team than many leaders do in months.

It said:

See me

I may be your leader, yet I am also a human being with a story – one that links with yours.

I see you

Every one of you has a story worth sharing and I'm interested in hearing it.

We see each other

We're all connected by special things in our lives that impact us. Our connection helps to build the trust we need to do this deep work together.

WAKE ME UP WHEN THE DATA IS OVER

Lori Silverman, author of *Wake Me Up When the Data is Over* works with some of the largest corporations in the world, using the art of storytelling to drive results. Silverman's book, gives real examples of organisations using stories to create organisational change, setting vision and enacting strategy.

Often working with sectors where data and logical rationality is seen as far superior to 'emotional rationality', Silverman ensures that we understand the cognitive work going on beneath storytelling:

'Lest all this seem too light and fluffy, with stories floating around in some ambiguous ether populated by group hugs and tired parables, keep in mind the secret is to integrate right-brain qualities of imagination and innovative thinking with left-brain analytical thought. The real goal is a whole-brained approach. Only because right-brain functions have been relatively overlooked is the emphasis now on cultivating our creative and intuitive side.'[93]

We win hearts through story. Great stories fire off electrical pulses in our brains and create neural pathways that help us make connections and decisions. Storytelling can evoke empathy, tension and delight. Research undertaken by the laboratory of Dr Paul Zak, neurobiologist and author of *The Trust Factor*[94], shows the impact of storytelling on the brain, through increasing the amount of oxytocin. Oxytocin is the molecule associated with trust and empathy. Stories with high levels of tension also increase cortisol. Zak's studies found that the more compelling the story, the more attentive the listener, the more likely to move to action.

In education, the pendulum swung too far to simply analysing data and evidence, which moved us away from remembering the power of story. Story allows us to see the world through experience and heart. Some of the most inspiring windows into schools come via the website full of students sharing their stories. This Ferocious Warmth approach of the new head of a girls' school brought it back to life over a period of three years. One of her strategies was to put videos out to the community, discussing school challenges and existing developments with school students. This informal story telling has increased connection to the school and the understanding of the transformational direction they're taking.

The movie *In My Blood it Runs*[95], a documentary told through the eyes of an eleven-year-old Arrente Garrwe boy, Dujeun, is a moving example of how understanding someone's story can give insight far beyond any statistical analysis. Dujeun is a charming and disarmingly articulate boy who lived in Hidden Valley Camp in Alice Springs with his mum and nan. He gets into trouble in school and the authorities and ends up moving 1200 kilometres north with his dad. It's a touching story of a 'failing and badly behaved juvenile' growing into a proud young healer and joyful child. It brings the data to life far better than any report.

SOMETIMES WE NEED THE COLD HARD FACTS TO JOLT US

Julie Kennedy, of Rowville Secondary College, powerfully linked the hard data with story to the whole school community at the start of a school year. With a population of over 2000 students, the school had been working incredibly hard to increase connectedness, with little success. Julie and her team wanted to introduce a large change in the way they structured the school into vertical houses based on principles of belonging, support and connection. Learning mentor roles were developed to ensure connection for all students. A huge amount of research and codesign went into developing this new system prior to its launch. When they were moving into the new way of 'being', Julie stood up in front of the whole student population and shared everything. First, the student connectedness data and then Julie then shared the story of how the school had been working for a number of years to improve the quality of the learning. She then wove stories that highlighted the benefits for them as students to feel more connected, both to each other and to the teachers. It was a transparent and heartfelt speech. The students then left the assembly with the ritual of leaving as houses for the first time to begin the process of connecting in a deeper and more meaningful way.

Data, evidence base, outcomes, measures. The logical, rational reasoning that drives improvement, programs and priorities. In a data-driven world, the Ferocious Warmth challenge is to link the cognitive with the emotions and feelings that connect us to our purpose and our joy.

Almost three years on, Julie's reflections on this initiative:

'Over the years I have had a great amount of pride that Rowville Secondary College teachers have been early adopters of evidence-based, high-impact teaching strategies. However, on their own they have had little impact on the connectedness and culture of our school. In a school of over

2000 people, it was commonly the "squeaky wheel that got the oil" and it was easy for underachieving or coasting students to fly under the radar.

'As soon as our major focus became building authentic and supportive relationships for staff, students and parents through the introduction of a vertical house system we started to see dramatic changes in our school culture. It was important to us that every child have an advocate at school, a Learning Mentor, who stays with that child for their entire time at school and who knows them academically, socially and emotionally. This relationship has also been rewarding for Learning Mentors who gain a lot of satisfaction from "making a difference!". We restructured the physical and human resources to support our direction. Creating house-based areas within the school has increased the sense of belonging and camaraderie amongst students and staff. We pushed away competing priorities (as best we could!). We have added to the rituals and traditions we use to celebrate and mark milestones and we build in fun when we can.'

Reflection pause ...

What stories do you share with the people you lead that seek to link the data or hard information but are guided by the emotions?

BRING PEOPLE INTO CHANGE

When I started teaching at Oakleigh Primary School, I came in as a Performing Arts Leading Teacher and a classroom teacher. One of my roles was to bring the choir to life again, after a few years of little energy from both teachers and students. I love leading choirs. My choirs always move and dance when they sing, which brings joy to everyone – singers and the audience – and me as conductor!

At the start of my tenure, someone directed me to a musty box and said: 'There's the choir uniforms. They were made by a parent years ago and the kids always sing in them.' My heart sank as I pulled out these choir uniforms seemingly from the nineteenth century. Long faded blue gowns with large white collars more suited to a cathedral than a bunch of primary school students. What was I to do? My whole being (and realistically, my ego) fought against asking students to wear these in public. I went to Phil, the principal, who you'll meet later, and asked him if I had to have the kids dress in this uniform? Would black and white clothes be OK? Phil, as a leader who was very tuned into treading the fine line between tradition and 'new ways of working', expressed concern that ditching them without some way of honouring the past would cause distress for the people who'd made them years ago. Moving from a new school to an established school of nearly 150 years was a great lesson for me in honouring the past and moving into the future, something I explore with schools all the time in my work now.

I pondered and brainstormed ideas. I discussed the conundrum with my colleagues and got their insight. I talked with the kids about how we might show that we were evolving as a group but still wanted to honour the past. Together, we came up with a plan.

The annual concert night came along and we were ready. The choir stood up and filed onto the choir stands in front of the stage in their choir gowns. A couple of the senior students spoke of the new choir, the history of the choir in the school and thanked all who'd helped the choir along the way. They also spoke of their joy of singing and invited everyone to enjoy their songs and join in. The choir clasped their hands angelically in front of them. It was 1993 and one of biggest hit movies was *Sister Act* with Whoopi Goldberg, where she turns a traditional nun's choir into a roaring success through dancing, harmonies and rocking voices. So that's what we did. We started off sweetly, the students singing beautiful harmonies to the song 'I Will Follow Him', and then the rock beat kicked in, the kids pulled off their choir gowns and starting bopping. Brooke, our amazing soloist, jumped up to the microphone and knocked everyone's socks off. The audience went crazy! Clapping, singing, moving along with us. The transformation was a complete success. The choir gowns were never seen again, and no one minded at all.

SHARE THE STORY OF CHANGE

Small change or large change, connecting our hearts to it is the key. Ownership of change doesn't come through logical argument; it comes through the head and the heart. Coralee Pratt, an experienced senior educator in the Victorian education system, called me in to the new school she was principal of. This very established school had been led by a much-loved principal for many years. As an experienced principal, Coralee knew to honour her predecessor's part. We created an event with her staff that shared the history of the school, highlighting the past decade or so – the achievements, the challenges, the learning. We discussed the key roles people had played in initiatives and the fabric of the school. The past principal was highlighted as being pivotal to their growth and evolution.

This process allowed people to share their insights and pride in past work, but also voice their appreciation for the contribution of former colleagues. It allowed us to look to the future and discuss, without judgement or apprehension, what was next for the school. It also gave Coralee further understanding of the school culture and what they truly valued, while allaying fears that everything prior to her coming would be changed or disregarded. It would be an evolution, not a revolution.

These types of discussions create connection. Connection to each other, connection to the work, and, most importantly, connection to our continuing evolution and growth.

Reflection pause... ...

Do I weave stories into my interactions?

Are the stories I share about hope and optimism, or problems and despair?

Do I share parts of my world with others through stories?

What rituals do we have to honour the past and look to the future?

chapter nineteen

FEROCIOUS WARMTH CONVERSATIONS

To get from good to great depends on the quality of the culture, which depends on the quality of the relationships, which depends on the quality of the conversations.

Judith E. Glaser *Conversational Intelligence*[96]

I can pretty much guarantee that conflict in a school stems from not enough quality conversations. We've either completely avoided the discussion or talked about the wrong things. One of the leaders I worked with had two people in an inherited team who hadn't spoken to each other because of a 'pumpkin' incident twenty years ago. (Don't mention the pumpkin!) Was it about the pumpkin now? No, but like a seed, the great pumpkin incident of 2000 wasn't discussed openly then, and grew rampant over the following years every time there was a disagreement! How many leaders over those twenty years shied away from the necessary conversations? How many people and standards suffered because of the lack of authentic discussion about the problem?

Many of the concepts we've explored give an insight into the strength of Ferocious Warmth conversations – owning our ignorant truth, enabling and enacting voice, creating psychological safety, challenging thinking with curiosity not judgement.

Here are three Ferocious Warmth conversation approaches that help to move conversations to extraordinary:

1. CREATE PARTNERSHIP NOT ADVERSITY

> SO MUCH ADVERSITY WOULD BE AVOIDED IF WE SIMPLY SAT DOWN AND LISTENED TO ONE ANOTHER MORE.

Deep and authentic conversations build strong relationships that can talk through the tough stuff. Discussions that honour opinions and seek to understand each other better help us achieve outcomes that support the most important reason for having them – the welfare and education of our students.

Unfortunately, things don't always run smoothly when we're passionate about our point of view. This can mean we come to conversations determined not to move an inch from our own perspective, but to expect the other person to change their view completely to ours.

2. BE OPEN TO INFLUENCE AND DIFFICULT CONVERSATIONS

Just like with learning, our conversations take a turn when we're addicted to being right. Our brains give us a rush of dopamine when we're right. 'See!' our brain shouts 'I'm right and it feels good!' If we're in a strong pattern of receiving this rush, we can also experience strong feelings of frustration and even anger when we don't get it.

The trouble is, when our need to be right overrides everyone else's, we head win-at-all-costs territory, which is detrimental to trust, collaboration and partnership. People wonder if talking with us is worth it. Why would people try to talk with someone who always thinks they're right? It ends up being very one-way that people either shy away from or approach defensively, expecting an argument.

If we're truly committed to working together, we need to drop our addiction to being right. We need real dialogue that dives into the diversity of thought in the room to explore it rather than shut it down. The more we can self-regulate our need to be right, the more can recode our brain to respond differently. We lose the fears of losing power, looking stupid and failing, and can teach our brain to find other ways to get our 'hit' of feel-good chemicals, through connection, creating something new, building trust, valuing others and learning new ways to solve problems.

Other people in the conversation also feel better about themselves – the culture starts to value opinions and people. The dialogue is about authenticity rather than power. Most of all: we build a culture of trust. With trust, anything is possible.

3. DEEP LISTENING — FROM NEUROSCIENCE TO INDIGENOUS WISDOM

One of my past mentors, the late Judith E. Glaser, dedicated her life to helping cultures shift through better conversations. Founded in the neuroscience of trust, her methodology of Conversational Intelligence™ shows that one of the most powerful ways to connect and build trust is to listen. Not just listening for the gap, or for what we agree or disagree with, but to listen deeply to understand, to empathise, to value, and to synthesis. This deeper listening helps to connect the heart and the head of both the listener and speaker. When our brain connects with others, coherent heart patterns occur that send signals to the prefrontal cortex that we are safe to engage. Part of Judith's approach is to encourage leaders to develop a 'third eye', one that brings together their intent from the head and the heart.

LISTENING DEEPLY FROM YOUR HEAD TO YOUR FEET

Science is catching up to what Australian Aboriginal people have been doing for tens of thousands of years – deep listening.

Emeritus Professor Judy Atkinson, AM is a Jiman (central west Queensland) and Bundjalung (northern New South Wales) woman, with Anglo-Celtic and German heritage. All her life, Judy has contributed to the understanding of trauma suffered by indigenous people, mainly children, stemming from the colonisation of Australia. Her work has been prolific and grown our understanding of generational trauma. Judy's TedX talk on 'The Value of Deep Listening – The Aboriginal Gift to the Nation' [97] is a raw look at the realities of this trauma and the ways we can heal it through deeper listening.

Speaking with Judy for just 90 precious minutes allowed me to open up my ignorant truth about many things. Through story after story, she spoke about the endemic failures she witnesses in the education system, the abuse of power over indigenous children and young teachers. I listened as she shared the challenges of helping the local indigenous community in a small regional town. She told me stories that made her question her own thinking, ignorant truth and bias. Judy robustly challenges whether the vast number of services provided are capable of delivering properly for indigenous children. All the children she has worked with in this small town would have, in her professional opinion, developmental complex trauma diagnosis (experience of multiple, chronic and prolonged developmentally adverse traumatic events, usually of an interpersonal nature).

I asked Judy, 'What is missing in the way we work with children who have experienced such trauma, if you could give people an insight from a leadership perspective?' Her answer was swift and definitive: 'Listen.'

I probed, wanting to find out more. Judy's TedX talk on deep listening shares the term used by the Daly River mob – dadirri – (da-did-di) to explain the Aboriginal way of listening, which prompted me to ask if she would talk about it further. 'Judy, what is it about the listening? What does deep listening look like in a scenario as raw as some of the ones you have witnessed?'

'First of all, I try to empty myself. I'm just present and people think I'm not doing anything but I'm actually watching bodies, I'm watching movement and I'm listening to words. There'll be times when I want to say something but I try to stop because I know in that conversation it will go deeper and deeper if I stop myself from speaking. Somewhere there will be a gem, there will be something that will come out that will teach me more than I already know.

'And it's about emptying my assumptions, my arrogance, my belief that I've got something I have to get in there and say. I can do the opposite as an activist, go into a meeting where I've got something to do and say and I can go wham, wham, wham! But in the listening, I'm watching the body, how the body is starting to move, what it wants to do. I might bring it out by just leaning forward and saying: "Is there something you have there? or "Is there something you can tell us about?"'

ALIGNMENT

Judy continues: 'When I first sit down I take a few deep breaths. Often I sit with my hand here on my bellybutton. That's where the soul lives and I'll just be holding it there. That is my gut. It tells me when my gut has got the right messages that I need to know. The other part of me is my feet. I'll get up and just walk a bit. There are four brains – the head brain, the heart brain, the gut brain and the feet brain.'

I was fascinated by this. As a facilitator and educator, I have always used movement within my teaching adults, as well as children. In *The Buzz* I suggest that anytime we feel stuck when collaborating we should move. The energy will shift. I asked Judy to tell me more about the feet brain.

'I was taught that when I was young by old men in Cape York who told me to take my shoes off. That I needed to stand and start talking. I was a pretty shy person at that stage and didn't do a lot of public speaking, but I started to talk about the child sexual assault issues we were seeing. They took me aside and they said, "Girly, when you get up to speak take your shoes off and just put your feet on the ground. Before you start to speak, just do a line through your body from your head down to your feet and then into the earth. Then you're grounded and connect to the mother." If you ever see me in a conference, I take my shoes off. The old men told me that I have a responsibility to speak out. I've never forgotten it.'

We often try to listen while totally out of alignment. Distracted by the email we just read, the list of to-dos we have to get through, the argument we want to win, the meeting we need to be at. Imagine the difference in the quality of our conversations if we talked less, listened more, held the space and connected to the other person, but also connected within ourselves to the earth. There is much we can learn from the indigenous approach to listening, to story and to holding space.

For years, Judy has been battling for the system to understand that trauma is infecting so many children. Her push for trauma-informed training and practices in education degrees has been a long-fought campaign. This is changing, as I notice many more schools I work in doing some kind of trauma-informed work. These deep listening skills can help not only students with trauma but any child or adult who seeks to be heard by us.

I asked Judy to give some advice to the readers of this book that might open up a different way of working with any disenfranchised children with strong trauma backgrounds. As well as increasing the listening, what would she say to us to create a different way of working with these kids?

'When you're dealing with a child whose behaviour is way off track, remember that this child has experienced something you know nothing about. [Our ignorant truth]. That behaviour is because of something they're too frightened to tell you. They don't know how to tell you. Rather than tell the child off, or send them somewhere else, remember that their behaviour is telling you something. Behaviour is language.'

chapter twenty

MOMENTS THAT MATTER

My last school leadership position was at Oakleigh Primary School in Melbourne, Australia. At OPS we prided ourselves on the close, strong community of staff, students and parents. The students came from over thirty different cultures. It was an exciting and extraordinary place to work. The school was the hub of the community.

OPS was led by Philip Hughes, a beautiful man who led the strong-willed and predominantly left-wing staff and community. We gave the department grief when the original iteration of nation-wide testing came up and over 80% of our families withdrew their children from the test. We stood outside the gates and handed union pamphlets to willing readers. The thought of standardisation and conformity was something that went against the grain for many at OPS – teachers and parents. The community spirit in the school was the strongest I'd ever experienced. A number of parents and students are still good friends many years later. We had an amazing welfare officer, Pam. Many refugee families came to OPS because of the reputation we had, due in no small part to Pam, of being a supportive and family-oriented school with teachers that gave their all to their profession and student learning.

Our Prep room was full of fun, energy and laughter. The two Prep teachers, Rob and Liz, were well loved by the children and their families. It was a beautiful melting pot of learning and connection. The Preps were so excited as they got the 'reading bug' and made their way down to us in the office for a big dance and celebration. A number of parents would gather in the Prep area every morning. Some of the women were new to Australia and had little in the way of family support. Rob, Liz, Pam and others would often just listen to their stories and life experiences or guide them to support services, if required.

HOLDING THE SPACE TO HEAL

Like any unexpected tragedy, no one was prepared for the calls one Saturday morning. One of our beautiful mothers had taken her two boys, one a preppie the other in kinder, drugged them to sleep and lay down with them in front of a train. We didn't know the extent of the domestic abuse the mother was experiencing until it was too late.

Our community was shaken to its core. None of us knew what to do. Phil moved on his instincts – his strong value of compassion and community. He knew the community would want to come together to talk, cry and grieve. The parents' room was opened up on the Sunday and many community members and staff congregated. We hugged and cried together. People came to connect with each other. This lasted a number of weeks, looking for answers or solace.

Back in the 1990s, there were no real protocols for what to do in a crisis situation. Leaders flew by instinct. Support psychological services and regional structures were relatively new within the system. Phil got on the phone to the one counsellor in our area, who came to the school, available for anyone who needed support. Phil was a calming presence, even in his own grieving.

Liz remembers: 'Phil allowed us to follow our feelings. He didn't try to impose anything on us, but anything we wanted, anything we needed, he gave, which to me was true leadership. He was so supportive. It was the moments of getting together and having those hugs with our friends, colleagues, parents and children that got us all through. It was so important. At any time we could say we needed to leave and someone would come and take over.'

As a community, we moved through the grief of losing Danny and his mum and little brother. We created a garden that is still there today, celebrating their lives. One of the most poignant and emotional memories of my time as a teacher is leading the whole school in singing Danny's favourite song in our assembly as a goodbye: 'Wally Wombat Shuffle'. I still feel emotional today when I think about that time. The toll on Rob and Liz was immense. Two brilliant teachers who felt they had not done enough. Of course, they'd done far more than many other teaching teams might have, opening up their classrooms in the morning, when others keep their doors firmly closed until it's time for the children to come inside. But that was not their way, and it was not the Oakleigh way. Anyone was welcome with open arms.

Leigh Sales' book *Any Ordinary Day*[98] is an extraordinary exploration of why some people seem to be able to emerge from tragedy and trauma in a better space than others. Before reading Sales' book, I had never heard of the phrase Post Traumatic Growth. While PTSD gets a lot of press, I had never encountered what might be considered 'the other option' – post traumatic growth. I just knew that some people move beyond tragic events in vastly different ways. Not only events we have been directly involved in, but vicarious trauma as well. In education settings, tragedies are dealt with far more often than any of us would like, as is exposure to dark and unfortunate situations that students may experience every day. It's a tough and heart-searing part of the job requiring leaders to be the glue that holds not only the school, but the community together. Too many tragic incidents take their toll on leaders. To maintain the emotional energy, self-care and self-compassion need to be moved up the priority list. Our leaders must feel strong enough to guide, be the central strong, calm presence, and have a plan.

This is what Phil gave us. He put in place strategies to help us deal with the immediate reality of the rawness of losing two little boys and a parent in such circumstances, but also longer-term supports and rituals to move us gently forward. Phil was the extraordinary moment for us on what started out an ordinary day. His actions, along with the already supportive environment of the school, allowed many of us to move through with post-traumatic growth rather than stress.

Unfortunately, many of you reading this book have needed to manage tragic situations within your school community. I am humbled by the continued strength of you all and hope that you are caring for yourselves to maintain this strength. It takes connection and bravery to step in and connect to people's raw emotions with empathy and kindness.

MOMENTS OF JOY AND CELEBRATION

The leader who walks through the school dressed as Jedi on May 4th, the teachers who jump into school celebration days with gusto rather than distain, and those who recorded daggy videos of lip-syncing songs during remote learning. All of these people help us to step into a space of joy and celebration. We can be so serious in schools. Yet there is so much to celebrate. Do you bring joy into your school? It's a missed opportunity to open our hearts and connect our brains.

MOMENTS OF PRIDE AND ACHIEVEMENT

Jackie was ecstatic. She'd managed to nail a really big presentation she'd been anxious about. This led to some exciting new developments for her faculty team back at school and an opportunity to further showcase the students' and team's work. But after she shared her joy with some of her peers for drinks on a Friday night, she felt deflated. Her friends listened to her enthusiastic download, one gave a short 'well done', no one else asked a question or made a comment, and they moved onto the next topic of conversation. Jackie sat, the joy inside fizzling out quicker than the champagne bubbles in the glass in front of her.

Sometimes we have trouble holding the space for other people's progress and achievement. Our own stuff gets in the way. It might be jealousy, perhaps its comparison issues, or our inner saboteur telling us that we are not good enough. Perhaps the judge in us sits there highlighting all the things Jackie isn't doing right!

Acknowledging others' joy and growth is a fertiliser for Ferocious Warmth. When we see others achieving and are genuinely happy for them, we give an enormous gift to them and ourselves. There is pride and delight in seeing others grow in front of our eyes. It feeds the soul of the Ferocious Warmth Leader.

courageous

chapter twenty-one

WALK TOWARDS THE HARD WORK

Fight for what you believe in, but do it in a way that people you lead will follow.

Ruth Bader Ginsberg[99]

'After my two terms at the school as acting principal I was going to leave. The behaviour was appalling, the culture toxic. But then my warrior kicked in. I was not going to walk away from this. I was going to do everything I could to make it better.'

A Ferocious Warmth principal, September 2020

Lifting skills and performance, re-imagining school or culture, connecting a community around a new vision, all take conviction and courage. How will you get your people onboard? It's a big job, and one of the most important on the planet. Ferociously defending that vision with warmth and empathy is possible. We don't need to become raving dictators to have people join us in the moral purpose. We do need to have strength of conviction, strategy as well as the people skills to create a coalition.

Jim Collins, in reflecting on the Stockdale Paradox we discussed in Chapter 3, The Paradox of Yet, found that Level 5 leaders he encountered had a strong resolve to do the hard work. On the Good to Great Ladder[100], Level 5 leaders turn things around and make a difference. Tapping into the skills of those they lead, these leaders face difficult circumstances and confront the brutal facts firmly. As Collins says, they know that if 'they don't confront brutal facts, the brutal facts will confront them.'

COURAGE TO BUILD THE RIGHT TEAM

Kaye Corcoran became principal of a school in regional Queensland in 2018, when the school's culture was stagnant and there were many brutal facts to deal with. Student, teacher and parent opinion survey data was extremely low and behaviour issues threatened daily to derail any learning. The leaders were constantly dealing with students exited out of class and both staff and students were in a battle for ascendency over one another. In the community, the school's name was mud. The paper in the regional area only reported on incidences of violent behaviour or suspensions. Anything the school was doing well went unnoticed, both internally or externally. Students and staff were merely surviving.

With courage and strength, Kaye knew she needed to bring people on the journey with her, starting by building a leadership team that had each other's backs. I was privileged to work with them as they went into a vulnerable place to grow trust and establish Minimum Viable Practices. These practices outline the very minimum we expect of each other in team. In this context the minimum was asking people to step up and show themselves as leaders. This school was tough. Over 3400 major incidences a year shows the level of out-of-control behaviour in classrooms, lack of focus on systems and management of culture.

I worked with Kaye and her leadership team not long into her principalship. I asked everyone to share what a trusting leadership team looked like from their perspective and did they feel that they had the trust of everyone in the room? There were quite a few positive and affirming comments made by members of the team. People stayed safe. When it came to Kaye, she paused and said: 'I am listening carefully to what you're all saying about how you see trust playing out in our team. But I want to be honest with you that after what happened last week, I don't feel like any of you have my back and I am not sure I trust that you will in the future.' In the stunned silence, there was time enough to remember members of the leadership team not supporting Kaye in front of the whole staff.

SET THE TONE

Kaye's courage to speak with honesty broke the veneer of 'nice' that threatened to keep less-than-useful behaviours under the table. It was forthrightly, yet respectfully said. From then on, we started the deep work of clarifying the beliefs and commitment required to drive the leadership team. Some of them stepped back and others stepped forward as they decided if they were up for the leadership challenge. They continued to evolve into a cohesive group, supporting each other to make the decisions the school needed them to make.

As a school with high turnover, due to the stress of the environment, Kaye was often left scrabbling to find staff to fill positions. She made some hard calls. Instead of taking whoever applied, she refused to fill roles if the applicants did not fit the belief system of the school, where every child and every day mattered. On hearing complaints from a number of students about a relief teacher and investigating further through discussions with teachers, she told him he would not be employed again, as he did not fit the criteria for a teacher at their school.

Often in corrosive or complacent cultures, courage is most needed. Courage to do the right thing, call the bad behaviour, see the people drowning in the toxicity or malaise and help them believe in themselves again. This is exactly what Kaye did for and with her students and her staff.

Kaye and her team of teachers have worked long and hard with the students to create the type of culture they know will help the learning. They have cocreated values and aspirations to live by. They've skilled themselves in Restorative Practices, such as with Adam Voigt and Real Schools, and Positive Education approaches to build stronger relationships and school culture. In an eighteen-month period, major behaviour incidences dropped by half, moral and learning outcomes increased. Still on the journey of improvement, they're now committed to being a thriving learning environment. Better outcomes will continue to come.

CLARITY GIVES COURAGE

One of most compelling aspects of Kaye's approach is her strong conviction about the type of school they should be creating with their students. Very early in the work, Kaye established clear understandings about how people should treat each other and that commitment was paramount. Transparent conversations about expectations helped people have certainty about what was needed to make a shift. Along with that clarity, Kaye sought outside expertise to help build the capacity of the staff in teaching and learning, collaboration and building relationships. Through many tough times for Kaye and the whole school, her strength and conviction for the hard, necessary decisions led the way for the school to transform. Student progress is lifting, the culture is calmer. It's becoming a place where learning can occur.

How we treat one another matters. Pitsa Binnion, Principal at McKinnon Secondary College, demonstrates conviction to stand up to bad behaviour: 'I don't put up with nonsense. When people are rude to others, or people are rude to me, I confront it. I'll not respond in an email to an email that's been rude. I'll ring that person, and say, "I don't deserve to be spoken to like that, neither do my team members, my people are doing the best job they can." If they're not behaving well, then you have to hold them accountable. You can't ignore it because it's not fair on everybody else that's doing the right thing. We all get a bit annoyed. If everybody's doing the right thing, and then there's one person getting away with it, I say, "Well, you're actually letting others down." It's non-negotiable. This is in the best interest of these children. They will never forget what you do.'

'Clear is kind, unclear is unkind.'

Brené Brown[101]

chapter twenty-two

WHAT DO YOU STAND FOR?

Some leaders I work with say: 'I need more ferocity!'. They are genuinely warm, people-centred leaders, but want more conviction to speak up for what they stand for. I ask them to reflect on what really matters to them then create declarative statements that show their beliefs in sticky messages that they can either say in their heads or out loud to others. This work helps them hold with conviction in the centre of their Ferocious Warmth. It has to be accompanied by a deep dive into the values that drive their leadership, so there's congruence between what they say and what they deeply believe. I learnt the concept of declarative statements from mentor, Matt Church. He helps thought leaders unpack their intellectual property into a way that evolves their thinking and understanding, partly by constantly exploring and unfolding their beliefs. As an entry point to this work, people are asked to write down at least 24 declarative statements about what they believe.

Beneath the stories in this book, can you hear people's beliefs? Our actions are the tangible evidence of our beliefs. If you haven't ever explored your firm beliefs about leadership, ponder the following guiding headings.

My beliefs about:

- Leadership
- Students
- Belonging
- Excellence
- Connection
- Collaboration
- Innovation
- Professional behaviour
- Learning
- Team
- Trust
- Forgiveness
- Transformation
- Community.

Are the belief statements you wrote above aligned with your values?

Do they reflect your moral compass?

Do they value results and relationships?

Do your actions reflect these beliefs? Or do you need to reimagine these beliefs, examining where some need to be unravelled or discarded to make room for new ones that help you be a more effective, balanced leader?

I asked Julie Kennedy of Rowville Secondary College how she reflects on her leadership beliefs, and what she stands for. She said: 'The book *The Wounded*

Leader[102] said that by writing we become responsible for our words. Many years ago, I developed an educational platform that documents what I believe about the nature of learning and the purposes of schooling. Having not kept a diary or journal before, I was surprised by the power of writing things down – it helped me think more clearly, reflect more deeply and make stronger resolutions. So now, I often write things down, draw diagrams or use mind maps to help me reflect, understand and solve problems. I love that "aha" moment when you discover something new about yourself, and I hope I never lose.'

> REFLECTION TIME BUILT INTO THE WAY YOU WORK CREATES GROWTH AND EVOLUTION.

STANDING FIRM

I asked Nathan Chisholm, Principal of Prahran High School, how he deals with feeling compromised in his beliefs, caught perhaps between a parent and a teacher. 'I think about my values and strengths and still myself into that space. I have a strong sense of what is right, particularly when it's around young people, so I'm not afraid to do what's right for the young person even if it upsets the parent or teacher. Yet I also have high levels of empathy so this work can take a toll, and it can be really difficult work. But I draw on a sense of knowing I'm the principal and the leader and I have to do what's right, not what's easy. Otherwise I'd be letting myself down, the kids and school. My moral compass keeps me on track.'

This can be draining work, especially when you're open-hearted, with high levels of empathy. Sometimes the community and students don't see leaders as open-hearted, simply because they don't or can't see the complex layers of an issue in the way leaders need to. Having horrible things said about you and to you can be soul-destroying. If we're too exposed, this can rock us. Best to stand firm on what we believe, including the best outcomes for the student.

Nathan continues: 'It can be difficult when you are coming from a place of care and love. You firmly believe what you are doing with the young person is right, but the family is refusing to see that and throwing comments about your integrity at you. To go back to the question, I think I draw from my moral compass, my sense of integrity, but there is a pragmatic nature to me as well. I accept the responsibility of the job. Some days it feels lonely. Some days are really tough, so I have to manage how I look after myself because some of that is the nature of the job. The buck stops here. I've got better at that over the years.'

This is an example of a Ferocious Warmth leader understanding that if we don't look after ourselves, our centeredness is diminished. As we've discussed, self-care is critical for balance and managing. Nathan has a strong team who he can download to when needed. They also adopt a pragmatic approach to the tough days. 'I've said to my team many times during 2020, this is such a tough time for all of us, but we have to believe that things are going to get better. That doesn't mean we can't say, "I'm having a rough day", but we stay determined to make things better.'

Ferocious Warmth. Realist optimism. Time and time again leaders are standing firm and doing the tough stuff. Bringing hope and resolve to others through their courage and conviction.

WHAT WE STAND FOR STARTS EARLY

My dad, Keith, started running his own electronics and security firm when he was 25 years old and a father to my four-year-old sister and two-year-old me. He came from a hard-working, yet poor family. Living on a farm that his father and mother worked, he learnt to drive the milk truck by the time he was 11 and started working on the weekends with an electrician. As a geeky kid who loved electronics, circuit boards and radio transistors, he left school early for an electrical fitter apprenticeship. As a little kid, I knew my dad worked hard. He wasn't home much, working long hours to get the business up and running, with Mum as administration support. His dinner often sat on the stove, the plate balanced on a pot of simmering hot water covered by a saucepan lid.

As the electronic security industry started to emerge, Dad's business created one of the first central monitoring stations. His company and their standards became well known to insurance companies and people who had substantial assets to protect through electronic surveillance. Some of these insurance companies only insured jewellers and high-risk executives if Dad's company was the one installing and monitoring the security alarms. His company was the first to create security agreements with clients to take responsibility for any mistakes on his part, providing the client held up their part of the deal. The biggest insurance company in the world was willing to back this security agreement, such was the integrity and excellence of the product and service. The capture rate for criminals was 80%, the industry's highest by a long way. His company also worked with police in crime prevention. The methodology and service Dad created was used to provide security to witnesses, investigators and prosecutors in a number of royal commissions. Dad become instrumental in the standardisation of the security industry as it burgeoned in the 1980s, lobbying government to create accreditation to keep, in his words, the cowboys out. He chaired many government and industry-directed standards committees, including Chair of the Australian Industry Standards Council for security.

I know I was infused by Dad's ethic of hard work. But reflecting on the values that drive my courage, I know it's much more than that. Every day I witnessed this hard work as he headed out the door, but joining him at work I was exposed to two major drivers: integrity and a 'just do it with professionalism' attitude. During the school holidays I worked with him, getting up early in the morning and heading off for the day. I'd solder circuit boards, crawl under houses to run cables for sensors, send a telex or answer the phones, climb up ladders in warehouses. With two daughters, Dad never told me in words or through behaviour that I shouldn't or couldn't do anything because I was a girl. This has stayed with me throughout my life.

During tough early days in the business, he would not always take a wage to ensure he could keep his apprentices and others employed. Mum also showed this resolve, going out to work elsewhere to keep things afloat. Dad's signature look was a three-piece suit. He wore all three pieces when talking with clients of high-end businesses or properties, or two pieces when walking into factories, and he always wore a tie. When installing security systems, he'd take off his jacket and put overalls over his suit. He was known throughout the industry for this quirk. Both of these examples, putting his staff first and the statement he made through what he wore, symbolised his value of professionalism.

Dad's leadership style is very different to mine. (He sometimes stands to the far right of Attila the Hun.) So even though we share many similar values, I have worked on some over the years that are different. I learnt the value of deep collaboration and creating an environment of voice and choice – the warmth element – through knowing that his more authoritarian style didn't bring out the best in me. I also know I need to watch the hard-work ethic doesn't take precedence over my presence with my family. It can be too easy to put the head down into some work and look up to find hours have gone by.

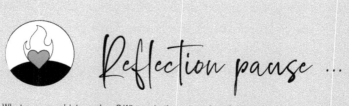

What are your driving values? Where do they come from? What stories can you find in your past that help you understand where they might have come from and why they're so important?

FIND YOUR PURPOSE

A bonus about working with leaders is that you get to work on yourself at the same time! When a Women in Leadership course in health that I co-facilitate occurs every few months, I use the time to re-evaluate my purpose as the participants undertake the same task. Dr Elizabeth Sigston, a senior leader, ear nose and throat surgeon, and executive coach (what a trifecta!) leads the group work. It is a powerful reflection process following the Be Do Have model:

- How do I want to be?
- So that I can do what?
- So that I/we can have what?

Currently, my professional purpose manifesto sounds like this:

To be authentic, compassionate and thought-provoking, to strive for excellence through learning, teaching and connection so that I can support leaders and their teams to challenge the status quo, deliver high quality and thrive while working together.

It will probably morph over the next little while, depending on the context and where the next part of my life takes me. I also find it useful to think of the big word that I want to drive my work for the year. This year it is elevate. I wanted to elevate my thinking, my relationships, my compassion and my impact. This has helped me whenever I've felt stuck and got me back on course. It's also guided my decisions and actions.

Is your 'being' reflected in decisions about what you do in your leadership work? What about the way you work with people? Your being is steeped in what you value most. It's your most authentic self. The values I choose to prioritise and enact help me decide how and where I work and with whom, which helps me see how I might make the world better. When I'm out of sync with that centred, value-driven behaviour, having the courage to reassess through the lens of my values gives me the conviction I need to make the harder decisions.

Reflection pause ...

What would be your purpose manifesto? What might be your big word?
Are you courageous in following that purpose and standing with conviction in your values?

chapter twenty-three

COURAGE
FOR CHANGE

'In the midst of hate, I found there was, within me, an invincible love. In the midst of tears, I found there was, within me, an invincible smile. In the midst of chaos, I found there was, within me, an invincible calm. I realised, through it all, that in the midst of winter, I found there was, within me, an invincible summer. And that makes me happy. For it says that no matter how hard the world pushes against me, within me, there's something stronger – something better, pushing right back.'

Albert Camus[103]

Connecting to our purpose and values fuels the courage to stand firm. When we're sure of what we believe and who we are, holding the line becomes easier. We start to be more certain about what we do and don't want, what we believe to be right and what doesn't sit with our values. One of my favourite examples of this comes from a good mate of mine, Adam Voigt, who runs Real Schools, a great organisation helping schools to build cultures that create belonging and positive relationships for all students. Adam is a fierce advocate for students and teachers. A former school principal and author of *Restoring Teaching*[104], Adam is well known for his strong position on education hot topics. Over the last few years, he's become a go-to person for the media for informed opinions on matters of education. His strong stances often bring him heat, but he stands there, firmly placed as a Ferocious Warmth leader, willing to listen, engage and discuss what he believes to be true. He is open to discussion and influence, but will go in to bat against inequity and injustice every single time. (And I know he would approve of my use of a cricket metaphor.) Reading some of Adam's responses to the interesting and colourful reactions he gets is a lesson in good humour, guts and conviction. He shares his insights with stories that connect people's hearts, and tells it like it is. His purpose is clear in his work and his writing: all students are worthy and deserve the very best we can give them, regardless of their circumstances. All teachers deserve far more respect and standing in our society.

CONVICTION THAT TRANSFORMS

Conviction is the steel spine of the Ferocious Warmth leader. It is drawn from a strong moral purpose and drive to make a difference. Through stepping into their own authentic self, Ferocious Warmth leaders clarify who they are and what they stand for. This seems to develop with confidence and is often coupled with a strong conviction for change and transformation. Like Adam, these leaders address head-on complex issues of disadvantage, discrimination, inclusion and access to education and health. Leaders with Ferocious Warmth care deeply about people and causes, and make things happen to shift mediocrity, status quo and complacency. I know many Ferocious Warmth leaders' family culture suffused them in the principles of social justice or they themselves were victim of an inequitable system. Others draw from values that speak of fairness and use of privilege for change. These early imprints set the course for a life seeking to impact positively on others.

Ferocious Warmth leaders can be seen in all sectors, leading change in their professions, standing up against the status quo that treats people inequitably. Elizabeth Broderick is an example of this type of leadership. She has championed change in attitude and policy through her work as Australia's longest serving Sex Discrimination Commissioner. She is also founder of Male Champions of Change, committed to changing gender imbalance in workplaces worldwide. She is one of the UN's Special Rapporteurs for Discrimination against Women and Girls, and a member of its workshop group.

Elizabeth has the Ferocious Warmth skill of inspiring people to think differently, without 'ramming it down their throats' or doing it through compliance and force.

She articulates her beliefs and the evidence base with conviction, all the while listening deeply to people's thoughts and challenges.

'Liz is collegiate, she's collaborative, and she keeps her eyes focused on what we're trying to achieve. I've never once seen Liz have to be forceful with people. I often watch her and marvel at the fact that she can do this with such influential people around the room. If you put these CEOs around a boardroom table in any other circumstance, there'd probably be disagreement all over the place, but she unifies us.'

Andrew Colvin, Former Australian Federal Police Commissioner and Male Champion of Change[105]

Leaders such as Elizabeth Broderick have the platform and ability to affect transformation at a national and international level. For most of us, transformation happens at the grassroots level. Our common goal? Better outcomes across all parts of society. It's the decisions we all make every day that lead to better education, greater community and belonging, and equity.

Antoinette Braybrook is CEO of Djirra. Djirra is an Aboriginal Community Controlled Organisation providing holistic and culturally safe spaces for women. It started in 2002 and is now a state-wide organisation in Victoria, Australia. At Djirra, women can get the legal and non-legal support they need and want. They work to free Aboriginal women and their children from violence, and to have a voice. Djirra works directly with women and their children, as well as with policy reform. Antoinette was recently inducted into the Victorian Honour Roll for Women. You get the sense that Antoinette would much rather focus on the many women and children she's helped over the years than herself. There is a fierce fire in the belly for Antoinette and passion for the purpose of the organisation. Her conviction is in evidence in an interview with Ella Bache's CEO Pippa Hallas[106]: 'I am inspired by my mother to live boldly and courageously. She has fought hard for equality and to have our voices heard; I honour and carry on that legacy. As Aboriginal women we are strong and we never give up. I want my family and my community to succeed and thrive. I hold this as a personal responsibility. This has always been my driving force, and it remains the same today.'

Antoinette firmly believes in building and maintaining strong relationships and trust. As a CEO she strives to stay accessible and visible to Aboriginal women. Her voice advocates for many who would otherwise stay silent. Her work is driven by a deep passion for the purpose of demanding change for Aboriginal women. In the Pamela Denoon Lecture for Australian National University on International Women's Day March 2020[107] Antoinette spoke of her legal speciality choosing her. It became obvious that her calling was working with Aboriginal and Torres Strait Islander women, 'advocating and keeping women's voices of family violence, incarceration, racism, child removal in front of white Australia'.

This is the Ferocious Warmth leader – conviction to transform and take a stand to protect and support those for whom the system does not work.

VALUES-DRIVEN CONVICTION — A STORY OF COURAGE

For over five years I've led a Women in Leadership program for The Monash Centre of Health Research Institute (MCHRI) and Monash Partners. The Executive Director of Monash Partners and Chief Executive of MCHRI is Professor Helena Teede, one of the most transformative leaders in medical research in Australia. Helena and I co-facilitate this program for doctors, surgeons, academic medical researchers and senior nurses with a number of brilliant female leaders from these professions. The program is Helena's brain-child. It's always well attended and gets consistently high-quality feedback.

As the professional leaders share their journeys and insights, Ferocious Warmth leadership stories fly thick and fast. The duality and tension of results *and* relationships, head *and* heart, logic *and* emotion is discussed openly and explored.

Unfortunately, due in no small part to the stress of the context, resources and high-pressure situations, health-care environments can be unsafe for many staff and patients. With endemic problems that many health settings are dealing with, Ferocious Warmth leaders are needed more than ever. These leaders model how to behave with professional respect and high standards, yet compassion. Historical leadership behaviours appear to stem from a belief that people work harder, and better, by shouting, belittling and generally behaving badly. The issue of disrespectful behaviour is discussed in researcher Matthew Grissiner's 2013 journal article:

'Disrespectful behavior can arise in any health care setting, and both the stressful nature of the environment and human nature play roles in this destructive behavior. We are driven to function in "survival" mode when forced

to cope with difficult personal frustrations and system failures. Disrespectful behavior is often "survival" behavior gone awry. Although personal frustrations and system failures do not excuse disrespectful behavior, they often create a tipping point by which an individual is pushed over the edge into full-blown disrespectful behavior.' [108]

As a young leader in the medical and academic field, Professor Helena Teede became one of the youngest professors in her field of endocrinology. She has led numerous units and been senior leader in a large health network. She sits on a number of committees of the National Health and Medical Research Council, which oversees grant money to research institutes around Australia. It is obvious that Helena is no light weight when it comes to transformation and commitment to the health of Australians. She's a fierce advocate for those she leads. When I run leadership programs, I always ask for people to tell us about the leader who has brought out the best in them and led them in a way they want to follow. In healthcare programs, Helena's name often comes up. Not only because some of the people she sponsors are in the room, but because she's able to balance setting high standards with creating an environment of support and growth. Helena's teams are the envy of many a female doctor and surgeon. A number of Helena's teams are younger females. She pragmatically and openly plans any family leave transition in and out of the team in conjunction and collaboration with each one, respecting their particular context. Her empathy and willingness to have open discussions with her team creates a safe environment for everyone to thrive.

This is not easy to achieve in a system fundamentally not built to cater for women who've been the main caregivers for their children, and suffers from serious lack of leadership opportunities for women in general. I have worked with female surgeons who have experienced very different reactions from their leaders. Many female surgeons never mention their children at work. One participant shared that when she left to have her baby, not one of her team asked anything of her when she returned. Nothing about the baby, her transition back or the supports she needed. The lack of humanness leaves me speechless. For another, the budget on her unit did not allow for any backfill for her maternity leave, so she knew that when she had another baby, her two male colleagues would have to take on her caseload. A recipe for guilt on one side, resentment on the other – even in the most supportive of men. For others, having a quick 10-minute break as a doctor can be a deal breaker for a breast-feeding mother when the breast-feeding room is 10 minutes away at the other end of the hospital. While there are other stories that show inclusion and evolution of approach, these are still very much the exception.

STANDING FIRM IN THE FACE OF BAD BEHAVIOUR

In a professional environment where toxic hierarchy, the status of 'elder statesman' and in many cases less-than-acceptable senior leadership behaviours can abound, one of Helena's stories is a favourite example of behaviours and action stemming from a strong set of values. As a young leader, Helena was in a meeting with two very senior medical leaders. She had brought two junior doctors and all were sitting at the meeting table. The two senior leaders proceeded to enter into a shouting match with each other, with no regard for the others. After this continued for a time, Helena stood up and interrupted them saying, 'This behaviour is not acceptable for my team to be exposed to. We are leaving this meeting. When the two of you are ready to resume respectfully, then we can reconvene.' Helena and the two junior doctors stood up and left the room.

Of course, Helena's heart was pounding and she was shaking internally. However, the fear of a possibly career-ending move was overridden by her steadfast belief that professional respect is critical to any conversation in the workplace. She was also compelled to act through her fierce protection of her junior doctors and minimising their exposure to such disrespectful behaviour. It is a perfect example of living the 'behaviour ignored is behaviour condoned' mantra.

Brené Brown would describe Helena's behaviour as Daring Leadership.

'Daring leadership is ultimately about serving other people, not ourselves. That's why we choose courage.' [109]

As an endocrinologist and health researcher, patient health has always been at the core of Helena's purpose. Does Helena ruffle feathers in the 'establishment'? I am sure she does. She disrupts the status quo. She is highly collaborative in a world where funding competition and academic jealousy can drive the agenda. Helena's purpose rests firmly with the health of the patient and wider community and she fearlessly pushes against people with self-serving agendas. She is fiercely protective of her team, yet encourages them to lift and step into their potential through stretching them.

Focussed, yet empathic.

Courageous, yet vulnerable.

Clear, yet collaborative

Wise, yet open to learning.

Understanding the drivers of our beliefs and values is vital to ferocious warmth. In discussing this chapter with Helena, she shared that she'd recently revisited her most important values. They came as no surprise to me:

- Courage
- Impact
- Kindness
- Support
- Collectivism.

As we discussed in both the Expansive and Connected elements, when we're already proficient professionals, self-awareness is step number one towards further growth. With our attention out doing the job, time to connect with self is often the first thing that gets dropped off the to-do list. For some, investigating our emotions and values never makes it onto the list because it can be too confronting. Connecting to self and self-awareness are developed characteristics of Ferocious Warmth leaders. Where do many of your values come from? What stories pop up for you when you let your mind wander to milestone experiences or events in your life? Just like the vision of my dad, standing at the back of his van, taking off his jacket after his important meeting, and putting on his overalls to get stuck into the hands-on work. His conviction about the right way for him to carry and present himself stayed true for the sixty years he worked, and still stands in his volunteer work today.

As you reflect further on your values and strong declarations about your current beliefs about topics you care about, what stories could you share about how you've stood firm? How have you shown courage when these have been compromised? What decisions has that led to?

UNDERSTANDING THE NUANCE

> THE COURAGE ELEMENT OF FEROCIOUS WARMTH IS THE PLACE OF THE BRAVE-HEARTED, NOT THE COLD-HEARTED.

Many people have been burnt by leaders with strong opinions about what they believe. These fearsome leaders use power-over as a way to get people doing what they want, rather than power-with. It is conviction without emotional intelligence or connection. Strength of belief without empathy. Ferocious Warmth leaders have strong conviction with authenticity and humility, not arrogance, hubris and posturing.

The warmth in our equation keeps us from ramming our point of view down other people's throats; instead, opening the space for dialogue and greater understanding of the reasons behind decisions. In cultures bereft of Ferocious Warmth leaders, full of fearsomeness and intimidation, conviction becomes a battlefield, with two sides not giving in. Ferocious Warmth leaders speak their conviction with humility and clarity, using the skills of listening and openness. They understand that their conviction still holds a big element of ignorant truth and are always willing to hear other thoughts.

"ONE THING BINDS FEROCIOUS WARMTH LEADERS IN A COMMON, COURAGEOUS LINE-IN-THE-SAND BEHAVIOUR THAT AFFECTS OTHERS' BASIC HUMAN RIGHTS AND ACCESS TO QUALITY EDUCATION IS NOT ACCEPTED."

authentic

chapter twenty-four

OWNING WHO WE ARE

Here's the thing... if you take the elements of a Ferocious Warmth leader –
Expansive, Connected and Courageous – you can't do them without Authenticity.
I challenge you to find someone who connects deeply with others, is a genuine
learner and stands firmly with courage in the thick of their purpose, who is not
authentic and real. Authenticity is the alignment of what we think, what we say,
what we feel and what we do. Authenticity builds as we become more certain
of ourselves and the impact we want to make on the world. The qualities that
often sit underneath this authenticity are humility and power. Another fascinating
duality of leadership.

TAKING THE SHACKLES OFF

Lu was told in her position as deputy that she needed to be careful about being
'too soft'. The principal of her previous school was more results driven and often
lacked the empathy needed to create a thriving environment so Lu felt that her
emotional intelligence was seen as a deficit. When she stepped into her own
principal role, she felt the shackles come off as she developed her own sense of
balance between ferocity and warmth, power and love. Within her authenticity, she
became aware of the need to be mindful to use her power for influence not for ego.
'I love hard' is a statement Lu uses to represent her leadership. Her authenticity is
evolving through her openness and caring as well as facing tough conversations
with courage and compassion.

A recent situation reflects Lu not only embracing authenticity, but also the duality of ferocity and warmth. Lu had taken a term off. When she returned she needed to deal with an underperforming staff member. The leaders had been doing some work with this graduate but were still very concerned. Coming from a high-challenge, high support approach, Lu sat down with her leadership team to identify the supports already in place. Capturing it visually on the whiteboard, they looked at the supports and asked themselves: 'What is it we need to do?' and 'At what point do you say "enough is enough?".' After this reflective work, they were confident that they were coming from a place of care and love for both the teacher and the students

A 'tipping point' came when the teacher's negative impact on the students remained too high without an appropriate change in her behaviour. Tough conversations were needed. In the end, the teacher left because everyone, including the teacher herself, recognised the supports she'd been given without change.

Lu's approach was authentic and humble. She's a deep, reflective person who seeks to come from a place of empathy when considering how to support others. The courage to be vulnerable and show who you really are can be scary, but so much trust is built when we step into that arena. It's turns out, Lu is neither too soft nor too hard.

AUTHENTICITY OWNS MISTAKES

Making mistakes is part of everyday life for a leader. Complexity, down days, new challenges and life in general is a recipe for mistakes and missteps just as much as highlights and touchdowns. Psychologists have found that competent leaders who own their imperfections become more likeable. This was originally named by psychologist Elliot Aronson as the 'pratfall effect'[110]. Experiments over the last 50 years or more indicate that people are put off by those seen as perfect and distant. Perhaps we're wary of the expert who has learnt rather than the one who is learning. Admitting missteps and imperfections as an authentic leader means taking responsibility from the heart. Our mistakes and failures are reframed when learning, not perfecting, is the goal.

I asked Dr Briony Scott what happens internally when she's faced with the reality of getting something really wrong. Her response: 'Our job needs us to be able to make decisions quickly and yet we can get it wrong. I find I get a wave of defensiveness, blame and justification, and then try to move to one of humility. We just have to sit in humility.'

SAVIOUR OR CURATOR?

We need humility to be learners, humility to acknowledge wrongs and humility to accept we can't do it alone. Humility helps us become co-creators with others, not the perfect leader with all the answers; the expert who is learning, not one who has learnt. We step into a mindset of curator not saviour. A curator brings out the best of others through authentic relationships that build potential and create change. They ask questions and curate thinking that leads to insight. A saviour rides in on that white horse and wants to save the day, which they might do for a while, but then everyone gets heartily sick of the horse, and its rider.

Saviour Leader	Curator Leader
Arrogant	Humble
I	We
Mine	Ours
Me	Us
Must	Let's
Tell	Ask
My way	Many ways
Solve	Co-create
Inform	Learn

AUTHENTICITY IS POWER WITH NOT POWER OVER

Dacher Keltner, researcher and author of *The Power Paradox, How We Gain and Lose Influence*[11] pulls apart the concept of power and what it does to some people. Studies show that the most impactful power is based on empathy and social intelligence, rather than fearsome leadership.

Strangely though, research also points to power doing weird things to people in these positions. Fearsome leaders are more likely to act selfishly, on impulse and with more aggression. Keltner calls this the paradox of power: the skills most important to obtaining power and leading effectively (empathy, modesty, humility, engaged in the needs of the people) are the skills that deteriorate once we have power. 'We gain a capacity to make a difference in the world by enhancing the lives of others, but the very experience of having power and privilege leads us to behave, in our worst moments, like impulsive, out-of-control sociopaths.'

Doh! What is that about?

There's that fearsome leadership pull happening, dragging us from the centre of the Ferocious Warmth loop. Keltner explores the power we often hold to – the Machiavellian philosophy of something to be grabbed and taken from others. He says we can outsmart this power paradox by changing our definition of power into 'the capacity of making a difference in the world'. The Ferocious Warmth leaders in this book demonstrate this redefinition of power. Their value sets and beliefs bring out the potential of others to do the same. A ripple effect occurs, building a power-with approach rather than power-over, what Keltner calls 'enduring power'. These leaders curate the skills of others. Keltner poses 21 Power Principles in his book, highlighting many of the Ferocious Warmth principles. One of most intriguing to consider is 'power is about altering the states of others.' State can refer to anything – beliefs, emotions, capability, knowledge. Educators can alter the states of their students in every interaction they have.

Together, the two principles of power is about making a difference in the world and power is about altering the states of others creates the potency of the authentic Ferocious Warmth leader.

> DOES YOUR POWER ALTER THE STATES OF OTHERS IN A WAY THAT'S GOOD FOR THE WORLD?

INFLUENCE AS POWER

The influence and power of the musical conductor has always thrilled me. While to many it seems that the conductor simply waves their arms about, if you've been in a band or orchestra, or sung in a choir, you'll understand a great conductor's influence on a group. The tonality, energy and vigour of a group of musicians can change completely. As a conductor of school bands, orchestras and choirs for many years, there is no better feeling for me than helping others make magic with a flick of a baton.

In a fit of back-to-my-roots and the joy of my younger years I decided to spend the day exploring my childhood passion for Baroque recorder music. (OK, this sounds deadly dull to many of you, I'm sure! But you do you, I'll do me.) My flute lay rusty on the piano, hardly played over the last ten years. I could still get a pretty good sound out of my recorders (I hear you groan!) and went and hung out with the recorder guild, who were having a masterclass with a global recorder guru playing Baroque dance music.

Put simply, it was an exquisite lesson in Ferocious Warmth leadership and the building of a collaborative and visionary culture. She altered our state. The leader was a highly skilled recorder player and conductor from the University of Melbourne, known globally for her solo playing and teaching skills. We started the day as a bunch of solitary players who happened to be playing the same music. Our conductor would lead us through a piece, then stop us, and quietly share a story of the court of France and Louis the XIV, who was known as the best courtier in Europe. As she weaved a vision for us, she highlighted the parts of the music where we needed to lift our energy, become perkier, hold a note, or fade at just the right time. We then played again, all striving to recreate this moment in a 17th Century French court.

Not once did she raise her voice, not once did we feel belittled by her for not playing to the level she wanted. This conductor took the human capital of that recorder group – reasonably skilled musicians in our own individual right – and built our collective capacity in one day. Through her expertise, collaboration and inspirational stories, she curated our skills and interest to create our version of a Baroque French court. Interestingly, at the start she didn't know approximately 75% of the group, yet her authentic head-and-heart approach made us listen, contribute and rise to the occasion. I felt her Ferocious Warmth. She was real and authentic. Transfer this scenario to schools led by Ferocious Warmth leaders and we get school cultures ready to transform and create environments that provide education in which all students thrive.

RIPPLES

Claire was coming back to her school after over 10 years of family leave and leave without pay. The term before she was due back, Claire came to a professional learning workshop I was running. Her principal, Steve, who she'd never met face-to-face, welcomed her warmly at the door. He asked her how she was feeling and told her how glad they all were that she could make it for the day. Claire said she was nervous and feeling a bit like a new graduate. Steve took her into the learning area, personally introduced her to a few people that she wouldn't have known and left them to chat. Some people came up and introduced themselves, smiling and helping her feel more at ease immediately.

Steve kicked off our day, working on the team learning culture and welcoming me to the school for the start of our ongoing partnership. He then paused, looked at his staff and said, 'I'd also like to make a special welcome to Claire, who will be returning to us next year after a decade away. It is fantastic that Claire can do this work with us, but I know that if I was in Claire's shoes I might be slightly nervous, so let's make sure Claire steps straight back into being a part of us, as we know how important that support is when we venture into a new journey.' Everyone clapped Claire. The day was a perfect foundation for her integration back into the school, connecting through many discussions.

Contrast this to another school where the opposite happened. Same scenario, yet there was an aloof welcome, even frosty. The frostiness came from the principal's side, not the returning teacher, even though another year of leave had been knocked back. I could feel the teacher wanting to make a good start of it. There were very few people left who she'd worked with before. After seeing what she could do to help set up the room for the day, the returning person sat by herself at a table, trying not to look terrified, hoping that someone who remembered her came and spoke to her. But everyone else sat down. I was fascinated and slightly embarrassed by their lack of welcome. I wondered whether it was symbolic of an 'I' culture rather than a 'we'.

As I set up, I sat down with her for a moment and asked her how she was feeling. She echoed Claire's nervousness. There was no mass or individual introduction to the rest of the staff (until I did it) and no painting a picture of mutual success. Nothing from the principal setting up the intention for bringing her into the team with open arms. Fortunately for her and the team, the work we did that day exposed her to many of her new and former colleagues, and the discussion on psychological safety exposed the need for belonging being our number one strategy for connection and collaboration. She came up to me at the end of the day with a smile on her face saying what a perfect day it was for her to dip her toe back in and learn so much about where the school had been. I'm glad she experienced that day. Her re-entry would not have been as joyful without that work.

THE LITTLE THINGS MAKE THE BIG THINGS

For me this is a snapshot that reflected the culture of the two schools and their leadership. Those little comments and gestures by Steve created connection and positive intent. They took him no time at all, but had a massive impact on Claire, and modelled positive culture.

Both schools are on a transformation journey. In Steve's school you can feel the collective efficacy. They're focussed on shift and how they can do it better together. They live the culture of 'we never arrive'. The second school is finding the journey trickier. The leadership (who tend towards results-driven) are still trying to connect people to the work. They are also quick to judge their staff pessimistically. As well, they're trying to shift a culture that is 'happy here, thanks'. Leadership hasn't figured out that the first port of call is to model behaviours that bring about connection, inspiration and belief for change, as well as acceptance and belonging. They will, though, as they build their own capacity along the way.

POSITIVE RIPPLES

As we know, teachers can have positive ripples on individuals for the rest of their lives. The teachers close to my heart taught me far more than the curriculum. John Savage taught me rigor and high standards were not only important, but attainable with hard work and dedication. Christine Gray taught me that women can be smart, professional, independent and intrepid all rolled up in the one person. Doug Heywood taught me kindness, patience, and the beauty and joy of making music with others. Jim Henderson, Hendo, as we affectionately called him, taught me that humour is a great way to help me learn, as he leapt on the tables and acted out the French Revolution with us. All of them gave me connection, valued who I was and pushed me gently yet firmly forward, both in learning and in being human.

Being a great leader is not that different to being a great teacher. The leaders that make a difference see us, value us and bring out the best in us. We remember great leaders long after they have left our stage, but their legacy continues in us. They connect our heads and our hearts to the challenges and joy of life. They help us see a grander vision than the one we might have set for ourselves. They see in us things we can't see ourselves and give us the nudge we need to aspire to more. They laugh with us and let us see their foibles, wrinkles and blemishes. They admit when they're wrong and seek to make things right. They reflect and learn from their mistakes and see the world with curiosity and wonder. These leaders push against inequity and never sit in complacency. They are in no way perfect, but constantly do the dance of balance ferocity and warmth.

I hope you continue to build the skills of a Ferocious Warmth leader. I hope you find alignment between your head, heart, gut and feet. We need more of you in our world – expansive, connected, courageous and authentic leaders. May all your ripples be positive.

A little something more

Including this poem is an indulgence on my part. It's not often that I'm working with a school and the local poet from the English faculty writes a poem based on the day. Andrew is well known in his school for capturing the ebbs and flows, and runs a poetic commentary on the person out the front, not always in a kind light. He writes it as he sees and feels it.

I spotted him at the start of the day, wearing a t-shirt that said: 'Ew, people' and a mug that said, 'I'd love to stay and chat, but I'd be lying'. We had a laugh and I asked him if I could take a photo. It was a deliberate and beautiful irony when the day was on collaboration and he would have to talk with heaps of different people!

At the end of the day he came up to me and said, 'I don't often share these with people who present to us, but I'd like you to have this.'

It's a cracker. Thank you, Andrew. I love how he's captured one of the turning points in working with a new school – will the influential soothsayer of the clan accept you?

PS: the 'writing sticks' he refers to are the markers and sketch-noting I asked them to capture the day with.

THE TRIBE

PART I

They gathered around the new electric fireplace
Staring in wonder at the bright coloured flames.
The wise woman arose
To the deafening silence of the tribe.

The dirt circles at their feet
Were scattered with strange scrapings
The tribe looked confused – dazed.
Some had their writing sticks at the ready.

The wise woman waved her wand
The tribe wandered and wondered
Single syllabic groans and grunts grew
As they gravitated into groups.

The fledglings of the tribe turned their ears willingly
Whilst the quarrellers quarrelled
Their eyebrows deep and their foreheads furrowed
In practised lines of discontent.

'We've always done it this way.'

The wise woman clapped her sticks
And the tribe returned to her face.
She chanted her spells full of buzz
Of 'agency' and 'change' and 'ideology'.

The old soothsayer arose
Ears pricked across the meeting place.
Would he accept or abhor?
Desire or dismiss?

The collective release of air was physical
Like a zephyr breeze across the camp.
The soothsayer had accepted the wise woman
And calm was restored.

And then the wise woman went into a trance
Calling on spirits from millennia in the future
And a strange musical tone erupted from her throat:
'Stop, collaborate and listen.'

But the tribe's attention started to wane.
They gazed up at the constellations
Praying to their gods for masterstock
Whilst using their writing sticks inappropriately.

PART II

With their bellies full and their hunger sated
The tribe returned for more words of wisdom.
Tales turned to comfort and safety and they learned:
'It's not easy being green.'

But colours turned to pictures turned to words
And the tribe again became confused
By the strange scratchings such as:
'Open Door Learning Walk Feed Forward Postcard.'

A story was told from long ago
Of a beast so large; so horrific
And the tribe was afraid of the beast
And named it the 'Terrorzone'.

But as the tribe DBJed
They giggled and laughed
As they were still immature and unsophisticated
And wanted lunch.

PART III

And finally the wise woman called out God's name:
"Hattie!" she screamed and the tribe hushed.
"Hattie!" she cried and the tribe bowed.
"Hattie!" she whispered and the tribe was reassured.

From the embers of the fire, visions arose.
Visions of purpose, visions of trust
And the tribespeople shared their visions
Of being brave and bold.

Seared in the flame's visions
Were words of alliteration
The clansman cooed of committed collaboration
And of co-creation and co-operation.

Tools were then provided to the tribesman
To create nets of the future
And after being embroiled in knots and gnarls
The magic of the psychological safety net was woven.

And the tribesman looked at each other anew
And at the wise women with adoration
For they had become
A 21st century tribe.

Andrew Brehaut, 2019

ENDNOTES

CHAPTER 1: THE WORLD NEEDS MORE COURAGEOUS AND CARING LEADERSHIP

1. Goss & Sonnemann, 2017
https://grattan.edu.au/wp-content/uploads/2017/02/Engaging-students-creating-classrooms-that-improve-learning.pdf

2. Youth Mental Health Report, Youth Survey 2012-2016.
http://www.blackdoginstitute.org.au/wp-content/uploads/2020/04/2017-youth-mental-health-report_mission-australia-and-black-dog-institute.pdf?sfvrsn=6

3. Niesche, *Improving Educational Equity in Australia.*
https://www.gie.unsw.edu.au/sites/default/files/documents/Gonski%20Equity%20Paper_web_2.pdf

4. Brotherhood of St Lawrence, December 2020. *The Great Disruptor: COVID-led Recession Deals Another Blow to Youth*
https://www.bsl.org.au/news-events/media-releases/the-great-disruptor-covid-led-recession-deals-another-blow-to-youth/

5. Chesters & Daly, October 2018, *Family and School Effects on Achievement Across School Career.*
https://education.unimelb.edu.au/__data/assets/pdf_file/0007/2903137/family-and-school-effects-on-educational-achievement.pdf

6. State of Victoria, Department of Education and Training, 2019, *Amplify. Empowering students through voice, agency and leadership.*
https://www.education.vic.gov.au/Documents/school/teachers/teachingresources/practice/Amplify.pdf

7. OECD, 2019, *OECD Future of Education and Skills 2030 Concept Note.*
https://www.oecd.org/education/2030-project/teaching-and-learning/learning/skills/Skills_for_2030_concept_note.pdf

8. Pat-El, 2015, *Culture of mediocrity? Identifying Self-Regulation Strategies of First Year Social Science Students.*
https://www.researchgate.net/publication/281440433_Culture_of_mediocrity_Identifying_self-regulation_strategies_of_first_year_social_science_students

9. Wehmeyer & Zhao, 2020, *Teaching Students to Become Self Determined Learners.*

10. NBC, September 2018, *Today Show.*

11. Heifetz et al., 2009, *The Practice of Adaptive Leadership.*

CHAPTER 2: FEROCIOUS WARMTH

12. Palmer & Stough, 2007, *Emotional Intelligence*, Genos Accreditation Manual.

13. Brackett, 2019, *Permission to Feel: Unlocking the Power of Emotions to Help Our Kids, Ourselves, and Our Society to Thrive.*

14. Kise & Watterston, 2019, *Step In, Step Up.*

15. Senge, 1990, *The Fifth Discipline: The Art & Practice of the Learning Organization.*

16. Ezard, 2015, *The Buzz – Creating a Thriving & Collaborative Learning Culture.*

17. Taleb, 2012, *AntiFragile: Things That Gain from Disorder.*

18. Kouzes & Posner, 2016, *Learning Leadership: The Five Fundamentals of Becoming an Exemplary Leader.*

19. Harris, Caldwell & Longmuir, 2013, *Literature Review: A Culture of Trust Enhances Performance.*

20. Ezard, 2017, *Glue – The Stuff That Binds Us Together to do Extraordinary Work.*

CHAPTER 3: THE PARADOX OF YET

21. Church, 2019, *Rise Up: An Evolution in Leadership.*

22. Collins, 2001, *Good to Great.*

23. Carver et al., 2010, *Optimism.* http://local.psy.miami.edu/faculty/ccarver/documents/10_CPR_Optimism.pdf

24. Nes & Segerstrom, 2006, *Dispositional Optimism and Coping: A Meta-Analytic Review.*

25. Godin, 6 September 2020, *Opimism as a choice.* https://seths.blog/2020/09/optimism-as-a-choice/

26. Collins, 2001, *Good to Great.*

27. Munby, 2019, *Imperfect Leadership: A Book for Leaders Who Know they Don't Know it All.*

28. Kise, J. A. (2019) *Holistic Leadership, Thriving Schools* Twelve Lenses to Balance Priorities and Serve the Whole Student.

29. Ng, 2017, *Learning from Singapore: The Power of Paradoxes.*

30. Godin, 2 October 2020 *The arc and the arch.* https://seths.blog/2020/10/the-arc-and-the-arch/

31. Czikszentmihalyi, 2008, *Flow: The Psychology of Optimal Performance.*

32. Glaser, 2014, *Conversational Intelligence, How Great Leaders Build Trust and Get Extraordinary Results.*

CHAPTER 4: STRENGTH AND SHADOW

33. Liebermann, 2013, *Social: Why Our Brains Are Wired to Connect.*

34. VIA Institute on Character, *Survey of Character Strengths* www.viacharacter.org

35. Gallup, *CliftonStrengths Assessment.* https://www.gallup.com/cliftonstrengths/en/252137/home.aspx

36. Quenk, 2000, *In the Grip: Understanding Type, Stress, and the Inferior Function.*

CHAPTER 5: THE IMPACT OF IMBALANCE

37. Cuddy et al., 2013, *Connect, Then Lead.* https://hbr.org/2013/07/connect-then-lead

38. West, 2020, *The Karpman Drama Triangle Explained: A Guide for Coaches, Managers, Trainers, Therapists – and Everybody Else.*

CHAPTER 6: UNCOVERING OUR UNMET NEEDS

39. Rumi, 2004, *Selected Poems*, translated by Coleman Banks with John Moyne, A. J. Arberry & Reynold Nicholson

40. Brown, 2015, *Rising Strong.*

41. Brown, 2018, *Dare to Lead.*

42. Riley et al.,2020,*The Australian Principal Occupational Health, Safety and Wellbeing Survey.* https://www.healthandwellbeing.org/reports/AU/2019%20ACU%20Australian%20Principals%20Report.pdf

43. Chamine, 2012, *Positive Intelligence, Why Only 20% of Teams and Individuals Achieve Their True Potential and How You Can Achieve Yours.*

44. Dweck, 2006, *Mindset: The New Psychology of Success.*

CHAPTER 8: RECALIBRATION — BACK IN BALANCE

45. O'Reilly et al., 2020, *When 'Me' Trumps 'We': Narcissistic Leaders and the Cultures They Create.* https://doi.org/10.5465/amd.2019.0163

46. *What is Emotional Self Awareness?* Online at: https://www.kornferry.com/insights/articles/what-is-emotional-self-awareness-2019

CHAPTER 9: EXPANDING SELF

47. *Meet the Robinsons* – Credit quote Walt Disney 2007.

48. Fullan, 2014, *The Principal: Three Keys to Maximizing Impact.* https://michaelfullan.ca/wp-content/uploads/2016/06/14_The-Principal-Handout_Spring-Summer.compressed.pdf

49. Robinson et al., 2009, *School Leadership and Student Outcomes: Identifying What Works and Why.*

50. *High Impact Teaching Strategies: Excellence in Teaching and Learning,* 2020. https://www.education.vic.gov.au/Documents/school/teachers/support/high-impact-teaching-strategies.pdf

51. Ottati, V. et al., 2015, *When Self-Perceptions of Expertise Increase Closed-Minded Cognition: The Earned Dogmatism Effect.*

52. Senge, 1990, *The Fifth Discipline: The Art & Practice of the Learning Organization.*

53. Robinson, n.d., *Open-to-learning Conversations: Background Paper.* https://www.researchgate.net/profile/Viviane_Robinson/publication/267411000_Open-to-learning_Conversations_Background_Paper_Introduction_to_Open-to-learning_Conversations/links/54d7cb6c0cf2970e4e755956/Open-to-learning-Conversations-Background-Paper-Introduction-to-Open-to-learning-Conversations.pdf

CHAPTER 10: BUILDING COLLECTIVE CAPACITY

54. Strauss, 2017, *Elon Musk: The Architect of Tomorrow.*

55. Knight, 2010, *Are You A Radical Learner?*
https://instructionalcoaching.com/are-you-a-radical-learner/

56. Hattie, 2017, *Collaborative Impact*
https://visible-learning.org/2017/05/video-john-hattie-collaborative-impact/

57. Donohoo, 2016, *Collective Efficacy: How Educators' Beliefs Impact Student Learning.*

58. Fullan, 2006, *Leading Professional Learning.*
https://www.aasa.org/SchoolAdministratorArticle.aspx?id=7620

CHAPTER 11: WHAT STOPS US LEARNING TOGETHER?

59. Wiliam, 30 May 2019, *Teaching Not a Research-Based Profession.*
https://www.tes.com/news/dylan-wiliam-teaching-not-research-based-profession

60. Edmondson, 2018, *The Fearless Organisation, Creating Psychological Safety in the Workplace for Learning, Innovation, and Growth.*

61. Clark, T.R., 2020, *The 4 Stages of Psychological Safety: Defining the Path to Inclusion and Innovation.*

62. Ezard, 2017, *Glue: The Stuff That Binds Us Together to Do Extraordinary Work.*

63. Brown, 2018, *Dare to Lead.*

CHAPTER 12: OWNING OUR IGNORANT TRUTH

64. Katie, 2008, *A Thousand Names for Joy: Living in Harmony with the Way Things Are.*

65. Russell, 2009, *Mortals and Others, American Essays, 1931–1935.*

66. Korzybski, 1941, *Science and Sanity: An Introduction to Non-Aristotelian Systems and General Semantics.*

67. Angelou, Maya, 1928-2014, author, poet, civil rights activist, singer, actor.

68. Church, 2019, *Rise Up: An Evolution in Leadership.*

69. Sergiovanni, 2015, *Strengthening the Heartbeat: Leading and Learning Together in Schools.*

70. Heifetz, R. Linksky, M., 2002, *Leadership on the Line, Staying Alive Through the Dangers of Leading.*

71. Brown, 2020, Linkedin.
https://www.linkedin.com/posts/brenebrown_a-huge-wholehearted-thank-you-for-supporting-activity-6592862869937799171-RHmq

72. Hofstede et al., 1997, *Cultures and organizations: Software of the mind.*

CHAPTER 13: COCREATING POSSIBILITY

73. Barker,1991, *The Power of Vision.*

74. What does the ICSEA value mean? https://docs.acara.edu.au/resources/20160418_ACARA_ICSEA.pdf

75. Vaughan et al., 2019, Students as partners in learning in rural and remote settings. *Leading Together.* Australian Educational Leader. http://www.acel.org.au/ACEL/ACELWEB/Publications/AEL/2019/4/View.aspx

CHAPTER 14: LEADING TRANSFORMATION

76. Di Prato, 26 September and 14 November 2020, *Brave and Afraid*. https://adrianodiprato.tumblr.com/post/630300215839178752/hope-and-fear-cannot-occupy-the-same-space

77. Big Picture Education Australia https://www.bigpicture.org.au

78. Kotter & Cohen, 2012, *The Heart of Change: Real-Life Stories of How People Change Their Organizations*.

79. Li, 2019, *The Disruption Mindset: Why Some Organizations Transform While Others Fail*.

80. IDEO, *How Experimentation Can Lead to a Successful Launch* https://www.ideou.com/blogs/inspiration/how-experimentation-can-lead-to-a-successful-launch

81. Flanagan & Gregory, 2019, *Forever Skills: The 12 Skills to Future Proof Yourself, Your Team and Your Kids*.

82. Simon H.,1984, *Models of Bounded Rationality: Economic Analysis and Public Policy* (Volume 1).

83. Ea, 2016, *The People vs the School System*. https://www.youtube.com/watch?v=dqTTojTija8&list=FLQNDpekpYLmXNk2H2pnNpWw&index=138

84. The Grove Consultants International, *Cover Story Vision*. https://www.thegrove.com

85. Rogers, 1962, *Diffusion of Innovations*.

CHAPTER 16: THAT WORD...LOVE

86. Brown, 2017, *Braving the Wilderness: The Quest for True Belonging and the Courage to Stand Alone*.

87. Gallup, 2017, *State of the Global Workplace*. https://www.gallup.com/workplace/257552/state-global-workplace-2017.aspx

88. Commonwealth of Australia, 2017, *Royal Commission into Institutional Responses to Child Sexual Abuse: Final Report.* https://www.childabuseroyalcommission.gov.au/final-report

89. Lewis, 1960, *The Four Loves.* Harcourt, Brace & World, Inc.

90. Farber, 2019, *Love is Just Damn Good Business: Do What You Love in the Service of People Who Love What You Do.*

91.von Goethe, J.W., 1795-6,*Wilhelm Meister's Apprenticeship.* https://www.bartleby.com/314/804.html

CHAPTER 17: PROFESSIONAL INTIMACY

92. Robinson, 2006, *Do Schools Kill Creativity?* https://www.ted.com/talks/sir_ken_robinson_do_schools_kill_creativity?language=en

CHAPTER 18: STORIES CONNECT THE HEAD AND THE HEART

93. Silverman, 2006, *Wake Me Up When the Data is Over: How Organizations Use Storytelling to Drive Results.*

94. Zak, P., 2017, *Trust Factor: The Science of Creating High-Performance Companies.* AMACOM.

95. Newell, M. (Director). (2019). *In My Blood It Runs.* [Film]. Closer Productions. http://closerproductions.com.au/films/my-blood-it-runs

CHAPTER 19: FEROCIOUS WARMTH CONVERSATIONS

96. Glaser, 2014, *Conversational Intelligence: How Great Leaders Build Trust and Get Extraordinary Results.*

97. Atkinson, 2017, *The Value of Deep Listening – The Aboriginal Gift to the Nation.* https://youtu.be/L6wiBKClHqY

CHAPTER 20: MOMENTS THAT MATTER

98. Sales, L. (2018). *Any Ordinary Day: Blindsides, Resilience and What Happens After the Worst Day of Your Life*. Hamish Hamilton.

CHAPTER 21: WALK TOWARDS THE HARD WORK

99. Bader Ginsberg, R., May 2015, Harvard University Speech. https://www.radcliffe.harvard.edu/news/in-news/ruth-bader-ginsburg-tells-young-women-fight-things-you-care-about

100. Collins, 2001, *Good to Great*.

101. Brown, 2018, *Dare to Lead, Brave Work, Tough Conversations, Whole Hearts*.

CHAPTER 22: WHAT DO YOU STAND FOR?

102. Ackerman & Maslin-Ostrowski, 2009, *The Wounded Leader: How Real Leadership Emerges in Times of Crisis*.

CHAPTER 23: COURAGE FOR CHANGE

103. Camus, 1950, *Return to Tipasa*.

104. Voigt, 2020, *Restoring Teaching: How Working Restoratively Unleashes the Teacher and School Leader Within*.

105. Breen, 2020, *Why Elizabeth Broderick Wants Men to Step up Alongside Women*. https://www.intheblack.com/articles/2020/06/01/why-elizabeth-broderick-wants-men-to-step-up-alongside-women

106. Ella Baché, 2020, 15 June, *BOLD Women – Antoinette Braybrook*. https://www.ellabache.com.au/blogs/ella-bache/bold-women-antoinette-braybrook

107. Braybrook, 2020, *Making First Nations Women Safe and Strong*. 2020. https://www.youtube.com/watch?time_continue=12&v=0QiizcD0lNA&feature=emb_logo

108. Grissinger, 2017, *Disrespectful Behavior in Health Care: Its Impact, Why it Arises and Persists, and How to Address it – Part 2.*

109. Brown, 2018, *Dare to Lead.*

CHAPTER 24: OWNING WHO WE ARE

110. Aronson, Willerman, & Floyd, 2014, The effect of a pratfall on increasing interpersonal attractiveness. *Psychonomic Science.*

111. Keltner, 2016, *The Power Paradox: How We Gain and Lose Influence.*

BIBLIOGRAPHY

Ackerman, R.H. & Maslin-Ostrowski, P. (2009) *The Wounded Leader: How Real Leadership Emerges in Times of Crisis.* Jossey-Bass.

Atkinson, J. (Speaker) (2017). *The Value of Deep Listening – The Aboriginal Gift to the Nation.* [Video]. TEDxSydney.
https://youtu.be/L6wiBKClHqY

Australian Curriculum Assessment and Reporting Authority. (n.d.). *What does the ICSEA value mean?*
https://docs.acara.edu.au/resources/20160418_ACARA_ICSEA.pdf

Bader Ginsberg, R. (May 2015). Harvard University Speech.
https://www.radcliffe.harvard.edu/news/in-news/ruth-bader-ginsburg-tells-young-women-fight-things-you-care-about

Barker, J.A. (Speaker) (1991). *The Power of Vision.* [DVD]. Discovering the Future Series.

Big Picture Education Australia
https://www.bigpicture.org.au

Brackett. M. (2019). *Permission to Feel: Unlocking the Power of Emotions to Help Our Kids, Ourselves, and Our Society Thrive.* Celadon Books.

Braybrook, A. (2020, 3 March). *Making First Nations Women Safe and Strong.* 2020. [Video]. Pamela Denoon Lecture. Australian National University. YouTube. https://www.youtube.com/watch?time_continue=12&v=0QiizcD0lNA&feature=emb_logo

Breen, M. (2020, 1 June). Why Elizabeth Broderick Wants Men to Step up Alongside Women. *In The Black.* CPA Australia. Retrieved from https://www.intheblack.com/articles/2020/06/01/why-elizabeth-broderick-wants-men-to-step-up-alongside-women

Brotherhood of St Lawrence. (7 December 2020). *The Great Disruptor: Covid-Led Recession Deals Another Blow to Youth*
https://www.bsl.org.au/news-events/media-releases/the-great-disruptor-covid-led-recession-deals-another-blow-to-youth/

Brown, B. (2015). *Rising Strong: How the Ability to Reset Transforms the Way We Live, Love, Parent, and Lead.* Vermilion.

Brown, B. (2017*). Braving the Wilderness: The Quest for True Belonging and the Courage to Stand Alone.* Random House.

Brown, B. (2018). *Dare to Lead.* Vermilion.

Camus, A. (1950). *Return to Tipasa.* (n.p.).

Carver, C.S., Scheier, M.F. & Segerstrom, S.C. (2010). Optimism. *Clinical Psychology Review,* 30, 879-889. http://local.psy.miami.edu/faculty/ccarver/documents/10_CPR_Optimism.pdf

Chamine, S. (2012) *Positive Intelligence,* Why Only 20% of Teams and Individuals Achieve Their True Potential and how you can achieve yours. Greenleaf Book Group Press.

Chesters, J. and Daly, A. (October 2018). *Family and School Effects on Educational Achievement Across the School Career.* Melbourne Graduate School of Education. https://education.unimelb.edu.au/__data/assets/pdf_file/0007/2903137/family-and-school-effects-on-educational-achievement.pdf

Church, M. (2019) *Rise Up: An Evolution in Leadership.* Thought Leaders Publishing.

Clark, T.R. (2020).*The 4 Stages of Psychological Safety: Defining the Path to Inclusion and Innovation.* Berrett-Koehler Publishers.

Collins, J. (2001). *Good to Great. Why some companies make the leap ... and others don't.* Random House.

Commonwealth of Australia. (2017). *Royal Commission into Institutional Responses to Child Sexual Abuse: Final Report.* https://www.childabuseroyalcommission.gov.au/final-report

Cuddy, A.J.C., Kohut, M. & Neffinger, J. (2013). Connect, Then Lead. *Harvard Business Reiew,* July-August 2013. https://hbr.org/2013/07/connect-then-lead

Czikszentmihalyi, M. (2008). *Flow: The Psychology of Optimal Performance*. Harper Perennial.

Di Prato, A. (26 September and 14 November 2020), Brave and Afraid and Australia's Biggest Unconference. *Permission is Triumph*. https://adrianodiprato.tumblr.com/post/630300215839178752/hope-and-fear-cannot-occupy-the-same-space https://adrianodiprato.tumblr.com/post/634734998561423360/never-let-a-good-crisis-go-to-waste-winston

Donohoo, J. (2016). *Collective Efficacy: How Educators' Beliefs Impact Student Learning*. Corwin.

Dweck, C.S. (2006). *Mindset: The New Psychology of Success*. Random House.

Ea, P. (2016). *The People vs the School System*. [Video]. https://www.youtube.com/watch?v=dqTTojTija8&list=FLQNDpekpYLmXNk2H2pnNpWw&index=138

Edmondson, A. C. (2018). *The Fearless Organisation, Creating Psychological Safety in the Workplace for Learning, Innovation, and Growth*. Wiley.

Ella Baché. (2020, 15 June). *BOLD Women – Antoinette Braybrook*. https://www.ellabache.com.au/blogs/ella-bache/bold-women-antoinette-braybrook

Ezard, T. (2015). *The Buzz – Creating a Thriving & Collaborative Learning Culture*. Lulu.com.

Ezard, T. (2017). *Glue – The Stuff That Binds Us Together to do Extraordinary Work*. Tracey Ezard Pty Ltd.

Farber, S. (2019). *Love is Just Damn Good Business: Do What You Love in the Service of People Who Love What You Do*. McGraw-Hill Education.

Flanagan, K. & Gregory, D. (2019). *Forever Skills: The 12 Skills to Future Proof Yourself, Your Team and Your Kids*. Wiley.

Fullan, M. (2014). *The Principal: Three Keys to Maximizing Impact*. michaelfullan.ca https://michaelfullan.ca/wp-content/uploads/2016/06/14_The-Principal-Handout_Spring-Summer.compressed.pdf

Fullan, M. (2006). Leading Professional Learning. *School Administrator*, vol. 63 n10, 10, Nov 2006.
https://www.aasa.org/SchoolAdministratorArticle.aspx?id=7620

Gallup, *CliftonStrengths Assessment*. https://www.gallup.com/cliftonstrengths/en/252137/home.aspx

Gallup. (2017). *State of the Global Workplace*. Gallup Press.
https://www.gallup.com/workplace/257552/state-global-workplace-2017.aspx

Glaser, J.E. (2014). *Conversational Intelligence, How Great Leaders Build Trust and Get Extraordinary Results*. Routledge.

Godin, S. (6 September 2020). *Opimism as a choice*. Blog post: https://seths.blog/2020/09/optimism-as-a-choice/

Godin, S. (2 October 2020). *The arc and the arch*. Blog post:
https://seths.blog/2020/10/the-arc-and-the-arch/

von Goethe, J.W. (1795-6). *Wilhelm Meister's Apprenticeship*. 'When we take people, thou wouldst say, merely as they are, we make them worse; when we treat them as if they were what they should be, we improve them as far as they can be improved.' [Sometimes quoted as 'Treat a man as he is, and that is what he remains. Treat a man as he can be, and that is what he becomes'.] bk. 8, ch. 4 (T. Carlyle, Trans). Harvard Classics.
https://www.bartleby.com/314/804.html

Goleman, D. (n.d.). *What is Emotional Self Awareness?* Korn Ferry. https://www.kornferry.com/insights/articles/what-is-emotional-self-awareness-2019

Goss, P., Sonnemann, J. and Griffiths, K. (2017). Engaging students: Creating classrooms that improve learning. *Grattan Institute Report No. 2017-01*.
https://grattan.edu.au/wp-content/uploads/2017/02/Engaging-students-creating-classrooms-that-improve-learning.pdf

Grissinger M. (2017). Disrespectful Behavior in Health Care: Its Impact, Why It Arises and Persists, And How to Address It – Part 2. *Pharmacy and Therapeutics, 42*(2), 74-77.

Harris, J., Caldwell, B. & Longmuir, F. (June 2013). *Literature review: A culture of trust enhances performance*. Australian Institute for Teaching and School Leadership, Melbourne.

Hattie, J. (2017). *Collaborative Impact: Research & Practice Conference 2017.* Cognition Education.
https://visible-learning.org/2017/05/video-john-hattie-collaborative-impact/

Heifetz, R. & Linksky, M. (2002). *Leadership on the Line, Staying Alive Through the Dangers of Leading.* Harvard Business School Press.

Heifetz, R., Grashow, A. & Linsky, M. (2009). *The Practice of Adaptive Leadership. Tools and Tactics for Changing Your Organization and the World.* Harvard Business Press.

Hofstede, G.H., Hofstede, G.J. & Minkov,M. (1997). *Cultures and Organizations: Software of the Mind.* McGraw-Hill.

IDEO. (n.d.). *How Experimentation Can Lead to a Successful Launch* https://www.ideou.com/blogs/inspiration/how-experimentation-can-lead-to-a-successful-launch

Katie, B. (2008). *A Thousand Names for Joy: Living in Harmony with the Way Things Are.* Harmony.

Keltner, D. (2016). *The Power Paradox: How We Gain and Lose Influence.* Penguin Books.

Kise, J. A. G. (2019). *Holistic Leadership, Thriving Schools: Twelve Lenses to Balance Priorities and Serve the Whole Student.* Hawker Brownlow Education.

Kise, J.A.G. & Watterston, B. K. (2019). *Step In, Step Up. Empowering Women for the School Leadership Journey.* Solution Tree.

Knight, J. (7 September 2010). *Are You A Radical Learner?* Instructional Coaching Group. https://instructionalcoaching.com/are-you-a-radical-learner/

Korzybski, A. (1941). *Science And Sanity: an Introduction Tt Non-Aristotelian Systems and General Semantics.* Science Press.

Kotter, J. P., & Cohen, D. S. (2012). *The Heart of Change: Real-Life Stories of How People Change Their Organizations.* Harvard Business Review Press.

Kouzes, J.M. & Posner, B. Z. (2016). *Learning Leadership: The Five Fundamentals of Becoming an Exemplary Leader*. Wiley.

Lewis, C.S. (1960). *The Four Loves*. Harcourt, Brace & World, Inc.

Li, C. (2019). *The Disruption Mindset: Why Some Organizations Transform While Others Fail*. Ideapress Publishing.

Liebermann, M.D. (2013) *Social: Why Our Brains Are Wired to Connect*. Crown.

Mission Australia in association with Black Dog Institute. (n.d.). *Youth Mental Health Report, Youth Survey 2012-2016*. http://www.blackdoginstitute.org.au/wp-content/uploads/2020/04/2017-youth-mental-health-report_mission-australia-and-black-dog-institute.pdf?sfvrsn=6

Munby, S. (2019). *Imperfect Leadership: A Book For Leaders who Know they Don't Know it All*. Crown House Publishing.

NBC. (September 2018). *Today Show*.

Nes, L.S. & Segerstrom, S.C. (2006). Dispositional Optimism and Coping: A Meta-Analytic Review. *Personality and Social Psychology Review*. 2006;10(3):235-251. https://doi.org/10.1207/s15327957pspr1003_3

Newell, M. (Director). (2019). *In My Blood It Runs*. [Film]. Closer Productions. http://closerproductions.com.au/films/my-blood-it-runs

Ng, Pak Tee (2017). *Learning from Singapore: The Power of Paradoxes*. Routledge.

Niesche, R. (n.d.) *Improving Educational Equity in Australia*. UNSW Sydney and Gonski Institute for Education. https://www.gie.unsw.edu.au/sites/default/files/documents/Gonski%20Equity%20Paper_web_2.pdf

OECD. (2019). *OECD Future of Education and Skills 2030 Concept Note*. https://www.oecd.org/education/2030-project/teaching-and-learning/learning/skills/Skills_for_2030_concept_note.pdf

O'Reilly, C.A., Chatman, J.A. & Doerr, B. (2020). When 'Me' Trumps 'We': Narcissistic Leaders and the Cultures They Create. *Academy of Management Discoveries, 3 September 2020.* https://doi.org/10.5465/amd.2019.0163

Ottati, V., Price, E.D, Wilson, C. & Sumaktoyo, N. (2015). When Self-Perceptions of Expertise Increase Closed-Minded Cognition: The Earned Dogmatism Effect, *Journal of Experimental Social Psychology.* 61. 10.1016/j.jesp.2015.08.003.

Palmer, B. & Stough, C. (2007). Emotional Intelligence, Genos Accreditation Manual.

Pat-El, R. (August 2015). *Culture of mediocrity? Identifying Self-Regulation Strategies of First Year Social Science Students.* Conference paper for EARLI, at Limassol, Cyprus. https://www.researchgate.net/publication/281440433_Culture_of_mediocrity_Identifying_self-regulation_strategies_of_first_year_social_science_students

Quenk, N.L. (2000). In the Grip: Understanding Type, Stress, and the Inferior Function. CPP, Inc.

Riley, P., See, S-M., Marsh, H. & Dicke, T. (2020). *The Australian Principal Occupational Health, Safety and Wellbeing Survey* (IPPE Report). Institute for Positive Psychology & Education, Australian Catholic University. https://www.healthandwellbeing.org/reports/AU/2019%20ACU%20Australian%20 Principals%20Report.pdf

Robinson, K. (Speaker). (February 2006). *Do Schools Kill Creativity?* [Video].TED Conference. https://www.ted.com/talks/sir_ken_robinson_do_schools_kill_creativity?language=en

Robinson, V., Hohepa, M. & Lloyd, C. (November 2009). *School Leadership and Student Outcomes: Identifying What Works and Why.* Ministry of Education, New Zealand. ACEL Monograph Series 41.

Robinson, V.M.J. (n.d.). *Open-to-learning Conversations: Background Paper.* The University of Auckland. (A revised version of material found in Robinson, V. M. J., Hohepa, M., & Lloyd, C. (2009). *School leadership And Student Outcomes: Identifying What Works and Why – Iterative Best Evidence Synthesis Programme.* Wellington: Ministry of Education. [Chapter 8, *The Knowledge, Skills and Dispositions Involved in Effective Educational Leadership.*]).

Rogers, E.M. (1962). *Diffusion of Innovations*. Free Press of Glencoe.

Rumi, J. (2004) *Selected Poems* (C. Banks (Trans.) with J. Moyne, A.J. Arberry & R. Nicholson). Penguin Books. (Original work from 13th century).

Russell, B. (2009). *Mortals and Others, American Essays, 1931–1935*. Routledge Classics.

Sales, L. (2018). *Any Ordinary Day: Blindsides, Resilience and What Happens After the Worst Day of Your Life*. Hamish Hamilton.

Senge, P.M. (1990). *The Fifth Discipline: The Art & Practice of the Learning Organization*. Currency Doubleday.

Sergiovanni, T.J. (2015). *Strengthening the Heartbeat: Leading and Learning Together in Schools*. Jossey-Bass Education.

Silverman, L. (2006). *Wake Me Up When the Data is Over: How Organizations Use Storytelling to Drive Results*. Jossey-Bass.

Simon, H.A. (1984). *Models of Bounded Rationality: Economic Analysis and Public Policy* (Volume 1). The MIT Press.

State of Victoria, Department of Education and Training. (2019). *Amplify. Empowering students through voice, agency and leadership*. https://www.education.vic.gov.au/Documents/school/teachers/teachingresources/practice/Amplify.pdf

State of Victoria, Department of Education and Training (2020, revised). *High Impact Teaching Strategies: Excellence in Teaching and Learning*. https://www.education.vic.gov.au/Documents/school/teachers/support/high-impact-teaching-strategies.pdf

Strauss, N. (2017). Elon Musk: The Architect of Tomorrow. *Rolling Stone*, 16 November 2017.

Taleb, N.N. (2012). *AntiFragile: Things That Gain from Disorder*. Penguin Random House.

The Grove Consultants International, *Cover Story Vision*. https://www.thegrove.com

Vaughan, T., Cleary, J. & Butler, H. (2019). Students as Partners in Learning in Rural and Remote Settings. *Leading Together.* Australian Educational Leader, vol.41, Term 4, 2019. http://www.acel.org.au/ACEL/ACELWEB/Publications/AEL/2019/4/View.aspx

VIA Institute on Character, *Survey of Character Strengths*
www.viacharacter.org

Voigt, A. (2020). *Restoring Teaching: How Working Restoratively Unleashes the Teacher and School Leader Within.* Adam Voight Education Solutions

Wehmeyer, M. & Zhao, Y. (2020). *Teaching Students to Become Self-Determined Learners.* ASCD.

West, C. (2020). *The Karpman Drama Triangle Explained: A Guide for Coaches, Managers, Trainers, Therapists – and Everybody Else.* CWTK Publications.

Wiliam, D. (30 May 2019). *Teaching not a Research-Based Profession.* Transcript of a speech made at an awards ceremony for teachers who had taken part in the *Glasgow in Partnership with Tapestry's Supporting Improvement: Pedagogy and Equity Programme.* https://www.tes.com/news/dylan-wiliam-teaching-not-research-based-profession

Zak, P. (2017). *Trust Factor: The Science of Creating High-Performance Companies.* AMACOM.

ABOUT THE AUTHOR

Tracey has been a teacher and learner all her career and is known for her Ferocious Warmth leadership approach and collaborative culture work. Tracey's collaborative framework for creating an environment of learning, trust and innovation is used in education and organisational systems throughout Australia. Her Buzz Diagnostic has been used by over 280 schools and has had over 8000 educators participate. Tracey has run leadership programs for education and system leaders for over 15 years in all education sectors in a number of states and in New Zealand. Tracey works extensively with schools, principal and assistant principal networks throughout Australia and leaders in other sectors.

Tracey is a former assistant principal in the government sector in Victoria, Australia. She has also worked as a project manager in the automotive industry, as part of the Teacher Release to Industry Program and as a business manager in a fine dining restaurant.

This is Tracey's third book. Her first books are *The Buzz – Creating a Thriving and Collaborative Staff Learning Culture* designed for education leaders to support schools to bring about transformation in the classroom and *Glue: The Stuff that Binds Us Together to do Extraordinary Work* for leaders across all sectors who want to lift beyond convention to create high performing teams.

Tracey was awarded a National Fellowship by the Australian Council of Educational Leaders in 2020.

Twitter: @traceyezard
Email: tracey@traceyezard.com

Lightning Source UK Ltd.
Milton Keynes UK
UKHW020844260521
384355UK00007B/75